The Perfect Fool

Stewart Lee was born in 1968 and lives in Stoke Newington, London. He has performed as a stand-up comedian in Canada, USA and Australia, written for T.V., radio, newspapers and magazines and collaborated on the libretto for Jerry Springer The Opera. *The Perfect Fool* is his first novel.

For more information on Stewart Lee visit
www.4thestate.com/stewartlee and
www.stewartlee.co.uk

The Perfect Fool

Stewart Lee

FOURTH ESTATE · London

This paperback edition first published in 2002
First published in Great Britain in 2001 by
Fourth Estate
A Division of HarperCollins*Publishers*
77–85 Fulham Palace Road
London, W6 8JB
www.4thestate.com

Copyright © 2001 Stewart Lee

10 9 8 7 6 5 4 3 2 1

A catalogue record for this book is available
from the British Library

ISBN 978-1-84115-366-7

Typeset in Sabon by
Palimpsest Book Production Limited
Polmont, Stirlingshire

The White Dawn
of the Hopi

A very long time ago there was nothing but water on the earth. By and by two goddesses, the Huruing Wuhti of the east and the Huruing Wuhti of the west, caused the waters to recede eastward and westward, so that some dry land appeared. The sun passing over the land noticed that no living being could be seen. When he mentioned this to the goddesses, the one in the west invited the one in the east to come and talk about it.

The Huruing Wuhti of the east travelled west over a rainbow and the two deities deliberated and decided to create a little bird. The Huruing Wuhti of the east made a wren of clay and covered it with a piece of möchápu cloth. Both goddesses sang a song over it, and after a while a live bird came forth. Since the sun always passed over the middle of the earth, the deities thought He might not have seen living creatures in the north or south. So they sent the little wren to fly all over the earth, but it returned and said that no living being existed anywhere.

But all the while the Spider Woman, Kóhkang Wuhti, was living in a little kiva somewhere southwest at the edge of the water, where the little bird had failed to notice her. Then the deity of the west proceeded to make many different birds and animals of many different kinds, covering them with the same cloth under which the wren had been brought to life. Then the Huruing Wuhti of the east made a white woman and a white man from clay, and taught them language, and gave them a small simple house in a good field in which to live.

But the Spider Woman heard the goddesses fashioning life from clay, and so she too created a man and woman of clay also. And she taught them Spanish, and fashioned two burros for them, and the couple settled down near her. The Spider Woman continued to create people in the same manner, giving a different language to each pair. But she forgot to make a woman for a certain man, and this is the reason why today there are always some men who are alone. Then, as she continued turning out people, she found that she had also failed to create a man for a certain woman.

'Somewhere,' she said to the woman, 'there is a man who went astray. Find him, and if he accepts you, live with him. If he doesn't, both of you must be always alone. You must simply do the best that you can.'

And the lone woman turned away from Kóhkang Wuhti, and began her search.

Hopi Indian legend, reported by
H. R. Voth in 1905

One

London. Long after midnight, the street people agree, there runs a train. An underground night train, unscheduled, undriven, and awaited by no one. The train that will take them away.

The Paste and Bucket man has heard it, whistling on the dead wind, once, his ear cocked, his head turned, as he flattened film star faces on to stone wall. A hundred art-deco-tiled yards downwind, the crazy fat naked woman has heard it too, singing in the ghost choir of the emergency third rail. Now she raises her head from her beer can and sniffs a new scent on the tunnel air, and hears a new sound.

And Mr Lewis has heard it too, borne on the air conditioning at 3 a.m., and bearing hard upon him. Stale wisps of wind wind over his saggy features. Yellow fingers push unhinged hairs off his grey face. He turns from searching the hands of the all but irrelevant platform clock, and sets instead to straining and twitching to name that sound, to number it and nail it down in the index of a mind tonight too scrambled to store it.

An unease had pricked the nape of Paste and Bucket's neck many times before. He'd wanted to ask for transfer, but on what grounds? Things come unglued as easily in Acton as in

Old Street, surely. But he could do without these whispering night winds. Decades of thoughts, days of conversations, years of sweat, and moments of regret had seeped through sole and seat into the woods and metals of these much put upon engines. And from the engines, the weight had sunk down into the rails, and from them into the system citywide, and now the city has its own secrets to tell. And Lewis knows the unnamed notion that nags him every night may thus reveal itself. Here, he reasons, or else northwards, in the track-ways of Hampstead Heath, or where the canal creeps through Kensal, or south-wards, reflected in a poisoned pond on Clapham Common, or east, between the moneyed monoliths of the Isle of Dogs. Or elsewhere again.

Tonight the crazy fat naked woman senses something coming for him too. And as a stale breeze ruffles her pink tutu, she shoots Mr Lewis an encouraging look from the slabs and starts to sing her lucky song: 'Would you like to swing on a star, carry moonbeams home in a jar, oh would you like to swing on a star, or would you rather be a pig?'

On the surface, laid out in the moonlight, the thousand resting carriages of Willesden depot, London's railway grave-yard. In the dead of night they roll in creaky and broken. Then the morning light revives them and they crawl back into service. But for now they stand in slumber as Peter Rugg patrols the deserted depot, copping a few sly feels of their threadless seats. An old greybeard, an ex-desperado, with crows' nest hair and a Crusoe beard. He had swung through swinging 60s' Notting Hill on a curling chemical chain, protected in a veil of musty woodsmoke. Those were the days, my friend, and anyone who was there cannot remember them. Now he is reduced to a single repeated act of penitent motion, by which to measure out the slow trickling away of his time. Dipping. Dipping down beneath the seat backs and seat sides of underground tube trains, dipping to find a long-lost, still burning cigarette butt, abandoned in someone else's Portobello flat, some time in the summer of 1972. Dip dip dip dip, all along the train. He

4

changes carriages and then he starts again. Dip dip dip dip, all along the train.

And as he dips, Peter Rugg sees Mr Lewis, sheltered between the sleeping engines, crouching over his maps. One, the London Underground Network, free at any station. Another, the Signs of the Zodiac, as written over the stars, torn from a Sunday supplement. He squints at the network. He squints at the starmap. If Victoria is Venus, if Betelgeuse is Baker Street, if stars are stops and black holes are tunnels, then he may yet be able to orientate himself. He had come to his senses in Archer Street, at the southern edge of Soho, clad in pyjamas and clutching a wedge of cash. And that was all he could recall. He squints at the netmap. He squints at the starwork. And as he raises his head to the vaulted heavens, tonight, between the slats of his fingers, the starwork squints back.

Another of the crazy fat naked woman's songs echoes down the line; 'Fly me to the moon . . .' Lewis scents the air. A thousand miles beneath his eyelids, for the first time, something solid and silver begins to spin in the twin orbits of gravity and memory. The surrounding stars pummel it with beams of light, refracting it into a shimmering web of energy. And things finally fall into place. '. . . and let me play among the stars . . .' And this is it at last. This is written in the wind. This is etched on the sky. Holding his head in his hands, and falling on the crumpled maps to weep, Mr Lewis finally starts to remember.

A shaft of sunlight slits the house as Bob Nequatewa opens the curtain and looks out into the pot-holed streets of Shungopavi, high on the Hopi mesas of central Arizona. Dogs cast about for breakfast scraps and babies bawl. Plastic crates and soda cans blossom like foreign flowers amongst an expanse of brown-green land and brown-grey buildings. In the distance, the sun rises over the other villages, huddled on the high cliffs, overlooking a flat plain of corn and grass.

Bob Nequatewa shakes a final unruly shank of cloth free of the window frame and the light floods fully into the house.

Dust particles burst into illuminated life and twinkle on the thermals while a bright-eyed boy scrutinises them, and stabs out a tiny fist to snatch himself some, a kitten boxing mosquitoes. Bob Nequatewa coughs, spits on his hands, brown and creased, wipes the palms on his blue denim dungarees, and leans a little ladder up against some shelves set into the plastered breeze block wall of his home. The boy turns from the light and wordlessly stands to steady it, as his grandfather shakily ascends. He stares up at the old man. Bob Nequatewa wheezes and grips a shelf for support as he clatters through battered boxes and bags for a small brown case, faded leather and tarnished brass. He hands it down to the boy, who buckles a little under the burden, and he points to the bed. The boy lays the case on the bedspread, an intricate patchwork of hand-stitched pieces, and returns to hold the ladder as Bob Nequatewa slowly makes his descent, sandalled feet slapping on the rungs.

Bob Nequatewa crosses to the bed, over the creaking boards, and looks down at the case, watched by the boy. He sighs. He walks to the window and looks out once more into the Shungopavi street, and then turns to consider the case again. The boy rubs his eyes and yawns. Bob Nequatewa ruffles his hair and smiles at him. He crouches by the case and places his fingers on the fixtures. He and the boy exchange a look, and the old man flips open the locks and lifts the lid. The boy peeps into the case, possum eyed, as Bob Nequatewa takes out the contents, one by one, and lays them out on the bedspread. A black and white striped hat, tapering to two gold tasselled points; white knee-pads with wrinkled leather straps; and a shrivelled loincloth so flimsy that now Bob Nequatewa can't suppress a smirk.

Clown clothes.

He hands the loincloth to the boy who holds it up in the sunlight, turns it round once, and then doubles up with laughter. The old man laughs too, snatching it back, and whipping the child's bare arm with it in a swift and sudden motion.

Outside, a car horn. The boy rushes to the window. A white 4-wheel drive has pulled up outside in the village, and already a crowd of chattering children has gathered around it. The writing on the side reads 'Phoenix Channel 8'. The boy looks back to his grandfather, and the old man folds the clothes back into the case, and offers him his hand. The boy takes it, and squeezes it tight. The car horn sounds a second time. Bob pulls the curtains closed again, opens the door, and mumbles under his breath:

'If it may be so, may I gain at least one smile.'

The Hopi clown's prayer. They walk out into the sunlight, and once more the room is dark.

Bob sits in the back of the vehicle, and as his bag is taken from him and stowed, he suddenly feels ill at ease. His grandson senses something is wrong, and tugs at his sleeve. Bob pinches the bridge of his nose, screws up his eyes, and tries to shut out the flickering and by now familiar female face that these days seems to greet him every time he lies down to sleep.

Tracy bursts into the bathroom with a crack of carpentry and a shower of splinters and sees the moon underwater. It bobs insipidly beneath regular flashes of the word MOTEL, captured in two-second red illuminations in the shallows of the bath, visibly cooling, and clouded with blood. Roscoe ran it an hour ago. He had drunk beer behind a bolted door, mixed the hot water and the cold water just so, and poured in a capful of foam. And she had sat on the bed in the next room, listening, smoking, and biting her bottom lip.

Tracy had heard the water stop running, the creak of the tap, a hammering of air trammelled in a pipe somewhere, and a voluminous sloshing as Roscoe lowered himself into the tub. The sound had made her remember a rare family excursion to Phoenix Zoo, the smell of candyfloss, and holding her mother's hand as she watched a hippo wade. To share in its weight, you would be invincible, she had thought. To be one with the creature. To take its power. To wear its muscle like

7

a shield. To be the Little Hippo Girl, snorting dismissively at curious onlookers. And if it all got too much, to sink into the glorious mud. Then her father had dragged her to see the turtles.

Roscoe didn't make another sound. After twenty minutes Tracy called to him: 'Take as long as you like hon . . .' Roscoe didn't answer. She imagined him in there alone, trying to soak off the scent of his ever having known her. 'I'll be out here, waiting.'

Silence. She lay back on the bed. In the open drawer of the bedside table a Gideon's Bible, and a crumpled comic book, left by the last to leave, one inch by two of black and white and yellow. 'Please pass this on to a friend when you have finished with it', read a message hand-written on the cover in deeply indented green ink, over a two-colour caricature of a dainty rosary and a dangling crucifix.

Are Roman Catholics Christians? was published by the Bible Messenger League, of Chico, California. Tracy knew it would be. She flicked once through the inky pages, lingering on a picture of a fat priest waving a cup and a wafer at a bearded man roped to a stake. 'Is this the actual blood and body of Christ?' he asked the captive. 'NO! It is symbolic', answered the smoldering martyr, as the flames fried his feet. 'ALL THIS HISTORY HAS BEEN COVERED UP.'

Tracy flipped open a battered brown briefcase, and placed the pamphlet alongside the others. *Man Or Monkey?, Satan's Slaves – The Devil's Music, The Truth About The Homo-sexuals.*

Her fingers fumbled over the bedside cabinet to flick off the lamp, burrowing through cigarette packs, rings, gum, a watch, a condom wrapper, keys. The room dimmed into the red road-sign throb. In the darkness she shivered and slid her hand down into her panties, feeling the cooling dampness.

'That was forty dollars we couldn't spare, hon,' she called, 'even for a room and a six-pack.' Roscoe didn't answer. But, earlier, he had said something about how a man could mistake something that sweet for love. And so when they had lain holding each other afterwards, she had finally made her confession.

And now she's standing in the bathroom, circled by splinters, staring at Roscoe's feet, curled above the surface, a drained grey white, the skin furled into fungal ridges. The water laps over the island of his belly, combing the black hair of his chest this way and that in tiny waves, like a breeze-blown field of crops. His nipples are blue and erect in the cold water. His penis, tiny and shrunken in the shallows, shrivels into his pubic hair. Hard to imagine how, hours earlier, she had taken it inside her. Now Roscoe's head is arched back too harshly, his mouth open too wide, his brown eyes bulging, his lips drawn too tight against his bones. Hard to imagine those lips kissing hers, not two hours before now. A mane of hair spreads suspended around his face, a dark but buoyant halo. The veins in his arms stand out in woodcut relief. A cigarette, left on the rim of the tub, has burned down unwanted and melted a permanent brown wound into the pink plastic. His hands float limply and apologetically, palms upward. And his wrists are slit. And the bath is full of blood.

Tracy sinks to her knees. As she leans in to kiss him she smells herself fading from his face. A cloud passes over the moon. Outside in the lot, the motel sign stutters and shuts down. A truck buzzes by in perfect stereo panning. A dog barks. From the bar across the highway the low indistinct jukebox throb, the click of pool balls, the crash of glass, and men laughing. A trash can rattles in the empty night. And Tracy is alone, in a dark room, with a dead man. Again.

Just outside Searchlight, Arizona, flies had massed on the edge of the highway, where the dirt had run red around her last lover, throat cut, and him lying between the cacti shadows. A big brown blur in the heat haze, he had stopped, stripped and strode out to die; and in Flagstaff another one had swung from a noose on a scrubby back-yard tree as neighbours struggled at sunrise to cut him down; and in a stationary car in a darkened garage in Phoenix, another. He had checked his hair in the rearview mirror a final time and stifled the last gasps of life; and another, the desert dogs scrabbling around his severed limbs, scattered on a railway track, someplace nowhere she can recall the name of.

She's packed up and gone, come the slightest signs of light. Four a.m. on a Wednesday morning.

'I don't believe it,' says Danny at last. 'That woman is actually going to fuck that pig.'

'So it would appear . . .' agrees Sid, brushing a wilted quiff out of his eyes, and dragging on a joint. Danny reaches over, takes the saggy roll-up between rotten teeth, and sinks back into the sofa. In the darkness the green-blue flickering of the TV screen throws Sid's face into pasty non-relief, and complicates the paisley patterns of the 60s rock posters on the walls. 'Luther Peyote & The Round Tabyls invite you to Step Outside Your Head! Why not ask your Bay Area Retailer for other exciting International Artists recordings?'

Sid retrieves the joint, runs a hand over his chin, and sucks. Outside the rattling windows there's a late-night South London silence, a constant subsonic machine burr punctuated by police sirens and the dog yowls of shouting old men. But inside the flat, the video soundtrack seeps into the room like a gas leak. Squawks of encouragement from a man and a woman in an incomprehensible Spanish. And a slurry of desperate, animal grunting. Beneath a tenth-generation copy snowstorm of interference and derailed tracking, the images fade in and out of clarity.

There's a chemical buzz off the dope tonight that Sid could do without. It's the best of Brixton skunkweed, envy of Amsterdam and curse of student halls. But it's not a sensation Sid actively seeks out any more. When he and Danny had been younger it had been different. Lolling into the sofa stoned had not been an end in itself, but an adjunct to some greater entertainment. Other people might even have been involved. But now it constitutes an entire, and utterly joyless, evening. Streamer traces of pig-skin pink colour swirl out of the screen and drape themselves around the light fitting.

'Do you think they're really nuns, Sid?' The woman gets on her hands and knees in the straw, and hitches up her habit, white ankles and calves streaked with barnyard muck.

'No, not unless there's some really weird Catholic sect down there in South America that your Jesuit teachers never saw fit to tell you about, no.'

'Ah, yes, the Sisters of Porcine Indulgence . . . I remember. They were very big back home, in the more rural areas obviously. But they couldn't get a foothold in Belfast for love nor money.'

How many nights of their lives have they spent together now, in various states of drugged disarray, watching trashy videos and forcing each other to listen to their favourite records? All that had really altered in their daily round these last few years was that they now had access to Abby's internet account. There was a whole world of information out there with which to while away the hours. And where did they want to go today? Probably to more websites full of obscure rock and roll trivia, to chat-rooms stuffed with slightly distressing conspiracy theorists, and to pages and pages of slowly scrolling pictures of anaemic-looking men and women doing disgraceful things with foodstuffs and household objects. And somehow, like a slurry of sludge sliding inexorably down a slate-grey slag-heap towards a sleeping schoolhouse, all this wretchedness and waste had slowly accumulated into the spectacular sum total of their fantastic lives. But it hadn't always been so.

Sid had first met Danny over a decade ago, playing bass and drums respectively for a fledgling band, the Lemon Pies. Their lone flexi-disc, 'I Have Embarrassed Myself', received a few late night plays. Sid had recently seen it offered for twelve dollars on an internet auction site and wished he had kept a few copies for himself. A subsequent radio session had revealed, so the critics of now long since deceased weekly music papers said, 'real songwriting skills'. And that was when the Lemon Pies had been asked to become the backing band for Timothy Waterhouse, a fallen boy-band puppet anxious for adult rock star status. Danny was against it and talked Sid out of making the move, appealing to his vanity and an ephemeral notion of 'credibility'. Back then it hadn't taken much to convince Sid that a pact with Timothy Waterhouse would be a pact with Satan. So he and Danny had left the Lemon Pies to sell their souls to corporate rock without them, confident that their integrity would bring its own rewards. Ten years later the other Pies were rich. Paul Foreman had even been featured in *Hello!* magazine, standing smiling in a Cotswold flower garden on the arm of a Dutch MTV presenter. Sid and Danny, meanwhile, played twice a week in a Dire Straits covers band in Streatham, and passed their time throwing shoes at the television whenever Timothy Waterhouse and the former Lemon Pies came on. Which was often. Sid had tried repeatedly to get the rest of the Sultans of Streatham to rehearse his songs, but unless they had the cool, clean lines of classic Knopfler, Ian the lead guitarist wasn't interested. And now, even the pleasure of telling strangers in pubs how he and Danny really nearly could have made it had long since faded.

The pig's grunts grow more frenzied, becoming squeals of incredulous animal pleasure. Meanwhile, the woman's moans become exhausted groans. 'It's not a silent order then . . . ,' says Danny, as they sit and stare, bottles in hand, ash falling to the threadbare carpet as the joint burns away forgotten. 'Sister Mary there is proving herself very inventive with the turnips . . . and the stick.'

Once, watching a video like this might have been fun. Now Sid and Danny tolerated the experience merely because they knew no better. How amusing it had been, a decade ago, to stay in night after night watching witless slasher films, terrible teen exploitation movies, full of push-up bras and Brylcreem, and ugly amateur erotica. How witty and clever they had been in their merciless destruction of the film-makers' naivety and cynicism. Admittedly, entire strands of late-night Channel 4 programming had been based on more slender conceits than two men making fun of cheap old movies, and videos harvested from the fringes of acceptable taste, but where once Sid had believed some things were so bad they were good, now he knew they were so bad they were simply just bad.

'How do you think you'd feel, Danny, if you'd done this? How do you think . . . you would . . . approach the rest of your life?' asks Sid.

Danny drags on the joint. '"Oh my God. I've had sex with a pig. I've transgressed every moral, social, physical and religious boundary known to man. I think I'll just become a heroin addict and kill myself." Does that answer your question?'

'Yeah. But maybe you'd think, "I've had sex with a pig. I've transgressed every moral, social, physical and religious boundary known to man. I fear nothing!"'

'Come and have a go if you think you're hard enough?' suggests Danny.

'Something like that . . .' Sid agrees, vacantly.

Scrabbling towards the delicious turnip the standing nun is dangling before its foaming face, the pig, against all biological programming, suddenly seems to understand what the camera expects from it, its tail quivering with confused energy. Sid shivers as he remembers too many frozen November afternoons spent scrumming down in Rugby matches, during despised games lessons at a minor Midlands grammar school, feeling a mass of heavier, fitter, boys forcing his face into the mud as his legs gave way beneath him. As the nun pushes her thighs back to meet the weight he wonders for a moment if Mr Tomkinson hadn't perhaps had a more sinister, hidden, training agenda. Snap out of it. 'When do you think this was made?'

'About fifteen years ago, Sid, judging by that hairstyle. A pig with hair like that today would never get laid by such a fantastic-looking woman.' And as Danny stares at the woman's contorted face, somehow it begins to assume a beatific aspect, eyes raised to heaven in silent suffering. He remembers child-hood genuflections before a thousand roadside shrines, at each sacred well from his home in the South, northwards, to relatives wrapped in war and intrigue. The Virgin Mary's face had been a vision of noble suffering, and before him was a deceitful cartoon of counterfeited lust, yet how close they seemed. And it has happened. 'Oh, Jesus, Sid . . . would you look at that,' he says, wincing at a close-up that the finest BBC wildlife documentary film crew would envy. But where once they might have laughed, now Sid and Danny crumble mute and broken back into their seats. Maybe they have finally found their own elastic limit.

'It'd be hard, though, wouldn't it?' Sid suggests, as if changing the subject. 'Going back to any kind of . . . life . . . after you'd done that.'

'I suppose . . . and it would take a lot to impress your woman there after this. I mean, "I bought you some flowers. I do hope you like them." "Yeah. Listen, sunshine. I've had sex with a pig. It'll take more than tulips to ring my bell. Get the fuck away with you." Where's the future in that?' Danny laughs. Sid feels a little sick.

In the old days, Sid would squander the critical vocabulary he had learned at college, but only half understood, by scouring lurid Italian horror films and low rent erotica for postmodern subplots that clearly just weren't there. And Danny had enjoyed bouncing back at him with proletarian bluntness. Sid set up his friend's punch-lines perfectly. Sometimes he wondered if they should have gone into comedy. He makes a listless attempt to set the ball rolling.

'Danny, I think that, within the boundaries of an essentially worthless piece of cinema, that pig is pursuing his own personal quest for meaning.'

'No, Sidney, the pig is pursuing his own personal quest for turnips.'

Sid laughs but, God, this has been a wretched night. He and Danny have spent so long filtering their viewing through the distorted lens of irony that he wonders if they are still capable of recognising real talent, real beauty, or even real suffering. He had been painted into a corner by his own refusal to seek them out, taking refuge instead in sneering and sniggering. There was a part of both of them which, when Fat Ian had asked them to join his Dire Straits covers band, had thought it would be an inherently amusing course of action. How they used to smirk at each other over the drum-kit behind Ian's back as he scrumpled up his stupid face in particularly flash bouts of soloing. But when they were onstage, dressed in their Dire Straits rock sportswear, there was no huge pair of inverted commas, suspended from the ceiling, to tell the audience that Sid and Danny's intentions were anything less than entirely earnest. Who is the most degraded here? The nun? The pig? Or he and Danny? At least the pig looks as if he's enjoying himself. Looking to his left now, Sid sees Danny squirm a little in his seat. He wonders if it is possible for a man to have an erection *ironically*. Surely such a thing would be beyond the ability of even the most perverted literary critic?

Why couldn't things be simple again? The first time Sid ever heard a song by his favourite singer, Luther Peyote, he had been twelve years old, and the music had flipped his wig in a spirit of honesty and innocence denied to the adult ear. When grown-ups purchased artefacts their tastes were infected with images of their own ideal selves, with second-hand ideas of critical worth and cultural significance. Oh, to be back there, a young boy approaching everything unencumbered, as if for the first time. Suddenly Sid is distracted by the skunk and the screen again. 'Pigs have weird cocks, don't they? All curly, like little drills . . .' There is a breathing space, while this wise observation permeates the mucous membrane of Danny's mind.

'That seems normal enough to me, Sid. Is your dick not curly like that then? Perhaps you should make your girlfriend get someone in her hospital to check you out. Patient number 95, Sid Parker, the one with the unusual straight wanger, the doctor will see you now!'

'It's a psychiatric ward, Danny.'

'Well, it won't do any harm. Just to put your mind at rest.'

And then, the beginning of the end. The swirling pump-house-engine penis jerks spasmodically four times and then jettisons an endless barrage of thick, globular semen. To Sid's dilated eyes, it threatens to surge out of the television screen and swamp all of South London. As he inhales again he sees the burghers of Balham wading to the tube station along a High Road slowly turning to treacle, sloshing with bestial residue. At Pixies' Wine Bar on Bedford Hill, Derek, the Scrabble-playing proprietor, blocks the steps to the cellar restaurant with sandbags, and the garrulous Indian woman in the Bonanza mini-mart on the corner of Marius Road begins a floor-mopping job of Sisyphean futility. Policemen redirect angry drivers off around the back of Tooting Bec Common and a yellow diversion sign warns of the South London Pig Semen Flood. At the Infants School on Elmfield Road an assembly hall full of slightly sticky children are warned that, due to unforeseen circumstances, they will not be allowed to play outside today. A young supply teacher blushes crimson as she is asked the first of a long string of difficult questions. And the Jewish delicatessen opposite the second-hand car dealers shuts its doors and ceases trading indefinitely.

At least, muses Sid, a flood of pig semen would lower the local house prices. He has rented the flat for nearly a decade now. At the start of the 90s Balham was still a cheap option, a part of town no one wanted to inhabit. But now wine bars and shops selling small wooden animals are supplanting the launderettes and off-licences. And Danny has slept on his sofa for most of that time, somehow never quite getting around to making a financial contribution, until Sid's requests for rent money had become a farcical monthly ritual. Both indulged it with a comforting sense of familiarity that proved, underneath the bitterness and bickering, that they were friends to the end. But the only reason Sid has been able to resist their landlord's often intimidating efforts to move them out is because they really have so little to lose.

Onscreen, the noise subsides, and the pig shuffles backwards a little on its hind legs. Someone throws the nun a grubby towel. A group of five or six people start clapping off screen. The tape fades to a flickering grey.

'Thank fuck for that,' says Danny, pressing the rewind on the remote. 'Now which sick bastard's idea was it to get us a copy of that, then?'

'Yours.'

'Ah well. Did you enjoy your stag night then, Ian?'

The boys' forgotten friend lies sleeping and snoring, slumped in an armchair on the other side of the room. Drunk and drugged at the end of a long day that's taken him from a greasy spoon breakfast, via the Vampire Ride at Chessington World of Adventures, to Wimbledon dog-racing track and an empty wallet, Fat Ian dribbles lager spit down on to his undulating belly, stuffed into a Dire Straits souvenir tour T-shirt, and fails to respond. Danny jabs at the sleeping man. 'You'll be married next month, Ian, try and enjoy yourself.'

From Sid's bedroom, a rustle of sheets, a lightswitch click and a woman's voice: 'Sid! Come to bed will you!' Sid shrugs apologetically and gets up as Abby puts her head around the door, crossing her legs, and hugging her breasts to her chest. Her drooping eyebags and skin the pallor of a thirty-six-hour shift are overwhelmed by the gentle upturn of her nose, the subtly inbred rosy arrogance of her perfectly cheekboned face. 'If I'm late for work again because of you two keeping me up, Huxley will have . . .' She tails off.

'Kittens?' suggests Sid.

'Your guts for garters?' says Danny.

'Yes. That's it.' She rubs her eyes. 'And put Ian in a taxi or something will you. Barbara will be worried sick about him,' and she shuffles back to bed.

'Can you ring one, Danno? Duty calls.'

'I don't know how you can after that, Sid. I feel sordid.'

Danny laughs, throwing a cushion after him. He watches Sid drag himself to the bedroom, listens for the light switch, and then leans over to within an inch of Ian's face. 'Ian, are you awake?' The fat man doesn't stir. Danny chuckles to himself, cracks open another beer, lights a joint, takes a crumpled tissue out of his trouser pocket, unzips his fly and presses play.

Somewhere west of the New Mexico state line, and north of the border itself, a deer raises its head from a mountain stream, as a single, sustained tone echoes out through the trees of the Coronado National Forest. The cottonwood leaves flutter a little as if blown by a light breath of wind. The same note chimes again, and the animal breaks into a run, skipping over rocks and fallen branches. Half a mile away, in an echoing metal-walled chamber, an old man sits on a stool, hunched over an electric guitar of indeterminate age and model, plucking the same string over and over, as if scared to move on to any of the others. A dented amplifier buzzes and howls at maximum volume every time the player leans forward or back, in and out of the invisible concentric rings of its magnetic field. At the rear of the room a tethered mule stamps its feet in fear. Yellow fingers pluck the note again, and the feedback subsides momentarily as the same single tone overwhelms the darkness of the room, flooding it with shuddering waves, before subsiding into the lightning storm of random noise once more. The mule struggles on its rope, backing away from the sound towards the back wall, where a makeshift bed lies beached amidst boxes and abandoned baked bean cans. The fingers fumble for the same single note once more, and the sound struggles again between the cataract roar of undisciplined electricity and the angel drone of the pure tone. Then the man picks up the guitar by the neck and throws it towards the wall. It clangs against the metal hull of the building, pitches a mathematically inexplicable second of butterfly wing chaos into the sound, and then, as the lead falls from the body of the instrument, tumbles to the dusty ground with a soft thump.

The mule bristles and is still. The man walks over to his bed, pulls a red blanket over his head, and sleeps.

In the darkness of the railway yard at the Willesden depot, Mr Lewis sinks to his knees. The words he has read every night, since first he began to suspect he was on to something, scroll again beneath his eyes: *'There came a clap of thunder so loud and terrible he thought the palace must fall. And suddenly the hall was lit by a sunbeam which shed a radiance seven times brighter than had been before. And in this moment he was illuminated as it might be by the grace of the Holy Ghost. Then it appeared, covered with a cloth of white samite; and yet no mortal hand was seen to bear it. And at once the palace was filled with fragrance, as though all the spices of the earth had been spilled abroad. It circled the hall along the great tables and each place was furnished in its wake with the food its occupants desired. And then it vanished, and he knew not how or whither.'*

Above him suddenly a star bursts, stuttering and streaking and kissing and shrieking. It throws the rolling stock shadows high. *'Let me see what spring is like on Jupiter and Mars . . .'* And Lewis sees this and takes it for a sign. The crazy fat naked woman sleeps at last, bare-arsed and undreamed of. Paste and Bucket is brewing tomorrow's coffee in a tarpaulin shack. Peter Rugg is excavating an uncharted wilderness of torn tartan seat covers. So only Mr Lewis has seen it and taken it for a sign. *'In other words please be true!'* And London stirs in its sleep as one, and the stars look down and wince. 'Oh, dear,' they seem to whisper, 'now there'll be trouble.'

'In other words, I love you!'

The Hopi Boy
and the Sun – i

A poor Hopi boy lived with his mother's mother. The people treated him with contempt and threw ashes and sweepings into his grandmother's house, and the two were very unhappy. One day he asked his grandmother who his father was.

'My poor boy, I don't know,' she replied.

'I must find him,' the boy said. 'We can't stay in this place; the people treat me too badly.'

'Grandchild, you must go and see the Sun. He knows who your father is.'

The boy made a plan, and slept.

Hopi Indian legend, reported by
Franz Boas in 1922

Two

In the silent, weightless, black vacuum, by the light of the silvery moon, a ceremonial chalice is drifting towards an outstretched hand, encased in heavy white space exploration gloves, the fingers opening and closing, rehearsing reception. For a moment it hangs suspended, revolving over the centre of the face of the moon, and then it spins out of sight. The white fist clenches shut, empty again. And a voice, outlining the parameters of a mission, or laying down the terms of an initiation, or an interrogatory debriefing, intones, 'You will communicate to us the discovery that you have made, and the circumstances which led to the same.'

High above Hampstead, north-east of the Willesden depot, the moon rises over a four-storey Victorian house, coaxing the slightest of sheens from the scuffed slate roof. A lightbulb blazes alone from the window of an attic bedsit. Mr A.R.Y. Lewis, its valued tenant of ten months, sits wide-eyed and unshaven on a wooden stool, scratching his stubble and gazing at the pictures pinned illegally to the wall; the space shuttle gliding in to land, an astronaut making his one small step, scrumpled newspaper clippings, a postcard of a ruined Somerset abbey, occasional tarot cards, a poster of a shining saintly icon emblazoned with gold leaf, holding a hawthorn bush and a silver cup. Empty spirits bottles, blister packs of prescription drugs and overflowing ashtrays crowd the surfaces.

Lewis runs a hand over a beery little paunch. He doesn't remember it being so pronounced. His body often feels unfamiliar to him, but he can only assume it is really his. He looks at a round-faced alarm clock and smacks his forehead with the flat of his palm. He's been sat since morning trying to make sense of last night's railway siding revelation. If it wasn't for the mud on his shoes, the dirt on his hands, the zone 6 tube ticket in his pocket, and the strange feeling of elation and relief that surges through him, he'd think it was a dream. This month's Prozac pack isn't even opened and when he cups his hands to his mouth and sniffs his own breath there's not a trace of anything. He looks in the mirror. Yes, that's him sure enough, he thinks. He says his name aloud, for reassurance. A.R.Y. Lewis. A meaningless collision of syllables, abandoned words, handed down to him from the discard pile at random, chosen in ignorance in an act of administrative expediency. The hair of his reflection is starting to grey around the temples. His sees a man who, if he'd only take more care of himself, might really be able to make a go of things. Or so Dr Quinton says at the hospital. 'A.R.Y. Lewis.'

He picks up a book and begins to read. *'The Queste del Saint Graal, despite its Arthurian setting, is not a romance, it is a spiritual fable . . .'* Funny. This doesn't feel like a fable. In a pile on the table next to the book, a collection of rail and air tickets tells the story of his own fruitless quest. Lewis had at least seen something of the world, on cheap day returns and bargain ferry breaks, since he'd first put a name to the silver shape that he'd seen so many times in his sleep. When Arthur's courtiers had their vision of the Holy Grail hanging before them, the king dispatched them out into the world to bring him home its precious cargo of the blood of Christ. And Lewis in turn had read the relevant literature, such as it was, privately published by paranoid amateur academics or sold in silvery embossed covers to airport bookshop thrill-seekers.

Lewis's studies had led him to dozens of the Grail's various alleged resting places. He'd been south to Glastonbury, and north of Edinburgh and on to Roslin chapel. He'd crossed the sea to Spain and France to search the Cathar castles, but none of them had the ring of familiarity he had hoped they would, and so he had turned back to the old texts, to comb them for clues once more.

Four a.m. the next night now and Lewis still sits at his desk, turning in his mind from yesterday evening's vision to two years of scrambled half-recollections. Stored in his memory alongside the spinning cup, there's always been the parallel recollection of the scraping sounds of something mechanical, something solid, enormous, white and weightless that he can't yet square with what he's learned. He shuts his eyes and the voices start again.

'T minus five.' Something retracting. A shuddering of metal. 'You are go for launch.' His hammering heart. 'Three minutes, twenty-five seconds and counting.' His fingers wriggling under heavy material. 'T minus three minutes, ten seconds.' A computer whir. The taste of vomit. 'T minus two minutes, forty-five seconds and counting.' An itch he can't scratch, a dry mouth panic. 'T minus one minute, forty-five seconds and counting.' Outside the tin wall, a hiss of something pressurising. 'One minute, twenty-five seconds and counting . . . T minus fifty seconds.' A hum of power. A desire to see the sky, to lie face down in grass and breathe in the smell of the earth. 'T minus seventeen seconds.' A deluge. A belated baptism. Something someone said once, something about 8,000 gallons of water per minute. 'T minus eight point nine seconds.' A sense of heat, elsewhere and unbridled. 'Ignition sequence starts. Six, five, four . . .' Suddenly he opens his eyes. The black bedsit room is gone. He buckles and gags, as trace elements of a suffocating skyward thrust shimmy through his synapses. He shuts his eyes and grips the arms of his chair, gritting his teeth, fighting against gravity. Something rises in his throat and blood rushes to his head. 'We have lift off!'

Lewis wakes later, lying awkward on the floor, his left arm numb under the weight of him, his skin wet with sweat, his breath acrid and burned. He shakes the voices loose from his head, puts on a donkey jacket, and descends the wooden staircase, creeping past the rooms of the sleeping tenants.

To what cause might he reliably ascribe the symptoms of his delirium? He remembers the Tuesday afternoon two years ago, when he found himself talking to a policeman on a side street off Shaftesbury Avenue, swooning with an aching head, barefoot, clad only in white pyjamas, and with no memory of how he had come to be there. People stared and pointed. A young French tourist with a bright yellow rucksack had laughed and taken a picture with a disposable camera. He found two thousand pounds in cash stuffed into his top pocket, and an anonymous typed letter suggesting he buy himself a copy of something called *Loot*, and find a bedsit that didn't require references and took the money up front. 'Good luck, dear unfortunate Brother!' was its final line.

He rounds the corner on to the moonlit main road, his breath forming frosty clouds in front of him, the sucking sounds of air-supply systems echoing somewhere at the back of his mind. Last Easter Sunday he had stood on high in the Whispering Gallery of Saint Paul's Cathedral. Looking down on to scurrying sightseers and square miles of mosaic, he had felt like putting himself to the test. If he jumped, surely he'd just bounce back up again in a single graceful motion, just like he had before, when he bobbed on the astral winds high above the surface of the moon.

A night-bus horn reprimands him as he steps into its path on Haverstock Hill. Momentarily, Lewis finds himself singing one of the old lady's songs, heard drifting over the empty depot the previous evening: *'Well would you like to swing on a star . . .'* Normally he'd never forget himself enough to sing. Something is up. Stopping to buy cigarettes at the Seven-Eleven, he heads for the Heath, a labyrinthine expanse of woodland and common, somehow spared the city's invasive expansion. Soon he is standing at the summit, bleached white in the winter moonlight.

Once he had found himself watching a war film in the window of an electrical shop. He knew the dialogue off by heart, but could have sworn he'd never seen it. And a woman had stopped him on Oxford Street again last week, caught him by the arm, smiling, then looked away. 'I'm sorry, I thought you were somebody else.' 'Maybe I am,' he had replied. But she could have been his sister, his first love, the mother of his child. He wouldn't have known.

The doctor had arranged a small burst of publicity in the local press eighteen months or so ago, hoping he'd be claimed like a lost dog. A forty-year-old Scottish widow who'd liked the look of him tried to pass herself off as a long-lost fiancée. An evening in Pizza Express followed by a reluctant viewing of an Arnold Schwarzenegger film had proved tricky. Then she said they'd met in Birmingham in 1983, but couldn't name a single city street, and had described the Bull Ring shopping centre as 'a great piece of architecture. I remember we both commented on it at the time.'

There had been a woman once, though, however briefly. Mid-November last year Laura, a late twenties bottle blonde, had moved into the ground-floor flat. They met unspeaking at the mailbox by the stairs some mornings, or passed each other silently in the hallway, in the manner of true Londoners. After a week or so, she came to 'borrow a cupful of sugar'. Why only a cupful? he had thought, how could she be so exacting about her sugar requirements? But they got to talking. She was new in town, down from Sheffield. Looking for work, something in the Media, the Arts. Was he doing anything Saturday? She wanted to see a comedian her friend had recommended.

A long tube and bus ride south-east, to a comedy club in a room above a pub in East Dulwich. Struggling for things to say to fill the dead air of the journey, he had had a realisation. Romance is a ritual trade-off of information. Where did you grow up, go to school? What A-levels did you do? Have you ever been to . . . ? Have you ever read . . . ? Did you like . . . ? Do you eat . . . ? And what do you do for a living? When the answers run out, love dies on the vine. After half an hour of being evasive, he had to come clean. 'I don't remember,' he said, 'I don't remember anything.'

Suddenly he was the little lost boy that she was on a mission to save. Where initially she'd been guarded, even reserved, now she was clasping his hands in sympathy, running her fingers over his face to make him understand how very deeply she felt for his plight. He realised he could choose to see his unfortunate predicament as a single man's boon, swapping his memory for a lifetime of compensatory sex and mothering. A more cynical man would have been moved to celebration.

Ten minutes into the first act, and he wasn't really getting it. 'Do you remember Spangles?' bellowed a whey-faced twenty-something into the mike. 'What were they all about? They were green, weren't they, some of them were anyway.' The audience laughed. But Lewis didn't. He couldn't remember Spangles. Or Chopper Bikes. Or John Noakes. Or the Clangers. And so he couldn't really see why it would be so very funny if the Clangers, whoever they were, had had sex, or smoked dope, but he understood it would involve them going to the all-night garage and asking for chocolate and rolling papers in high-pitched, unintelligible voices. But Laura only seemed to find this even more endearing.

'I love this room, don't you?' she had said, as she sank her third pint of snakebite during the first interval. What's to love? he had thought. It was a room above a South London pub, like any other, peeling paint, a beer-crate stage, and an Australian barmaid. 'Look at the little designs in the eaves,' she said, pointing. And carved into the corners of the ceiling cornices were tiny quadrilateral shapes, images of compasses superimposed over set squares. 'Freemasons!' Laura had said. 'They must have used this room as a meeting place at some stage. God knows what they got up to.'

'I'm sorry,' he had replied. 'I don't know what you're talking about.'

'No, of course you wouldn't, I'm sorry . . .' She hugged him to her. Her clothes smelt new, her hair dye chemically suspect.

The apparently traditional coffee question and a fumbled kiss on the doorstep, and she came upstairs. He had switched on the light before he'd really stopped to think about creating a good impression. Suddenly he wished he'd cleared away the Prozac packaging, maybe taken down some of the pictures. But Laura wasn't scared off. She studied his homemade gallery, her eyes wandering from Neil Armstrong to Joseph of Arimathea, curious at worst. 'What's all this stuff, then?'

'Just things that catch my fancy. They don't mean anything. I don't know why any of them appealed to me. Tea or coffee?' Back then, he hadn't been lying. Back then, his little theory had yet to form. Lucky really. If he'd told her he thought he'd once been an astronaut, and had held in his hands the Holy Grail, and within it the blood of Christ . . .

'Well, there's one thing you haven't forgotten,' she had said, later, clamping his rotating head between her thighs. But what did she expect? A dog may not remember Spangles but it still has instincts. But Laura had moved out again before Christmas. She didn't leave a forwarding address. *'Fly me to the moon . . .'*

He stops in a clearing, and sits on a bench to light a cigarette. The smoke curls up into the air and, as he looks through it at the glistening stars and out over the scattered orange street lights of the sleeping city, he starts to remember once more. Exhilarated, he feels as if he's falling again, the pitted, cratered surface of the moon rushing up to meet him head on, as it had done so many nights before.

'Looking for something?' A voice breaks his chain of thought. A man has sat next to him, fifty-five and fat of face, with pendulous St Bernard dog jowls, black hairs sprouting from ears and nose, Toby jug body smothered in a brown camel coat, bald head squeezed into a floppy felt hat. The man is offering a cigarette.

'Thanks.' He takes one, his own having long since fizzled out in the wet air.

'Well,' asks the man, reaching forward, cupping a gold lighter in leather gloved hands, 'are you looking for something?'

'I suppose I am. But I doubt I'll ever remember what it is.'

'Indeed. Well, I can assure you, young fellow, you won't find anything looking up at the stars, the treacherous old tarts!' The old man clears his throat, shakes a surplus acreage of chins, and continues: 'It would be lovely if we could all carry moonbeams home in a jar, of course, but those winking lights have been put there to taunt us, little shining points of unattainable joy and beauty, the flickering tits, no more than marsh gas, ingenious flatus, ignorant fatuous, wicked will o' the wisps, space farts that light the way to dusty death. If I were a younger man, why, I'd huff and I'd puff and I'd blow them all down, each and every one of the spangled trollops.' He inhales, swells up, and puffs out his cheeks, then totters in his seat a little, exhausted, and swigs at a hip flask of revitalising spirits before resuming. 'We must learn to ignore Heaven's tiny shiny Jack o' Lanterns, you and I, if we are to attain a truly higher state of grace. Obey the dictates of your own conscience. And let us invoke instead the assistance of the Great Architect! He will help you to repair your loss. Come, we shall both put our stargazing days behind us.' He clasps Lewis's hand. 'We may be the instruments of each other's salvation. Forget your moonbeam and stop up your jar. Here on earth alone, dear boy, may lie that which you seek.' Somewhere in Highgate, a church bell tolls out across the Heath. 'Turn again, Whittington, I implore you!' And the fat man leans over and kisses Lewis full on the lips. A pause. The man raises an umbrella over his face, anticipating a Hampstead Heath battering. 'I do apologise. I seem to have misread the situation rather seriously. I meant no harm . . .' But A.R.Y. Lewis

28

is laughing, spluttering up joyous nicotine phlegm, as he vanishes into the night.

The Hampstead Man composes himself. He waits a while then stands, suddenly sober, and strides purposefully away, whispering under his breath. 'Happy have we met, happy may we part, and happy meet again.'

Tracy stops at a railway crossing on a side road south-west of Shiprock. She grips the wheel tightly as she stares at the barrier through the dust-smeared windshield. The world stretches out around the vehicle, horizon to horizon, vast and uncontained. In her rear-view mirror the angular outcrop of Shiprock itself rises high into the sky, breaking the uniformity of the flatlands, like a brick dropped on to a bowling green. There was some local native myth attached to it, explaining away the geographical incongruity as the whim of some picaresque spirit, or the mechanics of some prophecy of salvation, but she is still too scrambled to recall it properly. She shuts her eyes. She thinks of Roscoe, dead in the bath half a day's drive behind her. Blood. Gut. Hair. The half-smoked cigarette. And she remembers the first time she ever spent a night with a man, a boy not unlike Roscoe. Six months later she had watched her father beating Chico around the head and face with a monkey wrench in the parking lot of Denny's, until she'd somehow managed to tear him away. The boy lost a lot of teeth, and an eye, and had seemed kind of slow ever since. But her father knew people, and had managed to smooth things over. Within a year of the beating, Tracy was gone for good.

Something stirs in her stomach and she feels an urge to retch. She snatches at the door handle and stumbles out on to the sand, the engine still running. A cluster of giant Saguaro cacti crowd the skyline around her as she lurches over the boiling blacktop and into the midst of the lofty succulents. They shouldn't be here, a day's drive north of their usual spawning ground, but they are here none the less. She places her hand between scrubby barbs, leaning on a green trunk for support as everything starts to spin. Half-buried rocks nudge out from the desert floor, suddenly the skulls of the dead, staring up at her, mouthing wordless accusations. She falls forward into a patch of open ground and turns to face the sun. A thirty-foot cactus looms over her, its two stubby arms held out at right angles in supplication, a perfect green crucifix, framing her body on the brown dirt below in the apex of its outstretched shadow, the sun hung midway behind it, crowning its head with a halo of radiant light. Flickering and blurred in the heat haze, the plants point truncated fore-limbs towards her, or over her shoulder, back to the wreckage she left behind her this morning in a motel miles back down the highway.

She sees the two-inch Christian comic books in her bag, two-tone angels sat in judgement, the gates of Heaven barred before her, and St Michael checking his log, before raising a cloaked arm and stretching out a pointed index finger to redirect her final journey southwards a way of paradise. 'For there is nothing covered, that shall not be revealed; and hid, that shall not be known.' And, under the influence of the little comic book, the tall cactus becomes an agent of Heaven, halo-headed and raised on high, staring down, awaiting explanation. Somewhere west, the train whistle blows. The railway track's growing rattle is the sound of a portcullis sliding down, of gates closing for good, of a cell door locking shut, night after night, day after day, till she's clasping her hands to her ears to block out the clamour.

And then it's passed her by. There is silence, the sound of the engine still spluttering at the crossing. She brushes the sand off her clothes and walks to the car. She flips open the trunk. Roscoe's toolkit glistens in the sun. It had lain there unused all the months she had known him, but had offered at least possibility of gainful employment when they ran out of pocket change and promises. She shuffles through the metal box, turning over grimy wrenches and hammers.

A truck passes by, somewhat in excess of the speed limit,

bobbing over the tracks without slowing. Something catches the driver's eye. For a moment there, he could have sworn, he saw a lone woman attempting to fell a thirty-foot cactus with only a handsaw.

In the back seat of the 4-wheel, Bob Nequatewa wakes with a start and cries out. His grandson looks up from a magazine and clasps his shoulder.

'What's the matter, Bob?' asks the driver, not unkindly. 'Feel a disturbance in the Force?'

'Something like that . . .' says Bob Nequatewa, and shuts his eyes. This will be the last time he will wear the clothes of the clown. He is going to Phoenix to make his final perform- ance, a travesty of all he ever learned. But, hey, there's folks on the reservation could use the money.

Like a good clown, Bob Nequatewa has clowned his way through life. Now all those whose laughter he once worked for have long since left. But once . . .

'Yaahahay!' he would shout, announcing his presence on a rooftop, black and white, and all but naked, overlooking the whirling *katsina* dancers. He always arrived late on the festival days, past noon, lagging behind his destiny. Then he would struggle, falling and tumbling, into the square, clambering over stray buckets and bales and grappling with the dancers, clutching at their bright feathered costumes and props, saying, 'This is mine!' and 'This is mine!' and 'This is mine!' But now Bob Nequatewa looks down at his crumpled body and no longer feels any need for such elaborate metaphors for life. He is a living example of the struggle, a barely living example. If the Owl *katsina* were to whip him for his disobedience today, he would probably buckle and break.

He looks back at his grandson, staring out of the window at the moving landscape, and remembers the day when, as a young boy himself, he realised he wanted to be a clown.

It was the middle of a hot dry summer. In those days the clowns were as priests, shaman-satirists, perfect fools, and

31

when one of them passed away the funeral was a great public occasion. Bob had stood holding his mother's hand, her best shawl slung over her usual work clothes, as the body of the old clown, clad in full festival costume, was carried on a stretcher of skin through the village, by four younger clowns, hair in bunches with black and white face paint. The town crier called out over the rooftops of the pueblo, ordering the mourners to gather in the square. The clowns carried the body along the west side of the plaza, and up on to the flat roof of the highest house, and the people assembled in the shadow of the building.

When everyone was there, looking upwards and shielding their eyes from the sun, the clowns picked up the body, an arm and a leg each, and stood at the edge of the roof. 'Yaahahay!' they hollered, and swung the body out over the plaza as if to throw it down on to the onlookers. Then again, with gasps of amazement from the people as they pulled the corpse back from the brink at the last possible moment. And then again, to the same astonished response. And then a fourth time. But this time the clowns let the corpse fly. And the body of the old clown soared high into the sky, passing momentarily over the face of Father Sun, and then fell down into the square, smashing and shattering in the sand. The clowns hollered, 'Yaahahay!'

And then everybody laughed.

And that was the day Bob Nequatewa realised he wanted to be a clown.

'If it may be so, may I gain at least one smile.'

This will be the last time he will wear the clothes of the clown. There is nothing left to be done and nothing left to be said. Beside him, his grandson taps him on the arm. 'Are we almost there yet, grandpa?'

Beneath the traffic rumble of Fleet Street and the café chatter of Covent Garden, an oak door swings open in silence on to a subterranean room. Still shaky from his late night out on the cold heath, the Hampstead Man enters, sweating under his heavy camel coat. He hangs the coat on a peg, sits on a small wooden bench, and considers. It had been expedient to sound Lewis out a little by following him to the Heath. But, henceforth, his assistance will be as unobtrusive as possible, though a loss so important could not fail to be generally and severely felt. And in the event of success he would communicate the discovery that he had made, and the circumstances that led to the same. Poor Lewis's sense of longing steered him skywards. The Hampstead Man had merely pointed him back towards the earth. 'Turn again, Whittington!' he had said, more to amuse himself than anything.

There was a nobility in service of the Craft that was not to be underestimated. The Hampstead Man knew that the prize his masters hoped Lewis would lead them to was probably of no real value. An old vessel, long since fallen from use, with a few insignificant organic flakes floating inside it. Had he not been taught that there was a holy beauty in anything functional? But the cup's symbolic importance was, in this case, paramount. To bring it home once more where it belonged, from whence to commit it again to an eternal safekeeping, was to follow the will of the Great Architect, and to follow the will of the Great Architect was to set things right, and to be of use. What higher calling could there be? It was the Hampstead Man's duty to knock off all superfluous knobs and excrescences; to further smooth and prepare the stones; to adjust the rectangular corners of the buildings; to assist in bringing rude matter into due form; to lay and prove the horizontals; to adjust uprights while fixing them on their proper bases; for thus, by square conduct, level steps and upright intentions, one might hope to ascend to those immortal mansions whence all goodness emanates. And so he would continue to make diligent search, throughout the Universe, until time or circumstances shall restore the genuine article. Such was the predominant wish of his heart.

*   *   *

Six p.m. at Pixies' Wine Bar, and underneath a wall-mounted green garden ornament statue of a leering wide-mouthed goblin, Danny and Sid are chatting to the regulars. They have suffered a half-hour rhapsody from the women present about Timothy Waterhouse's marvellous performance on TV last night, and are now answering questions about their own, rather more mundane, musical careers.

'Put it this way,' Sid says to Alicia, a forty-seven-year-old ex-air hostess who once got two thousand quid out of a Channel 4 documentary crew by convincing them she was a women's bare-knuckle prize-fighting champion, 'nobody suffers Alfredo's Licensed Kebab and Vegetarian House of Delicious Mediterranean Eats and Live Music, 1137a Streatham High Road, for the sake of the food. And nobody takes a bus that far beyond the end of the Northern Line to check out its music, unless your idea of quality is an endless stream of tribute bands paying tribute to artists who, at best, deserved only the tribute of being battered to death with sticks.'

'Right, but it has a late bar and needs live music for the licence?'

'You guessed it. But it's hardly worth being tortured by the kind of acts they book at Alfredo's just to get an after-hours' drink, even if you are a certified alcoholic. How's this for an all-star line-up, right? Wednesdays it's Shepperton Starship, a group of elderly men from Shepperton who, aided by a Dutch Grace Slick un-look-a-like, faithfully re-create the sound of Jefferson Starship, but will not touch any of the band's earlier, Jefferson Airplane, classics because "this band is about quality musicianship and adult-orientated power rock at its best, Sid, not 'groovy beat music'. We build our city on rock 'n' roll!" Then on Fridays, it's Shakin' Steven . . .'

'Shakin' *Stevens* . . .'

'No, Ali,' says Danny, with a mouthful of crisps, 'Shakin' *Steven,* a fat bloke called Steven from Dollis Hill who does a tribute to Shakin' Stevens. And has motor neurone disease.'

'No!'

Danny admits that he's made up the bit about motor neurone disease, but that the rest is true. The regulars discuss the ridiculousness of the continued existence of Shakin' Stevens, and how he is essentially just a tribute act to Elvis himself. Sid, typically, reminds them that in the early 70s the raw rock and roll of Shakin' Stevens and the Sunsets was seen as a viable alternative to the progressive rock dinosaurs of Yes or Genesis.

'Fuck that,' Danny interrupts, swallowing and gesturing at Alicia with a large crisp. 'It's life imitating art imitating Elvis, isn't it? It's a veritable postmodern hall of mirrors. It has to be seen to be believed, I assure you. But only once.'

'What's tonight, then?' says Derek, turning away from beating his wife at Scrabble again and leaning over the bar to join the conversation.

'Tuesdays? Tuesdays and Thursdays are the highlights of the week,' boasts Danny. 'Tuesdays and Thursdays is our lot . . . the Sultans of Streatham. Relive the magic of Dire Straits twice a week for a minimal cover charge!' Everybody laughs. 'Be sure to arrive early to witness the collapse of all Sid ever held sacred.' Alicia sneezes the best part of her fifth vodka and Red Bull out of her shining nose. Sid feels the colour rise in his cheeks. Why does Danny do this? In private he's capable of being supportive, sympathetic even. But once they're out of the flat he becomes a caricature of himself, particularly if women are around. His accent drifts west, his nostrils flare, and he resorts to the ever-less convincing option of playing the wild rover. Oh, no, never no more. Please. It must be wonderful, thinks Sid, to be able to buy into a broad cultural stereotype whenever you feel the urge to grow bigger. Sid wonders sometimes if he really knows Danny at all, and if Danny really knows himself between the blarney and the bitterness. While Danny rises, ruts and flourishes, Sid can only retreat into sexless grammar school neutrality, bobbing out from beneath what remains of an overhang of hair. Thus, he had spent most of the early 90s standing in the corner at parties, being patted pitifully on the head by female trainee solicitors, while Danny was in an alley outside, trousers down in the drizzle, doing something dirty and wrong up against a drainpipe with a woman he wouldn't even swap phone numbers with. Danny senses his friend's weakness and goes in for the kill. 'Of course, Sid's just biding his time. His "real" area of interest is late 60s psychedelic music, and he genuinely thinks we'd be more successful if we tried to play our own twenty-first-century British version of . . . who's your favourite band, Sidney?'

'Luther Peyote and the Round Tabyls.'

'Long-haired types, were they, Sid?' says Derek. 'Bongo music?'

'Not really. It was more . . .' Sid trails off. What was it? How could he begin to explain in mere words, to this ragbag of musical illiterates, the full significance of Luther Peyote and the Round Tabyls?

Sid had first heard Luther in the Virgin Megastore, Wolverhampton. Unlike the muscle-bound crunch of the metal and punk staples his schoolfriends and he were weaned on, the guitar sound that suddenly took over the shop's speakers was thin and anaemic, as if mocking the very notion of rock music with its proud weakness. There was a kind of hissing noise running all through the song, a wobbling rhythm, like bent thunder, and strung senselessly over the surface of the sound, a caterwauling, coyote-shrieking singer, who threw infinitesimally complex phrases into the mix with a cavalier disregard for phrasing and metre. Apparently, 'Totems lost are now arising, circles ringed in evil hour, ancient seed of unclean angels, through the eggs into the flower.' What could the man possibly mean? But it made perfect sense to his twelve-year-old self. Years later Danny suggested to Sid that Luther was really singing 'throw the eggs into the flour', and that the song was actually a recipe for flan. When he wants to wind Sid up he still calls Luther the Flan Man. Admittedly, there were Dutch Eurovision songs that made more sense than Luther's more elliptical lyrics, but Sid was already smitten. Standing there on the shop floor, he hadn't been sure if he loved or hated the record. In fact, the music had made him a little nauseous. But suddenly he felt his ears fold in on themselves and suck in the sound, as the very wrongness of what he was hearing began to thrill him and give him wings, and for a second he thought the whole store would melt and turn to mud.

The wild-haired man in the paisley patterned shirt, who worked behind the counter on Saturdays, had put the music on. Sid asked him what it was, and he wordlessly flashed him the cover: '*Chainmail Moccasins* – Luther Peyote and The Round Tabyls.' And underneath the lettering an enormous multicoloured eye stared out as if daring him to part with his paper-round money. The shop assistant had given him the signal. With one brief flick of the twelve-inch sleeve, he had lifted the flap of the secret speakeasy of record collector hell; it beckoned, and invited Sid in. On the wall behind the counter, the fake social realism or sword and sorcery sleeves of dozens of new wave and hard rock albums wilted into insignificance. Sid handed over the money. Four pounds and ninety-nine pence. And he was lost. His life was never to be the same again. He had Luther Peyote to blame for a thousand wasted weekends trawling record fairs, for the fact that be-jumpered men in second-hand shops knew him by name, for his chronic inability to put anything by for a rainy day, and for the fact that he disappointed his parents by quitting the church choir and buying himself an electric guitar. Luther Peyote had single-handedly condemned Sid to spend eternity walking the world in search of a hit as powerful as that first dose. Well, if not the world, then at least the multicoloured aisles of the appro-priate music stores. But for that one childhood moment, when he'd glimpsed a vision of Heaven and Hell on the first floor of the Virgin Megastore, it had all been worth it. Abby, in her less patient moments, had invoked her professional authority and called it a form of autism. But she would never understand. None of them would ever understand.

'Anyhow,' Danny interrupts Sid's thoughts, 'Sid thinks a

"bongo music" band would pull even more punters than a Dire Straits tribute group. So I figure I may as well stick with the Sultans of Streatham. The alternative is too terrible to contemplate.' Everyone laughs again. At Sid. His fists clench and unclench uselessly. At this precise wrong moment, Abby enters the bar, brushing wind-wet hair off her face. 'Sid,' she says, her hot breath clouding the air in front of her. 'They've pulled in one of my outpatients for causing trouble in Leicester Square. The police want me to go up town and vouch for him.' Sid's face falls. The prospect of Abby's presence had at least threatened to make the dreary experience yet another dismal trudge through the empty, tundra-like expanses of Private Investigations a little less unbearable this week.

'Let the mad bastard rot, I say!' shouts Danny.

Abby ignores him and kisses Sid goodbye. 'See you later. I'm sorry.' He watches her leave. Abby never comes along to see us any more, he notes.

'Now be fair, Sid,' says Danny. 'That's a pretty good excuse. And it's not like she's going to be having it away with the kind of feller who stands around outside Burger King with his knob out shouting at pigeons, now, is it?'

An hour later, ten stops up the Northern Line, Abby waits at the counter as two policemen lead her patient out of the cells. Peter Rugg is dressed as usual, a Hawkwind vest under layers of mutually inappropriate shirts, black jeans gone brown, gathering at the knee, open-toed sandals flopping to reveal two different football socks, half a dozen necklaces of coral and keys, feathers and pebbles, and a blue woolly Birmingham City FC bobble hat. He looks like the kind of acid-casualty 60s survivor Sid used to insist on taking her to see playing to all but no one in some North London dive, back when she could still stand to spend a whole evening with him. Peter Rugg shakes a dog mane of hair and hails her from within a foaming beard.

'Dr Quinton! I knew I could count on you! Now, if you'd

just explain to these gentlemen that there's been a grave misunderstanding then they can set the Wanderer free! These wallies have grasped the proverbial stick by the proverbial wrong end, well and truly, I say.' One of the policemen sighs, and approaches her with a clipboard.

'What's Peter been up to this time, then?'

'You know the Prince Charles Cinema, love, corner of China Town?'

'Yes.'

'Well, he was in there, running around, kicking people out of their chairs and trying to pull the seats off the hinges, generally acting threatening and violent.'

'It was there, Dr Quinton,' the old man shouts, round-eyed, 'or something like it. I smelt it. I thought I'd find it the night before last out west, see, when I saw about a million trains. All those juicy seats and no fucking arses in the way. But no. It weren't to be. But somebody was smoking it up there in the cinema tonight, I tell you, smoking it for sure, or something like it, and I smelt it out with my psychic nose!' Peter Rugg fixes the officers with a resentful stare. 'And I would have found it, too.'

Abby stands between Peter and the policeman. 'Mr Rugg suffers from a somewhat problematic delusion, officer. If you'll let me explain . . .' The policemen silently raise their eyebrows and gesture for her to continue. 'In 1972, you see, Mr Rugg dropped a burning cigarette end down the back of a seat.' The policemen smirk knowingly at her little white lie, but she continues. 'It caused a fire, burning down the home of a friend of his. Mr Rugg has spent the rest of his life trying to find the cigarette end in question, usually down the back of seats, to put things right. It's a form of obsessive compulsive disorder exacerbated by trauma and guilt.'

The policeman hands Abby the relevant paperwork. 'Jesus!' He turns back to Peter Rugg and uncuffs him. 'Have you got any idea how many cigarettes are smoked every day in London alone, Mr Rugg?'

'Well, officer, I estimate it's about twenty-five million, but I don't have access to the exact figures. I wrote to the government. They know, of course they do, but they won't tell the likes of us, will they? Scared of what old Peter Rugg might find out, they are.' Peter Rugg taps his nose knowingly. The policeman winces. 'Never give up hope, officer. What are we without hope, eh?' The policeman shrugs.

Abby picks up a pen. 'Peter? Fancy a cup of tea after all this is over?'

'No. Milkshake?' Milkshake then. Whatever it takes. She bends over the desk and writes. The policemen look at her legs and make approving faces, rocking backwards and forwards on the balls of their boots. Peter Rugg looks at the floor, scanning the skirting for cigarette butts.

Minutes later, Abby follows him through Leicester Square, heading towards Burger King to make good her milkshake promise. Hundreds of Euro-teens crowd around a Spanish man singing Oasis songs in a paella-mouthed accent, to the rapturous applause of the nationally displaced. It's one of the most awful sounds Abby's ever heard, but the pound coins are collecting all the same, tossed into an upturned sombrero at the singer's feet by children who don't fully understand their value. Maybe Sid should consider a change of direction. He could probably pretend to be Spanish at least as convincingly as he pretends to be a member of Dire Straits. She stands and watches a moment longer while Peter, as usual, scrabbles around on the pavement, searching for dog-ends and putting them into a plastic bag.

'I'll check 'em when I get home, see,' he explains. Suddenly something catches his eyes from across the square and he takes her hand and drags her through the crowds of inter-railing revellers to the front of the Swiss Centre. Beneath the clock, a barrel-gutted Mohican punk in a Motorhead T-shirt and a tartan kilt is entertaining a small crowd of swaying drunks, blasting out a formless dirge on an ancient-looking set of bagpipes.

'Billy!' shouts Peter, and pushes through the onlookers. Abby follows.

Billy sets down his pipes and smiles. 'Ruggsy! The Wanderer!' Abby clocks the tracklines up the piper's arms, something too shiny in his eyes, as the two men embrace. 'I've been doing like you said, Ruggsy,' he says, and reaches behind him.

'You're a star, Billy Bagpipes, a regular highland thing!' The piper hands Peter a bulging black bin bag. Peter sets it on the pavement and opens it. It is full of dog-ends.

'They're not all rollies, mind, Peter. I think I picked up a few wee fag butts by accident you know, but I wasn't necessarily at my best when I was looking, know what I'm saying.'

'Don't worry about it, Billy, that's marvellous. What did we agree, now?'

'Twenty quid a bag, Ruggsy, I believe.'

Abby watches despairingly as Peter fumbles through his pockets and hands over the fee. 'Don't spend it all on short-bread, now, Billy. Get yourself in a hostel for the night, eh?'

Abby brings two milkshakes over from the counter and sits down next to the overflowing bin bag. Drunk diners eye her suspiciously. Peter returns from a circuit of the room, his hands full of ashtrays, and empties them into the bag. He sits down. 'Thanks for coming and getting us, Doc. Much appreciated.'

'I can't keep doing this, Peter.'

'Yeah, I know. But I have to find that bloody rollie, see, you know. I explained it to you.' He sucks noisily on the shake. People stare.

'Finding it, even if you could find it, which you never will, won't help you, Peter. It won't undo the fire.'

'Two points, Doc. One, I will find it. Mexican grass, see? Very distinctive smell. I can tell now it ain't in this bin bag just from one sniff of it, but Billy's a good boy. He does what he can, but he doesn't know, not like me.'

'And your second point?'

'Eh? Oh, yeah, right. Secondly, I know that finding the pesky

41

joint that undid me won't "undo" the fire. But I am a shaman, see? I'm working through a ritual here. I've got a system. And when I find that joint the planets will align, water will turn into wine, people will shit pressed flowers and cum gold leaf, and global harmony will reign supreme. Biff! Bang!! Pow!!! You'll see it happen. Shazam! By the power of Castle Greyskull! Suddenly everything will settle. The world will take wings! One day you'll wake up smiling, all tingly and happy with your fanny on fire, and you'll think, "Stone me! Peter Rugg must have found what he was looking for! The Wanderer has worked his magic. The old psychedelic wally-lord, he's disappeared in smoke!" And when I finally find that joint, a whole chapter of my life will be closed, too. The End! Bam! If you enjoyed this title here are some others you may like.'

'It's been a long chapter, Peter. A lot of dog-ends.'

'Don't think I don't know, Doc . . .' he sucks up more of the shake, '. . . and I'm getting heartily sick of the job in hand to be quite honest. I'm gettin' a crick in me neck, and the stink of my room! Fuck! There's things I wanna do, places I wanna go, people I wanna meet. But it's hard to find the time when you spend all day searching down the back of train seats for a thirty-year-old joint.'

'So, why not just stop?'

'I can't. I have to see it through. What you don't get, Doc, is this. I don't need treatment. I just need to find that joint. I'm supposed to see you again tomorrow morning you know, Doc, but I'm wasting your time, really.'

'Not really, Peter,' says Abby, staring at an onion ring. 'Tonight you saved me from something truly terrible.'

Three

Tracy spent the morning burning up the highways at legally inadvisable speeds, and swerving round gesticulating truck drivers, oblivious to anything that might be approaching, as if welcoming the opportunity of collision. But now she's been calmed by cigarettes, by FM radio, by the scrub and sage blur, by the empty planes of the Arizona desert, and by chopping down a cactus with a handsaw. Yes, that felt good. To her right, hints of the solid buttes and soaring pinnacles of Monument Valley peek over the horizon, and roadside Navajo trading posts flash blue jade jewellery from under flapping awnings. She cruises under the midday sun at an easy pace, to an undisclosed point in the distance, where two-lane blacktop bisects the brown acres, slides between the staggering rock stacks, and slips silently under the curtain of a stonewall azure horizon. She had peeled back the car top an hour or so ago, and the wind in her face creates an illusion of cleansing. But Roscoe will be found soon, wrapped in swaddling and laid to rest, another corpse to bear on her back for ever, another wasted year, and another point off her licence come Judgement Day. What did the Christian comic books say? She remembered a cartoon of a naked, Flintstone-faced man, rising shocked from the grave to face the heavenly jury.

'Judgement? You don't understand! Heaven and Hell are here on Earth – I've always said that!' If she let herself, she'd weep for ever. Instead, she must plan a new identity, a new life, and find a hiding place for a year or so. She imagines a sheriff's office somewhere not so very far away, a map full of pins, and a web of coloured string that connects them, each and every one, waiting for her to walk straight into its state correctional cast-iron centre. But not now, not after she's come so far . . . As she passes the sign for Kayenta the sun is at its highest.

She pulls off the 160 into a gas station next to a cinema and fills up. The local Burger King advertises an exhibition of the work of the Navajo Code Breakers, and Japanese tourists file up in good faith to learn how the Native Americans saved the nation from subjugation by the land of the rising sun. Through the window, she sees a photograph of the ruins of Nagasaki displayed next to an advertisement for a Cheeseburger Meal and Free Drink. Outside the gas station, a revolving tin sign flaps and clatters endlessly in the dry wind, alternately advising of GAS and FOOD. Simply standing still for a second on the shadeless forecourt is enough to make skin smoke. In the washroom she ties her black hair back up off her face and runs her hands under the cool water. Once they were neat and groomed, croupier's hands for a season or two some years back, but this morning she's chewed the corners of her fingernails down to the bloody quick. She scrubs at them with liquid soap. She looks at herself in the mirror. She's holding up well for her thirty-five years, she thinks, and most of them spent shrivelling under the sun in Arizona, Nevada, Southern California and Mexico, or freezing in the bleached, nocturnal, air-conditioned environs of casinos and table-dancing clubs. Unmade-up, she has a natural, easy kind of charm. 'A person would trust this face,' she thinks. 'It don't look like the face of a killer.' And then she catches herself out, 'And it ain't.' Someone has left one of the Christian comics hanging from a string by the cistern. *Doom Town – The Story*

Of Sodom, and an orange skull rises over an unlit cityscape. The usual ballpoint message: 'Please pass this on to a friend when you have finished with it.' Tracy pulls it loose and puts it in her pocket. Another for the collection.

In the store, she pushes her sunglasses to the end of her nose, and hugs biscuits, soft drinks and cigarettes between her bare arms. She pays the clerk at the counter, an elderly Navajo man who eyes her suspiciously. They fumble with the change and bump hands and heads as they both reach to pick a fallen cent or two off the top of a stack of *National Enquirer*s. She regrets having given him longer to form an impression. 'A pretty girl, but clumsy and nervous,' he'll tell the police, 'with dry skin. And ugly fingers,' he'll add, if she's very unlucky and it makes the local news.

When she goes back out to the car a young man is sitting on the back seat, all tight drainpipe blue jeans and splayed legs, a dirty dog on heat, in a cowboy hat and faded denim shirt. He stretches out over the door, languidly, and bawls an affected drawl. 'Morning, ma'am. Travelling alone?' Tracy doesn't answer, and just eyes him, left hand on her hip, her little grocery bag dangling limply from the other. He continues, unfazed. ''Cos if you are, I figured maybe you could use a little company, to make the days pass faster, and maybe make the nights pass real slow, you know what I'm saying.' He slides his hand into his shirt, idly pulling back a flap of material, revealing a hairless boy's body and an almost invisible brown nipple. 'I'm Brad. But you can call me whatever you like, whatever makes you feel good.'

Tracy sets her bag on the tarmac. 'Listen . . . Brad. I've loved many men in the last fifteen years, all of them better men than you, and every single one of them is lying somewhere between here and Mexico City, throats slit, wrists slashed, necks broken, arms and legs separated from their bodies by speeding locomotives, heads crushed by passing trucks, guts contorted by deadly poisons, hearts broken and dead, all dead, everyone of them dead.'

45

Brad's eyes widen a little under the brim of his hat. 'Ma'am?'

'Now, do you really think you still want to come with me?'

He pauses, straightens up in her back seat and buttons up his shirt. 'No, ma'am. I'll probably wait and see if I can get me a different ride.'

'I think that would be best.' She picks up her bag again and jangles her car keys at him coercively. Brad hops out of the car and walks towards the road, turning only to call back, 'You be nice to your boyfriends, now, lady.'

Tracy climbs into the driver's seat. She goes to light a cigarette. Behind grimy glass the garage man is making a phone call, looking at her as he speaks. She accelerates off the forecourt, out on to the highway. The dust from her back wheels makes a caged coyote outside the store spin round in discomfort, snarling. Brad looks down at it, looks up the road after her, picks something black out of his nose and licks it off a nicotine-stained finger.

Two a.m. at Alfredo's, before an audience that almost reaches double figures, and Sid limply plucks out the jaunty bassline of the Sultans' climactic closing number, 'The Walk Of Life'. Glancing behind him at the band, Danny thunking out the pedestrian bash and pop rhythm, Andy dozing through the lead breaks while dreaming of joining a stadium metal band, Fat Ian manfully strumming, and all of them stooping ashamedly in stone-washed denims, white vests and bandanas, he winces a little. And then he stares out at Alfredo's clientele, two unlucky Streatham High Road whores who failed to score, spraying last week's profit margins up against the bar, and three elderly Irish drunks, straining to disagree with each other about absolutely nothing of any importance over the inoffensive un-rock of Dire Straits' back catalogue. And Sid wonders who here should be the most ashamed, these broken late-night drinkers, or these broke moonlighting musicians.

Finally, the song scuttles to an end. Three stained women, huddled round a sleeping, tomato-sauce-smeared man, stand up and applaud, spilling their last dregs of house red. For a moment Andy seems delighted, acknowledging them with a clenched fist victory salute, but as they burst into laughter even he realises they were just being sarcastic.

Fat Ian steps up to the mic: 'Thank you, London, and good-night! It's time to go home. You've been enjoying a "walk" through the back catalogue of Dire Straits in the company of us, the Sultans of Streatham, and that was our last number tonight, "The Walk of Life". See you every Tuesday and Thursday here at Alfredo's!'

They begin to clear the gear. 'I bet they can't wait,' mutters Danny, unscrewing a cymbal. 'I happen to know that y'man there with the caliper and the big piss mark on his crotch thinks our interpretation of "Brothers In Arms" is the bollocks.' No one laughs. Alfredo comes onstage to pay them, mumbling something about adding the balance on to Thursday's money and a cash-flow problem, his wobbling tits straining at the buttons of a dated dress shirt, his fingers kneading the air in apology like stubby salamis.

Travelling home to Balham, Sid had volunteered to sit in the back of Ian's spluttering Bedford van. Usually he'd be up front with a Luther Peyote tape in the stereo, forcing the others to appreciate the subtle intricacies of some country rock raga, but tonight the gulf between his ambitions and his reality seems too great to endure. Squeezed alone between the drums and amps, Sid's mind wanders as he recalls a long drunk night spent alone in Edinburgh once, for some forgotten reason. It finally lurched to closure at a strip club, or 'go-go bar' as the Scots euphemistically called them back in the puritanical late 80s, nestled at the foot of a winding stone cobbled stair, some-where between the gates of the castle and the gates of the meadow. The dancer had been introduced to the ten or so spectators by the barman as Jeannie, a plain porridge-fed girl of no more than nineteen, and she had put her 20 pence into the jukebox to select a backing track, before clambering from the surface of the bar up on to the stage, a tiny, two-foot-square shelf nailed up into the corner of the back wall by the door to the toilet. As some self-consciously sleazy, five years out of date, electro-pop crackled into plodding half life, Jeannie's black plastic boots, hotpants and bra glistened in the lights, and it became clear her chosen theme that evening was a sexless variant of S&M. Taking a toy rubber whip out of the crumpled Scot Mid supermarkets plastic bag at her feet, Jeannie cracked it listlessly, clipped the fluorescent light fitting above her head, and abruptly ceased to go-go anywhere at all, as a thousand tiny slivers of shattered glass shimmied slowly down through a dense fug of cigarette smoke and embarrass-ment, sprinkling like spiky spring catkins on to her semi-naked skin. Without even giving poor wee Jeannie the option to climb down and shake herself clean, the barman simply passed her up a dustpan and brush, and gestured at the wreckage. And Sid had sat, sipping a half of Heavy, watching a virtually naked teenage girl crouch on her hands and knees above a dozen staring drunks, brushing broken glass into a blue plastic pan, wisps of ginger pubic hair wriggling free of the sides of her straining PVC knickers, as the tiniest pinpricks of blood blos-somed like roses on her white back, while Soft Cell's 'Tainted Love', Jeannie's song, Jeannie's big production number, which no one even had the sensitivity to turn off, mocked her unre-pentantly from the jukebox.

'I can take you away from all this,' he had wanted to say, 'to Balham . . .' Indeed, it had been the most degrading sight he had ever witnessed. Until last night, that is, when he saw the video Pat had loaned to Danny. And until tonight, when he saw Andy really, seriously imagining, for a moment, that anybody in their right mind was going to give the Sultans of Streatham a genuine round of applause.

If Ian loses control of the van, he thinks, or flips on a speed bump on Balham Park Road, or careers through the Oxfam shop front window and explodes, they'll all be sweating it out later with Jeannie, and the nun, in their own special circle below. 'Here there be Entertainers', the inscription will read. And child murderers will look down on them contemptuously with a curious mixture of pity and disgust. And 'The Walk Of Life' will play continuously, for all eternity, on a slightly warped 7-inch single.

'I'm not being ungrateful, Danno, not at all,' Sid says, having spoken of his vision, and dragging the last of Danny's drums into the flat. In the harsh light, Sid's collection of psychedelic 60s American garage band posters vie for attention with Abby's drug company promotional yearplanners. 'It's just that when I ran away from home to join a rock and roll band . . .' Danny holds his tongue, and allows Sid to entertain this illusion. Fact is, Sid had left university with a good degree in English Literature, and he could really have done something with his life. But a decade of trying to make it in various useless bands is like being institutionalised. After a few years, one simply becomes unfit for work. '. . . I wanted to take a journey to the centre of the mind . . .'

'Like Luther Fucking Flan Man!' Danny spits, boiling over.

'All I'm saying is, I had higher ambitions than the Sultans of Streatham.'

'You don't know you're born! When I was your age I used to dream of a regular Tuesday night residency playing Dire Straits covers in front of three drunken whores and a sweaty pimp in a Greek restaurant in Streatham.'

'Well, you've got what you always wanted, then,' says Sid, and dims the lights as he searches out some comforting old vinyl, 'but I haven't.' He pulls the Round Tabyls' 1967 debut album, *Chainmail Moccasins*, out from its alphabetised resting place, the same copy he'd purchased all those years ago. Someone had played him a CD reissue at a record fair, but he knew every crack and pop of the record's scratched surface, and somehow the seamless digital reproduction just didn't sound right. The clanging mono chimes of Luther's de-tuned twelve-string picking its way through the side-long epic, 'Step Outside Your Head', spill out into the flat. Sid had ripped the song off to write 'Sitting Outside Your House' for the Lemon Pies. The band had later flogged it on to Timothy Waterhouse as a B-side for a cover of a Kinks' song, without giving Sid a credit. A lawyer friend of Abby's had advised him he couldn't really afford the cost of taking them to court. Sid sits down defeatedly and starts to roll a joint, as he hears Abby stir next door. 'Keep it down, will you, Sid. They kept me there till midnight and I'm on a 6 a.m. shift tomorrow.'

'Sorry, love.' He reaches behind him and turns down the music. 'Sorry, Luther. But look, Danno,' he begins again, 'I mean, how did we let this happen? We've turned into circus chimps.'

He makes a final nip and tuck to the joint and hands it to Danny to light. Danny inhales. 'Circus chimps are better paid, Sid. And they get all the tea they can drink.' Danny leans back in the armchair, reflectively: 'I'm sorry to disillusion you, Sid, but personally, I don't care what the fuck we play as long as it pays. I'm just hoping not to die in rented accommodation.'

There's an easy silence for a few minutes or so. Finally Sid speaks. 'You know what I was thinking about on stage tonight, Dan?'

'Dignity? Self-respect? No, I know, don't tell me, pigs' cocks?'

'No. I was wondering what really happened to Luther.' What really happened to Luther? It was a long and sad story that Sid knew perfectly well from dozens of filed clippings and neatly bagged fanzines. Luther's real name was Doug Rooney. His mother had been an opera singer, and his father was a history teacher. As a boy in Tucson he'd read *The Sword in the Stone* at school and become fixated on the stories of King Arthur. As a teenager he'd scored some peyote from the local natives, and had suffered a vision of a rock and roll music that united the ancient myths of America's European invaders and the culture of her original inhabitants. He'd meant to change his name to Uther Peyote, crossing the name of King Arthur's father, Uther Pendragon, with the name of the

Navajo's most sacred sacrament, but there'd been a mistake at the pressing plant on his first 7-inch single. And so it was *Luther* Peyote and the Round Tabyls who took to the stage clad in chainmail and Indian head-dresses, got beaten up regularly by local red-necks, and cut three of the finest acid-rock albums of the late 60s, before Luther and his supplier were busted for drugs. Luther pleaded insanity to try and buck the possession charge, and got himself locked away in a mental institution, but the electric shock therapy he received inside had quickly made his pretence a reality, and he was never quite the same again. 'The trouble with pretending,' he said to *Beatfreak Magazine* in 1983, 'is that sometimes you can pretend too good.' After a failed mid-70s comeback, Luther used the money he'd got from 'Foot Of The Vampire' featuring in a teen-slasher movie soundtrack to buy himself an abandoned US airbase somewhere south-east of Tucson and slip into utter obscurity. And unlike most other 60s' casualties, Luther had never seen his back catalogue re-embraced and re-evaluated by a new generation of would-be geniuses. Indeed, the only Luther Peyote riff that ever got ripped off turned up on the B-side of a Timothy Waterhouse single. And Sid sits there, slightly stoned, and wonders once more, whatever happened to Luther Peyote.

'Maybe he's out there, Dan, holed up, alone in his empty aircraft hangar, wishing someone would call and just ask him to join a band again.'

Danny snorts dismissively and points at Sid with his bottle. 'If he is still alive, Sid, if, then I guarantee you Luther Peyote is completely out of his tiny twelve-string guitar classic 60s psychedelic Arizona acid-rock-and-roll garage band beatnik goatee beard and sunglasses-after-dark mind. His brain is fried to a crisp, and he's so full of drugs he rattles when he walks. Got it?'

'You don't know that, Danny. It's all relative. I mean, look at us.' Both are still dressed in their Sultans of Streatham stage clothes. They laugh. Abby shouts for them to shut up. Sid lifts the needle off the record, shrugs at Danny, and goes to bed.

In the darkness he quietly kicks off his Dire Straits costume. 'Sid,' says Abby from the bed, as a pair of white socks flop into a pile in the corner, 'do you think you are going to keep on with the Sultans of Streatham for ever?'

'Abby, love, can we have this conversation another time?'

She sits up in bed. 'Sid, I saw a fairly bad busker in Leicester Square tonight who appeared to be making twice in one evening what you do in a week.'

He sits down next to her. 'OK. Just leave it, will you.' He feels the percentage chance of sexual intercourse rapidly diminishing.

'Do you think maybe that you just keep on with Ian because you know it's going nowhere? It's safe, isn't it? You'll never achieve anything so you know you won't ever be judged.'

Sid gets under the covers. 'Abby, you spend all day working with these enormous psychotherapy concepts and then bring them home and clobber me over the head with them.'

'I'm not a psychotherapist, Sid . . .'

'Whatever.'

But Sid can sense a way out. 'You're like one of those Scrabble players, like Derek, who learn all the one- and two-letter words but don't even know what they mean. It's about as fair as if I were to quiz you about great dead rock stars of the late 60s.'

'Yes. Well I'd know all the bloody answers, wouldn't I, living with you for three years.' There's a dead silence a million miles wide. 'You know what your problem is? You're scared of commitment.' Sid grimaces. That is such a girls' thing to say, and as such the male mind is incapable of dragging out any argument that can match it. Sid knows that Abby knows that the phrase 'you're scared of commitment' has long since been rendered impotent by misuse and that, at best, it can only be but a prelude, a parping ceremonial trumpet announcing that the real battle is about to begin. She turns on to her side to face him. The real battle is about to begin. 'You're scared of commitment to your music and you're scared of commitment to me. You only have to look at your bloody record collection to see that.' Sid sits up, astonished. Now, this isn't playing fair. His record collection is the most committed thing anyone could ever hope to see. Once Sid gets into someone he is compelled to track down everything they've ever done at whatever cost. Old hippies behind stands at record fairs look to him for answers. Sid's record collection is an object lesson in commitment. But Abby hasn't finished with him yet. 'Sid. Everyone you really like is dead. Their accounts are closed. They will never let you down with a dodgy novelty single or a cash-in comeback tour. If you weren't scared of commitment you'd take a chance on raving on about someone who was actually still alive.'

Sid's mouth opens and closes. He thinks of the creaking shelves of vinyl and CDs outside, suddenly sensing some kind of secondary pattern emerging from within the rigorous alphabetisation. Potted biographies bloom and wither in his mind, all ending with the same fatal full stop.

There's six CDs and four albums by the New York saxophonist who took late-period John Coltrane to its logical apocalyptic nursery rhyme conclusion, and committed suicide in 1970; a wedge of vinyl by an unsung hero of the British blues boom, who got mixed up in black magic and threw himself under a tube train, Finsbury Park station, 8 May 1974; too many albums to mention by the angel-voiced Greenwich village folk singer who overdosed on the eve of his greatest work, and everything his similarly ill-fated son ever recorded, before he swam out into the river to die; five CDs by the siren of the British folk rock movement who fell fatally downstairs April 1978; a four-album 80s' box set of the trademark 'tortured romantic' who died once of an anti-depressants overdose in November 1974, and a second time more recently when some wanker licensed his music to a car commercial; the sole album by the American blues singer, disfigured during childhood in a fire, who died homeless on the streets of New York in 1998;

that CD compilation by the Cleveland punk who tried to combine Dylan *and* distortion, before dying a drug death in 1977; three different versions of the sole album by the Moby Grape guitarist who fled Bellevue mental hospital by motorbike in 1968 wearing only his pyjamas, and passed away still in state care in a trailer in Santa Cruz in the mid-90s; and everything, including the rare Lawson Square Infirmary 12-inch, by the underrated Australian country rock singer whose heart gave out, aged thirty-six, on 2 February 1999. Hmmmm. Maybe Abby had a point, but Sid wasn't about to concede it. 'No way, Abby. No way. Because . . . who's my favourite artist of all time?'

'Luther Peyote.'

'Luther Peyote! And your theory is fucked, actually, because Luther Peyote is not dead!'

'He's the one who sings like he's got a dog stuck up his arse, right?' Sid's suddenly quite impressed that Abby has at least taken in something of the essence of Luther. 'He may as well be dead,' she continues. 'Even you don't know exactly what's happened to him, and you know what? You like it like that. God forbid that Luther Peyote should ever reappear. That would kill you.' And she turns away on to her side. Sid closes his eyes. Something is dying on the vine.

Tracy pulls off the highway into a nameless trailer park, almost hidden in the scrub beneath the shadow of a big brown hill, miles from the nearest sign. Most of the little caravans are empty now, yellows and blues peeling in the sun, a web of wires and power lines criss-crossing their cracking roofs. Roscoe had talked about them moving back there.

She slows through a central aisle, distended dogs and dirty children scuttling roach-like out of her path. Through the frame of the windscreen, she sees Roscoe's grandmother, sat as usual in a canvas chair outside her door, a floral print dress fluttering in the feeble breeze, revealing swollen tree-trunk legs, her sightless eyes flickering white and useless. She cracks the shells of pistachio nuts with nimble fingers, or crushes them open with her teeth and spits the pieces out into the dirt. Tracy stops the car opposite her trailer and gets out. Mrs Allen hears the door slam. 'Ross? Ross? Is that you?' She grips the arm of the chair and rises breathlessly. 'You in trouble again, Ross? You need a place to hide? 'Cos if that's so you can turn tail right now and head right on out of here. If your momma were here . . .'

Tracy takes her by the elbow and sits her back down. 'No, Mrs Allen. It's me, Tracy.'

Bob Nequatewa wakes and sits upright in bed. The white starch motel room sheets bounce the bright morning light around the room, and he squints and shudders and shakes his head. He positions himself on the side of the bed, rubbing the soles of his feet exploratively on the unfamiliar flooring, and then stands and walks to the window. In the next bed, his grandson opens his eyes and watches silently. Bob Nequatewa pulls up the plastic blind and looks out. Phoenix, Arizona, is jerking uneasily into life, trucks passing, people shouting, some splashing from the pool, the hiss of sprinklers and the smell of pancakes and syrup. He shuts his eyes, pinches the bridge of his nose, and feels the morning sun on his face as he tries to shake himself free of last night's dreams.

Kóhkang Wuhti, the Spider Woman, and her unfinished pair of people. The lone woman wandering. The Hopi boy whose father was the Sun, leaving home and setting out on his quest. There is no place for these stories any more. Bob Nequatewa wishes he would forget them.

It has been a long time since he'd thought of Hopi history, and when he'd packed his clown clothes into his case yesterday morning he'd done so with little thought for their spiritual significance. For him, the hermetic seal of the world of the Hopi had long since started to leak.

It was at the end of the 60s when the hippies had first started arriving, uninvited, at the reservation. The flower children naively imagined that native culture might offer them something more significant than the world they'd left behind, but found instead a ritualised, ordered society in many ways more formal than their own. Tribal elders tried to shoo them out from sacred ceremonials, and drive their caravans off their land, but Bob had already felt the bulkhead breaching. Even then, the younger people were drifting away from the reservation and out into the wider world. There were forces at work that would not be resisted. It had been like that for a long time.

In 1891 the Hopi had confronted a small detachment of US cavalry at Oraibi, sent from Keams Canyon under the command of one Lieutenant Brett. Brett had come to arrest Hopis suspected of destroying surveyors' marks, and his soldiers had forcibly restrained a batch of young men who attempted to forbid them to enter the village. It was then that the Hopi had unleashed their secret weapon, a young man dressed as an old woman who mumbled at the soldiers in a language they could not understand, followed by a man in a black mask who sprinkled them with an inoffensive liquid. The Hopi had sent out personifications of Kóhkang Wuhti, the Spider Woman, mother of the twin war gods, and of Masau-u, God of Death, to intimidate the soldiers. There could be no more powerful gesture of intent. But the symbols meant nothing to the white men. They saw only a pantomime dame and a masked man with some water. As a show of strength, Brett destroyed a nearby peach orchard with shots from a cannon, and soon the disturbance was quelled. It had taken only the destruction of some fruit to induce the apocalypse. Sometimes Bob wondered what, if anything, had been learned from this sorry incident.

Somewhat disillusioned, as a younger man he had often travelled to Tuba City, to run with the despised Navajo, who seemed to him more equipped to embrace the Americans. The Hopi hated the Navajo, but the Navajo were only winning the long-standing land dispute because they were happy to employ white lawyers, rather than waiting, as the Hopi did, for the will of the Gods to intercede in an issue they felt no outsiders were entitled to adjudicate. Outside Old Oraibi, up on the Hopi reservation, was a sign: 'Warning. Warning. No Outside White Visitors Allowed. Because Of Your Failure To Obey The Laws Of Our Tribe As Well As The Laws Of Your Own This Village Is Hereby Closed.' But down in Tuba City the Navajo would sell tourists baseball caps bearing their most sacred symbols, if the money was right, and turn out substandard Hopi *katsina* dolls to anyone willing to pay for them. A group of young Navajo had introduced Bob to the peyote ritual, and among the freaks of Flagstaff and Tucson, Bob had found a ready market for the magic cacti buttons. The peyote church wasn't part of Hopi culture, but to the hippies hanging around outside the bars that bordered the railway line, a real Indian dealer smacked of authenticity, and Bob had marked up his prices accordingly, or else offered his wares for free to women that were grateful in the right way. He and his accomplices had quite a scene there for a while, selling nights in earthen Navajo hogans with a well-supplied guide as part of the complete peyote package. Until he got busted, that was, briefly imprisoned, and finally returned home to sit out the rest of the century resigned to life as it ought to be lived. After a few months of whispered comments and suspicion, the Hopi had finally let him return to clowning. And there were moments, standing on the roofs of the houses, looking down at laughing children in the plazas below, when he felt once more the same thrill that the wide world beyond the mesas had also offered him. That said, when a white woman at the cultural centre had told him she felt at home there because she had a Red Indian Spirit Guide, he'd had to restrain himself from punching her out.

There is a knock at the door. Bob opens it. A young girl in a simple uniform stands uncertain. 'Mr . . . Mr Neq-ua-te-wa? There's a fax here for you from Channel 8.'

'Thank-you.' Bob closes the door, reads the note, screws it up and throws it into a waste bin.

*   *   *

'Tracy? You that coloured girl?' asks Roscoe's grandmother, leaning blindly forward out of her chair.

'No, Mrs Allen. Ross and I came round last March, remember? I made a salad and Ross barbecued some steaks. We drank wine and you smoked a cigarette. You showed us pictures of your husband.'

'Paul? Paul was a fine man. A gentleman.' Tracy pulls up a wooden box and sits down, looking up at the old woman's canyoned face. 'And where's Ross, missy? In jail again, I guess.'

'No. No, Mrs Allen. Ross has . . . gone away.'

'Gone away? Locked away, I shouldn't wonder. He never had a lick of sense anyhow.' Mrs Allen cracks a shell and spits.

'No, Mrs Allen. Not locked away. Gone away. See, a friend of his from Phoenix found him a two-year contract, drilling oil up in the north-west. When he comes back Roscoe says he'll be rich. Roscoe says, when he comes back, he'll take care of you, buy you a TV and all.'

'What use is TV to me, girl? And I ain't got two years left, Ross knows that.'

'He sent me to tell you, to say he loved you and was sorry.'

'Yeah? Well, Ross never was too good at writing, now, and I never was too good at reading.'

'Like I say, Mrs Allen, he said to say he loved you, and that he was sorry. I guess we're both kinda sorry.'

Mrs Allen stops chewing and stares blindly through Tracy, and out across the plain. 'You ain't got nothing to be sorry for. I can tell you're a good girl, just trying to do what's best. I understand.' She takes Tracy's hand. 'You'd best be on your way,' she says. Tracy lets go the old woman's hand and walks to the car. 'Besides,' Mrs Allen says under her breath, 'I got a radio. Ross made the news already.'

Outside the motel, police cars, curious locals and a lone ambulance line up drearily in the midday sun. The crew lean on the bumpers, waiting for the all clear from the police photographer. 'Driving dead men to morgues is all it is, dead men to morgues,' says the driver to a stretcher-bearer, bouncing keys percussively on his thigh, 'I can take ninety-degree corners in first gear and steer that cracked blacktop at night . . . but there's certain kinds of passengers that don't deserve the benefit of our special training, know what I'm saying?'

In the motel room bathroom, a flash-gun flips a hard white burst off the mirror and Sheriff Hopkins shields his sunken eyes. 'Woah! This is real Weegee stuff,' gasps the photographer. 'I gotta run me off a black and white roll too.'

A glob of chewing tobacco oozes from the sheriff's mouth, swings momentarily on the rim of his lip, and falls soggily to the lino. As the sheriff's elongated, gallows-tree shadow falls across the floor before him, Dr Littwick looks up from dusting for clues, pauses to remove his glasses from the end of his pointed nose, and polishes them. He strokes the top of his bald head while tutting a meek and ineffectual rebuke. Deputy Cowdrey, an unreasonably young-looking thirty-something, bustles in behind them, waving a fluttering fistful of statements. 'It's a suicide, Sheriff Hopkins,' he starts, 'a regular open and shut suicide. We ain't required here.'

'I'm nominally still in charge here, Deputy Cowdrey, yes? So I'll decide if and when we ain't required.' The deputy looks suitably ashamed. 'And, anyhow, I think on closer examination you will find there are a couple of irregularities.' Hopkins sucks something up from his throat, hacks, and spits it out. Cowdrey winces.

Littwick snaps on a rubber glove and dabs at the contamination. 'It's a brave or foolish officer, Deputy Cowdrey, who dares to make such a quick judgement, surely you know that by now.'

Hopkins fixes his deputy with one eye open, one eye closed and continues. 'You'll see the proprietor says the deceased had a woman in here with him last night.' The sheriff sways back and forth self-satisfiedly, like a flagpole in a light wind, before continuing again. 'You know, Cowdrey, whenever a poor young man chooses to take his life, with a senseless and foul act of obscene self-mutilation, that goes against God and against Nature, there is usually a woman involved somewhere. But is it possible that even a woman, I ask you, would just run off and leave somebody lying here like this?' Cowdrey wanders to the end of the bath, and looks at Roscoe, cold and congealed now in a stagnant ruddy swamp, while Hopkins stands centrestage, waiting to be proved right.

'So – they had a disagreement,' the deputy suggests. 'An argument. She said "That's it, honey, I'm leaving." He said, "You can't. I love you. Don't you understand? I'll kill myself!" And he did.' Hopkins chuckles to himself at the evident stupidity of the deputy's theory. Cowdrey continues. 'Maybe he'd cried wolf one too many times? Maybe she didn't take him seriously the once she perhaps should have done? It's a tragedy, Sheriff Hopkins, you don't have to tell me it's a tragedy, but isn't this just . . .' he searches for the word, '. . . domestics?'

Hopkins shakes his head and sighs. 'Domestics! A man is dead! With all due respect, Deputy Cowdrey, I think what we got here is a little more serious than a domestic. They checked in under the deceased's name, together, then in the morning she's taken off all alone, leaving a supposed suicide behind her. Don't it remind you of anything?' Hopkins pauses for effect, and spits out another nub of wet tobacco. Littwick bristles silently and scrapes the mucus from his work once more.

'Nope. You got me, Sheriff Hopkins,' Cowdrey apparently concedes. 'It don't remind me of nothing.'

And the sheriff begins to circle the blood bath theatrically, a regular third act detective. 'The circumstances of the suicide – missing female witness and all – are exactly the same as a supposed suicide in Black Mesa three years back. Now, back then you'll remember I had you run a check on the state files. Sheriffs' departments as far afield as Littlefield and Pirtleville had logged four other comparable supposed suicide cases between them running back fifteen years. Do I have to spell it out, son? What we are dealing with . . .' and Hopkins stops, puts his hands behind his back, and assumes the most commanding pose available from a limited repertoire significantly hampered by his puppy dog belly and a tendency to slouch, '. . . is a very cunning serial killer.'

Cowdrey has heard all this before, every Friday in the bar opposite the office. He and Littwick have laughed about it over last orders for nearly half a decade now. Hopkins wanted just one *True Detective* case to make his name, before retiring into an as yet unplanned sheriffs' hall of fame. And they would laugh at his frustrated ambition, before ordering a final beer.

And, sure enough, here's Hopkins now, sitting on the rim of the bath, head in hands, and Littwick flicking at his thigh with a plastic brush to shoo him away. But this time Cowdrey won't be deterred. 'No, sheriff. At best we're dealing with a frightened woman, who's fled the scene of a regrettable accident. You're looking for . . .'

'A woman, Cowdrey, you said it yourself – we're dealing with a woman! Don't forget that. A woman!' He steps through into the bedroom, staring at the crumpled bedsheets, as if they give evidence of his theory. Cowdrey follows. 'Now, I'm not saying we should try all women for manslaughter, Deputy Cowdrey, no. It ain't their fault. They didn't ask to be angels and they didn't ask to be whores. That's just the way God made them.'

'Mrs Hopkins back from her mother's in Prescott yet, Sheriff Hopkins?' Littwick calls through from the bathroom.

'You watch your mouth, boy,' says Hopkins, staring out of the window towards the horizon. 'Deputy Cowdrey, you take control of the station for a day or so. I'm going off alone to follow up a few leads.'

Cowdrey interposes himself between Hopkins and the view. 'Sir, excuse me, but this is ridiculous.'

Hopkins pushes past him, through the door, out into the sunlight. 'I'll call in, Cowdrey, when I have something.'

'Yup,' says Littwick, leaning on the frame of the bathroom door, 'it's *Monday Mystery Theater* time again.'

Hopkins clambers into the patrol car, clicks the seat-belt into place, puts on his sunglasses, stares around him a little, and turns the key in the ignition. As he drives away, a dust-cloud sprays out over Cowdrey, and leaves him coughing and spluttering. As it settles, the body of Roscoe MacLean, Caucasian, age thirty-two, eyes blue, height six-two, is borne with stately dignity to the ambulance, by two men discussing baseball scores, and cursing his weight.

In the hospital waiting area a young nurse struggles with an obstinate, ragged-arsed man. 'Come on, Mr Rugg,' she pleads. 'Your appointment with Dr Quinton is in half an hour and we need to do a preliminary examination.' But Peter Rugg, as usual, has a more pressing appointment with some furniture. On his hands and knees among the surgical stockinged legs of a gaggle of geriatrics, he slithers on his thirty-year-old rainbow jumper between the red plastic sofas, dipping his hand down the back of each in turn, one after the other after the other. 'Mr Rugg,' she cries, 'what have you lost?'

'Can't you see, darlin'?' he says, standing, brown teeth breaking into a smile behind his beard. 'I've lost my mind.'

Dr Abby Quinton stands watching the scene impassively, dressed in the regulation knee-length white coat. She wonders what she will say to Peter Rugg today. His lucid explanation of his behaviour in Burger King last night has all but convinced her of the irrelevance of any professional help she can offer. Maybe he's telling the truth. If Jesus came back today and was committed to her care she'd recommend the strongest medication. She's a resourceful, patient girl though, that nurse. Abby makes a mental note to commend her at a later date. Peter Rugg, meanwhile, has started lecturing the other patients, in sonorous, mock ministerial tones, standing on a seat near the tea machine, arms outstretched, duffel coat billowing around his spindle body like some travelling Victorian huckster, howling in cockney hippie tongues. 'We walk in the shadow of deception, all you ladies and gents, listen in! There's a white bird as sleeps beneath the sand, and when it spills its guts out at last, then all your secrets, O proud men of glory, will spill out with 'em.'

Why do they always get religious? Abby wonders. Why not just become obsessed with geology, or French foreign policy in the fifteenth century, or different varieties of gnats, or pop music like Sid and his borderline autistic friends. 'Is it a book, or a film?' Abby hears an elderly onlooker shout, as Rugg gesticulates skywards with trembling bony fingers. 'You'll have to give us more of a clue than that, mate.'

Abby heads down the corridor, a little unsteady and still slightly sleepy, Peter Rugg's prophecies fading in the distance: 'Beneath the sand he sleeps, awaiting the Templars. Dried blood will scatter upon the desert winds, the serpent smiting the heads of his enemies, whack! Just like that! Stitch that! Nice one, Mr Slithery Snake!' The nurse finally wrestles Rugg from his makeshift pulpit, and his audience make a disappointed noise. Abby yawns. She can't stand staying at Sid's flat these days. She used to sit up with him and Danny, join in their stupid arguments, indulge Sid's 60s' 7-inch singles, and endure Danny's flirtations with mock irritation. But now the sound of the boys' laughter drifting through the bedroom door at 2 a.m. is just noise, and when Sid comes to bed in the early hours, he does so like a dog that's shit on the carpet and knows it's in for a beating. Her old friends from college are engaged to lawyers and accountants. Once they'd envied her the bass guitarist, back when the Lemon Pies got played on Radio One, and there was the odd poster around town for gigs in the back rooms of Camden pubs. And, to be honest, she'd enjoyed a strange sense of vicarious, counter-cultural superiority by association with her black-clad boyfriend. But even though she had always quite liked Dire Straits, this feeling had begun to fade the day Sid joined the Sultans of Streatham. Sid had given up his dreams, sinking into the same Sid-shaped space on the sofa night after night after night. These days, Abby thought, she had more admiration for Peter Rugg, chasing the impossible cigarette butt out into the wild blue yonder, than for her broken boyfriend. And not just for Peter Rugg. Sometimes she even felt a surge of inspiration from the exhilarating delusions of her second favourite problem patient.

The astronaut had presented himself two years ago now, an articulate, clearly professional man, well spoken and in good physical health, but with absolutely no recollection of any personal details whatsoever, not even his name so he had chosen one off the staff war memorial by reception, just to be able to complete the relevant paperwork. Initial consultation sessions had uncovered little and a press campaign to identify the unknown amnesiac proved futile. To top it all, the poor fellow was obviously clinically depressed, with no interest in anything. He couldn't hold down any kind of job even though he was clearly quite adept and capable. Prozac only exacerbated his delusions, culminating in the moment, last March, when he announced that he had once been an astronaut. Abby conceded this was more original than Jesus or Napoleon Bonaparte, but the patient's belief that he had orbited the moon conspired to make everyday life here on planet earth seem rather stale and unprofitable. But, nevertheless, there was something mildly thrilling about the tenacity with which the patient clung to this most untenable belief.

Abby stops and opens the door to the consulting room. Inside, the astronaut sits at a table, piling paper cups up into a fragile white tower, now some two or three feet in height, with shaking, unsteady fingers.

'Good Morning, Dr Quinton,' mutters the man, and as Abby leans forward to shake hands, her sleeve clips the top of the tower. It trembles, teasingly, for a second, and then, one by one, the paper cups tumble in tiny arcs to the floor, bouncing on impact, and then rolling to separate corners of the room. Abby watches the accident happen in spectacular slow motion and the patient's lips harden into a scowl.

'Good morning, Mr Lewis,' she says.

Four

'I appreciate how you feel, Mr Lewis, but I hardly think . . .'

From his stiff-backed seat at the consulting room table, Lewis squeaks the rim of a polystyrene cup full of weak tea. The noise seems to agitate the prosecution, so he does it again, sighs, and resumes his defence.

'I understand your scepticism, Dr Quinton, but it doesn't make my experiences any less real. I still have the memories, and suddenly they seem clearer than my recollection of . . . of whatever it was I did yesterday. "Oh, Mr Lewis, we're organising an outpatients' coach trip to Brighton at the weekend, would you like to come?" I've walked in Space, for Christ's sake, Dr Quinton, where only meteors and moon-beams go. I've seen my home planet from above and from beyond. I've known at first hand my own wonderful insignif-icance in the grand scheme of things. I have been as one with the cosmos. Ice-cream, fish and chips, and flickering amuse-ments? I can't really see the point.'

There's a pause. Lewis squeaks his cup in the silence. Abby shifts on her seat. She can almost smell his craziness. 'Well, maybe you should give Brighton a try, Mr Lewis,' she suggests. 'You can have a very nice relaxing weekend there, away from everything.' Abby's consciously breaking one of the key rules in the book, just for the fun of the little thrill it gives her, and she can't believe Lewis won't be at least a little embarrassed by the come-on that's buried in her therapeutic suggestion. But no.

'Doctor. Please. I've walked on the moon.'

She feels foolish. And blames Sid. She suffers a sudden flush of shame, and then a stab of frustration, and decides to take it out on the patient. 'You've consistently argued your case very eloquently, Mr Lewis. But it seems to me, that, deprived of any genuine recollection of your own real personal history, however mundane it may have been, your subconscious is overcompensating rather spectacularly by saddling you with the most fantastic life story one could possibly construct. And the fact remains that it is exactly that, a life *story* – it's impossible for you to have been to the moon. It's not the sort of thing you can do on a whim, like a stroll around the heath . . .'

'I'll tell you a story,' the patient says, sinking back into his chair. 'When Yuri Gagarin parachuted out of the Vostok's re-entry capsule, after making the first manned space flight in April 1961, he landed in a field in front of a Russian forester's wife and her six-year-old daughter. And *they* didn't believe *he* was an astronaut, until a military helicopter arrived to spirit him away.'

'Well, in that case, Mr Lewis,' says Abby, after a pause, 'I await with no small amount of excitement the arrival of your own personal military helicopter.' She's surprised at her gleeful sadism, but continues in the same vein. 'And until such time as it darkens the North London skies, I am afraid we must assume that unlike the rather better known Yuri Gagarin, you never left the surface of mother earth.'

Lewis slumps deflated. 'I'm sorry,' Abby says. And she is, now. She wonders what possessed her, and what circumstances have driven her to take such a perverse pleasure in tormenting her patient. She turns back to Lewis who looks up, imploringly.

'But I have the memories, Doctor. And they're the only memories I've got,' he says, with equal measures of anger and despair. 'So until such time as you manage to determine whether I might have been an astronaut, I'm afraid I myself must choose to believe that I was. And you'd be surprised how easy it is to do so.'

'Easy, Mr Lewis?' she says. 'It doesn't seem easy.'

'Like I said, you'd be surprised. Otherwise I have to accept that I'm completely and utterly mad.'

As Lewis leaves the office, until next week, and steps into the corridor, a familiar man stands up from an orange plastic seat, throws back his ratted hair, and points at him with a blackened fingernail. 'Oi, Wally!' he shouts through a scraggy beard. 'Answer me this! Did those feet in ancient times walk upon England's mountains green, or did they not walk about there at all, and walk about somewhere else instead?' Throwing an arm around Lewis's shoulder, Peter Rugg follows him towards the exit, into the centre of the waiting area. 'Or did those feet in ancient times zip around real speedy like on a pair of shiny new skates? Voom! After all, they were Jesus' feet weren't they, Wally, and if he'd a wanted skates he could a magicked 'em up, outta nowhere, five loaves and three skates, paf!, sporting goods superstore, skates, geddit? Wadda ya think, pal? Did those feet walk and such like, or did they not?'

'I'll let you know, I promise,' Lewis answers, shrugging Rugg off, wrapping his coat around himself, pushing open the swing door, and wondering where he'd seen the man before.

'If you're going out, eh, Wally, bring me back . . . oh, a bow of burning gold,' Peter Rugg calls after him, as he descends the steps to the street, 'some arrows of delight, packet of fags, pint of milk, *Daily Mirror*, box of matches, and a chariot of fire. Oh, and Wally, keep the change!'

A tube ride south to Tottenham Court Road and Lewis slides through a revolving airlock into the chrome interior of the Café Cyberama. Here, among the multi-megabytes of incessant international chatter and tawdry sexual prevarication, he has systematically searched out extremes of ill-supported opinion to confirm, deny and mostly merely confuse all of his most paranoid personal imaginings. But now, in the light of his vision of the night before last, while he shivered beneath the stars at the Willesden depot, and following his uncharacteristically frank, if not bruising, encounter with Dr Quinton, one particular line of cyberspatial inquiry urgently requires a more dogged pursuit.

When he first got behind the wheel of a car again, a Mini bought with mysterious untraceable payments into his bank account, Lewis knew he wasn't going to need many driving lessons. 'Oh, Mr Lewis,' said the instructor as he slipped effortlessly into first gear, 'it appears you've done this before.' Likewise, keyboard skills came back to him as easily as eating and sleeping, but trying to remember where he might have picked them up has long since proved fruitless. Writing the definitive English novel perhaps, or debugging troublesome programs for grateful multinationals, or maybe just working on a supermarket checkout.

But now, at last, Lewis was starting to rule out some of the more mundane options. He positions himself at a computer screen. Around him students with too much spare time swap *Star Trek* trivia with their stateside counterparts, and a bespectacled fifteen-year-old calls up a grainy X-ray image of a bent Baywatch Barbie, stuffed up the rectum of a forty-two-year-old male.

Lewis finds his regular discussion group, the Magic Bulletin Board, and logs in under his usual user name. 'Moonhead.' He types the sentence he's been turning over in his mind all morning. He had not dared mention the idea to Dr Quinton lest she arrange to have him sectioned. 'Sphincter Boys please. More information required re Masonic Moonlanding.'

A few minutes south, via a worldwide circuit of buzzing cable, Danny is hunched as usual over a computer keyboard, giggling, pulling on his mid-morning joint. Sid slumps on the sofa, drinking coffee, and Danny swivels his hips sarcastically to the wobble-board rhythms of another of Sid's lost Luther Peyote classics, leaking like battery acid from the speakers.

Suddenly he shouts out. 'Hey! The Sphincter Boys! He's asking for us. It's that Moonhead guy again, regular as a bowel movement.'

Sid sighs, disapprovingly. 'Oh, Christ. Leave it, Danno.'

'Lay off, Sidney,' says Danny, reaching up to the bookshelf above the table. 'You should show an interest. I'm just gonna tell him what he wants to hear. A friend in need . . .' Danny flicks along his flatmate's self-consciously esoteric and largely as yet unread library of smudgy underground literature: *A History of Hallucinogens, Memoirs of the Dog Boys, Freemasons from Atlantis, Black Helicopters Over Dallas, A Guide to the Punishment and Correction of Young Ladies, Infernal Machines and How to Build Them, Failure Justified, An Anton LaVey Reader* and, finally, *Krazies – A Guide to the Fringes of Human Belief.* Danny pulls down the book and opens it.

'OK, last time we spoke to y'man Moonhead I was just starting Chapter 6, so . . .' Danny condenses the text as he begins to type: 'Moonhead – re: the discovery and subsequent concealment of the fantastical Christian artefact, the Holy Grail, and its precious cargo of the last precious drops of blood of our saviour Jesus Christ our Lord. Further to last week's conversation we have unearthed some more information which we feel may be of interest to you.'

Sid stands behind Danny, and reads over what he has written. 'Just leave him alone, Danno. It's not fair. Week after week. It's like taunting a kitten.'

Danny ignores him, browses through the book's blurred photos and unconvincing sketches and continues to type: 'Full of cold war fears of Armageddon, American Freemasons arranged for Neil Armstrong to safeguard Grail by putting it into a pre-planned orbit of the moon, while exploring the planet's surface during the 1969 moon-landing. Two decades later disgruntled European Freemason faction secretly fund space shuttle shot of their own to recapture it.'

Sid feels Danny's enthusiasm for this absurd story soften his irritation a little. 'Christ, Danno. The blood of Jesus – in space?'

Danny points at a drawing of Neil Armstrong on the moon's surface holding his Masonic apron, and Buzz Aldrin carrying a Masonic flag, and then a photo of the Scottish Rite Temple, Washington DC, where the writer alleges the moon Mason flag now hangs. Danny laughs, 'This is all clearly . . . what is the technical term – shite? Oh, here we go, look!'

Onscreen, Moonhead has written back: 'More information please.' Danny skim-reads and replies: 'It is rumoured Euro-Masons put unknown British Astronaut into space 1998. He recovered Grail, but shot down in US airspace and bailed out near Mexican border. Body never recovered.' Danny leans back and drags on his joint. His unseen correspondent continues, responding with disconcerting swiftness. 'More please. What happened to the Grail?' This clearly matters to Moonhead.

Danny passes the smouldering joint to Sid, scans the book once more, and writes: 'Grail alleged held by Masonic sympathetic officials in US Air Force, in hangar of an airbase in Arizona.'

Sid is mildly interested now, and sucks on Danny's joint as the story unfolds before him. 'This is such wank.'

'What airbase? Must know. Please.' The words flash up, disembodied, pitiful now almost.

'Well, Danno?'

'Don't know. That's the thing about these books. There's never any actual real information in them, just a load of speculative, unsubstantiated, dope-smoker crap.'

Again, a palpable, human urgency seeps through the electronic text. 'Repeat. Must know. Please.'

'Poor sod. You've really driven him up the wall now, Danno,' Sid chastises him. 'Can't you just make something up to put the mad fucker out of his misery?'

'S'pose. Do you know the name of any American airbases?'

'Roswell?'

'Too obvious,' shouts Danny. 'A dead alien and the Holy

Grail under one roof, it's too good to be true. Even old Moonhead wouldn't swallow that. I know – what's the old airbase the Flan Man retired to?'

Danny reaches up to a stack of Luther Peyote biographical information, neatly filed away by Sid. Sid tries to snatch the pamphlets back. 'But Danny – this is lying.'

'What fuckin' airbase was it, man?' Danny shuffles through Sid's alphabetised clippings and leaflets, scattering paper over the keypad. Sid looks down at him, scrabbling through the uncorrelated information.

'OK, OK,' he says, leaning over Danny's shoulder, taking the keyboard, and, without having to consult anything other than his own obsessive memory for Luther Peyote's life story, he reluctantly types the name: 'Coronado airbase, Chiricahua, Arizona, USA.' The words flicker on the screen.

'That should shut the mad bastard up,' says Danny, with an air of triumph. And Moonhead's name winks out of the chat-room window.

'It has,' notes Sid. 'He's logged off.'

In the Café Cyberama, Tottenham Court Road, user number 19 has left without paying his bill. A coffee cools unfinished and a cigarette burns to waste. A flushed and bewildered teenage boy nurses a smacked ear over a downloaded picture of a misused doll. On a napkin, a densely etched doodle of an angular ceremonial cup is framed by a perfect lunar circle. A waiter scowls and puts it into the brimming ashtray. As he heads back to the bar, a fat man in a camel coat rises from behind an unfurled *Daily Telegraph*, walks to the terminal table where A.R.Y. Lewis, his Hampstead Heath listener of two nights earlier, had been sitting, and quietly pockets the crumpled piece of paper.

'Without even having the courtesy to bid us thank you and goodbye,' says Danny, across town. 'I dunno. You do some fucker a favour . . . Hey, did I tell you Pat sent me the address for a site of naked women with beards?'

*   *   *

Tracy pulls off Highway 160 to check her map. Folding it out over the dash she swigs on a can of diet coke and looks at her watch. She traces a line south with a broken fingernail and opens her purse. A few crushed notes and some loose change stare back. She drives on and folds the map into her bag alongside the detritus of the past few days; takeaway pizza menus, a bus timetable. She feels the Christian comic book she had found in Kayenta in her pocket, and opens the briefcase on the back seat to deposit it among the others.

Finding the pamphlet had stirred the mud of her memory. A stack of titles flickered behind her eyelids, tracts she'd been made to read, memorise and repeat: *The Death Cookie*; *Have You Been Brainwashed?*; *Holocaust*; *Allah Had No Son*; *The Correction and Discipline of Christian Children*; *The Truth About the Homosexuals*; King James' quotations quiver in speech balloons, hissing from the mouths of marbled two-tone Saints and Sinners, Angels and Devils, Pimps and their Fallen Whores.

The Truth About the Homosexuals. That had been the one that broke her. The True Romance comics-style story of a mustachioed, Aids-ridden hipster in sunglasses and a cowboy hat, who won the heart of an innocent young schoolgirl. `Wow! I never dreamed he'd ask me. I don't want to mess up this date!` Finally, a doctor broke to the girl the news of her impending death. `You see, Sally, God didn't want you to die, but you reached out and chose death yourself.`

It was 1980, a world of white socks and stonewash, and ex-hippie teachers who read them Dylan lyrics in Literature classes and smoked pot after school. Metal braces glistened from pretty faces, and yesterday's hair gel was tomorrow's greasy skin condition. Standing on the desks at the centre of the room, two of the boys plucked at the text at random. Tracy's classmates roared approval.

'Get this!' cried Gary Parker. `"In Leviticus 20, God demanded the death of any man who had sex with an` animal. Both he and the animal must die!" Seems a bit unfair on the animal, huh?' Everybody laughed.

'I dunno, Gary,' added Dean Lucas. 'Some of them lead you on, with their big fuckin' eyes.'

Outside the circle, Tracy was slumped at a desk, her head in her hands. 'For Christ's sake, Gary,' shouted Anna Tashain, putting a comforting hand on Tracy's shoulder, 'can't you see she's upset? Just put the book away, man!'

'What's up, Tracy, did we touch a raw nerve?' And everybody laughed. And then Dean let her secret spill. 'No, no, it ain't that. Check the credits, back page. Wooah! Heavy.'

Gary read aloud. '"Bible Messenger League Publications, PO Box 660, Chico, California", and then there's a rubber stamp that says: "Your local distributor is . . ."' And then Gary had turned to Tracy. 'This shit is left all around town by your Pop? No wonder you never put out!' Everybody stared at Tracy, some shocked, some stunned, most trying not to laugh. That was where the trouble had started. And within a year she was gone.

At the Navajo town of Tuba City she pulls into a diner and goes inside. The elderly Native American woman behind the counter recognises her from the days Roscoe had spent working with her son in the garage across the road. 'Morning Tracy,' she calls out. 'And where's your handsome young man this morning?'

'Oh . . . he's gone, Alice,' she says, finding a seat. 'He got a job over in Santa Fe.'

'Oh, I'm sorry to hear that. Still, at least you'll be able to visit, I suppose. Now, what can I get for you today . . .' she pours coffee, '. . . bacon and beans, bacon and links, bacon and eggs, bacon and hash browns, bacon and pancakes . . .'

'I'll just have the coffee, I think.' She drinks in silence, staring out of the window at men loading up trucks in the lot, laughing, their arms straining at crates, their bodies bowing under the weight. She sees them crushed and broken, their limbs littering the rail track, and then dissolving in the dampness of the motel bathtub. She counts up her cash. A stocky, plaid-shirted man, his black hair tied back in a pony tail, calls out to her from the shadows. He sits himself slowly down at her table. 'Tracy,' he begins.

'Little Joe.'

'I ain't seen you around awhiles, Tracy.'

'No. I was off east with Roscoe.'

Little Joe considers. 'I hear you telling Mom he's gone.'

'Yes, Little Joe. He's gone now.' A fly buzzes between them.

'Remember when I fixed your TV set, Tracy?'

'I remember, Little Joe. You fixed it fine. Got me the best picture I ever had.'

'That's right, Tracy. I sure did.'

Little Joe looks into her half empty cup. 'Remember when I fixed your radio, Tracy?'

'I remember, Little Joe. You did good. It's never let me down since.'

The big man toys with the sugar bowl for a minute or so, and looks up. 'I always liked you, Tracy.'

'You're a sweet man, Little Joe.'

Alice silently pours a refill. Little Joe struggles for something. 'Is Roscoe coming back?'

'No, Little Joe. Roscoe's not coming back.' Tracy reaches across the table and puts the palm of her hand to his cheek. 'You're a sweet man, Little Joe.' She leans over and kisses him on the forehead. Little Joe's brown eyes glaze. He sits adrift, frozen to his seat. Tracy stands. She turns. She leaves.

'Tracy,' Little Joe says, to no one.

'Mr Nequatewa.' Bob Nequatewa sees the lone woman walking away from the Spider Woman's lair, away from Kóhkang Wuhti, and out into the world. 'Mr Nequatewa.' He sees the Hopi boy sleeping alone, dreaming of his father who was the Sun. 'Mr Nequatewa.' Then he opens his eyes, and sees the scene he has been trying to block out.

In an air-conditioned office in Phoenix, Arizona, Bob

Nequatewa sits at a marble table surrounded by his betrayers, his grandson at his side for support. Outside the sun glows like electric honey off the roofs of metallic buildings. Before him, Al Stapleton, the tanned TV host, of whose good intentions Bob has been repeatedly reassured by Claudia the researcher, is talking.

'As you probably know by now, Bob, the theme of Friday's show is clowns and clow-*ning*, so we've gathered together clowns from all walks of life and we're gonna ask you how and why you got into clow-*ning* and what sort of shit really cracks you up.' Bob sees that Al Stapleton himself is wearing a wig and make-up. He says nothing. Al continues, 'But I don't want you to worry about any of that, Bob, don't worry about be-*ing* funny. *Saturday Night Live* this ain't. *Good Morning Arizona* isn't about set-up gags and rehearsed stories. It's about *real* people. And *real* people are *rrrrrr-eal* funny. Just be yourself, and something *hil*-arious is sure to happen, OK?'

Bob looks out of the window at a jet slowly crossing the blue sky. Claudia, the woman whom he'd talked to on the telephone, leans over to him and squeezes his forearm. 'Anything the matter, Mr Nequatewa?'

Bob sighs. 'I wonder . . . what does Mr Stapleton really know of the Hopi clowns?'

'Well, Bob . . .'

'The Hopi clown is not like a comedian or a rodeo circus performer. He is a Perfect Fool, showing the people that man can never be perfect. He teaches us how man clowns his way through life, and hopes that this knowledge will lead man to some sense of right. He opens a door into a greater reality than the ebb and flow of everyday life. This is accomplished by the following means.'

'Mr Nequatewa,' interrupts Al's assistant Irma, a formidable forty-something, forcefully. Bob ignores her.

'First, there is the element of shock. Pueblo clowns, in the course of the contribution to the *katsina* ritual, might, for example, engage in sexual displays which are normally quite taboo. This breaks down the ordinary round of everyday existence, shocks people out of their petty daily concerns, opening the mind to greater considerations than mere humour.'

'Mr Nequatewa, we have a lot to get through and . . .'

'Your early white anthropologists had some difficulty appreciating this too, Mr Stapleton. John G. Bourke's 1881 publication *The Urine Dance of the Zuni Indians* was virtually a forbidden text.'

'Well, Mr Nequatewa,' interrupts Al, 'I doubt we'll be asking you for a Urine Dance on *Good Morning Arizona*.'

His lackeys laugh. Claudia shudders a little. 'Good,' says Bob. 'It is a Zuni dance, and as a Hopi clown I am not entirely familiar with the steps. All I am saying is, I wonder, does Mr Stapleton really understand the role of the clown in pueblo society?'

Al turns to Irma. 'Irma, do I really understand the role of the clown in pueblo society?'

'You'll be fully briefed, Mr Stapleton.'

'See, Bob? I'll be fully briefed. And hey, trust me, I do this five days a week fifty-one weeks of the year. I think I'll be able to get through a show about clowning, huh?'

Everyone laughs. Except Claudia, who nervously looks up through a blonde fringe and catches Bob's eye. 'Do you have any other worries, Mr Nequatewa?' she asks.

'Do you still require me to dress up?'

'We would prefer that,' says Irma. 'All the other clowns will be appearing in their fancy costumes. We reckon it's gonna look pretty damn terrific.'

A pause. Al speaks, as he shuffles his papers. 'Is that it then, Bob? Any other questions.'

'Yes,' says the old man, taking his grandson's hand. 'When do I get paid?'

Sheriff Matthew Hopkins is half a day clear of the murder at the motel, heading south-west on a whim. He winds down the window and feels the hot wind blow off the dry land and buffet his face. The first of the killings had been fifteen years ago now, a body found in a back yard somewhere just outside Jerome. Neighbours said the victim had recently struck up a strong friendship with an unknown woman of indeterminate origin. She left the morning of the supposed suicide having placed an anonymous 911 call to alert local ambulance services, establishing a pattern that was to repeat itself a further seven times over the following decade and a half. It was almost as if she wanted to be caught.

What Cowdrey, Littwick and the other doubters failed to appreciate, Hopkins realised as he drove on, was that police work was all about patterns. Even unrelated incidents of petty vandalism and domestic violence added up to a needlepoint picture of sorts, albeit one that showed only that people were basically fucked up. Hopkins knew that Cowdrey and Littwick had him down as a religious nut, and that they sneered when he quoted scripture, and yet privately he wasn't really sure if there was a God or not. But when he busted twenty Mexicans living ten to a bed in a barnyard somewhere, or looked at crime scene photos of splattered brains and broken heads, or smelt the scent of pot drifting over the high school fence, he knew that what people needed was discipline and a sense of duty, whether its heavenly source were real or a myth. Hopkins imagined if he looked long and hard enough, sooner or later God would reveal himself to him, in a column of fire or a burning bush, but until such time as he chose to, it couldn't hurt to back the winning side. And, likewise, he knew that sooner or later he'd find the fugitive female, and she'd confess and prove him right, and he would be garlanded with fragrant apologies.

In fifteen years he hadn't seen so much as a blurred security camera snapshot of the cautious and cunning killer but, all the same, he felt like he knew her. Sometimes he dreamed of meeting her, of stopping her on a sidewalk somewhere and calling her bluff as she gratefully gave herself up to capture. His wife, Grace, had said once that she felt like he was having an affair with a woman he hadn't met. Sometimes she said she'd rather he took another woman on the side than expend so much energy chasing the unknown killer. Hopkins had taken other women on the side anyhow. He'd assumed she never knew, but now Grace was gone, to her mother's in Prescott, and Cowdrey and Littwick had yet another reason to laugh up their sleeves. He should phone her.

Hopkins pulls up at a gas station and walks to a call box. He flips a coin between his fingers. Grace will insinuate and accuse, and he will defend himself. The usual pantomime will be played out. It will culminate, as it always does, with the usual accusations; that, twenty years back, he had driven their daughter away. And, as usual, he will have nothing to say. Hopkins puts the coin back in his pocket and returns to his car.

Night has fallen. And so have Danny and Sid, crashed out stoned on the sofa as outside the street lights wash the sky orange. Shortly before midnight, rustling plastic bags and rattling keys, Abby enters weighed down with case notes and supplies. Unwashed cups and plates are spread out over all available surfaces, and stinky pants pile up at the foot of the washing machine, daring it to swallow them.

'Well, well,' she says, unloading, and assuming a position at the centre of the rug, 'and what have you two hard-working lads been up to all day?'

'Ah,' says Danny, stirring first. 'Sorry, Abs. We were on the internet feeding obviously false information to all the paranoid nutters and . . .'

'Christ. Is that your idea of entertainment? You sick tasteless bastard . . .' Abby feels something begin to crumble within her. She looks at Sid. 'Sid?' But Sid is half asleep, or pretending to be, as if his assumed stillness will enable him to escape her predatory attention.

'Your missus is off on one, Sid!' says Danny, poking him.

'Fuck you, Danny!' Now Abby can't stop herself, and feels

months of irritation spilling out in an almost soothing wave of wrath. 'Do you actually pay any rent here or what? I've literally spent all day at work trying to sort out some poor tragically deluded man and yet you are happy to waste your lives indulging the fantasies of the de facto mentally ill for your own fucking pleasure. You make me sick. And it's my bloody computer and the e-mail address is in my bloody name and I pay all the bloody phone bills . . .' Abby snatches a cigarette up off the table. She is shaking with anger now, on the verge of tears of suppressed frustration. Bad omen, thinks Sid. She never smokes. Abby inhales, pauses, considers, and concludes, 'OK, Sid, that's it. I've had enough. I'm leaving.'

There's a moment's silence.

Abby takes another drag and exhales. 'I can't go on with this. I'm leaving the flat and I'm leaving you.' This is a surprise to Sid. A minute ago he'd been turning over in his mind the mess Danny had made of his Luther Peyote clippings, and wondering whether to buy a special box to keep them in, or whether it would be better to borrow a scanner and store them on computer discs. Now, completely out of nowhere, his girlfriend appears to be finishing with him. Or something. He looks at Abby. He looks at Danny. The television buzz fades into the distance. His vision fuzzes. Fibres of the threadbare carpet rush up to meet him. He breathes in and steadies himself. He considers the situation carefully and responds thoughtfully. 'Is it your time of the month, Abby?'

Abby bites her clenched fist. Danny stands. 'Shall I just go . . .' But Abby pushes him back down on to the sofa.

'There's no need, Danny. I'll come and pick up any of my stuff that's here tomorrow. If you think I'm spending another night here, you're sadly mistaken.'

'Abby . . .'

'I mean, Christ, Sid, I was lying in bed alone last week listening to you two sitting up watching a porn video.'

'Now come on, Abs, be fair on Sid,' interrupts Danny, diplomatically. 'It was Fat Ian's stag night.'

'Yeah, and Danny actually got the video, not me,' protests Sid, up and pacing around now.

'Yes, Abs, that's right. And I forced him to watch it. At knife point. And he didn't like it at all. In fact he said to me, "Danny, why am I watching this film of a woman having sex with a pig when I have my own beautiful girlfriend waiting for me in my bed? I must be mad!"'

Abby chokes on the smoke of her unwanted cigarette. Each waits for the other to offer some crumb of compassion, through a long and terrible silence. Finally Sid speaks, but not to Abby.

'Well, thanks, Danno. I think you might have swung it for me.' Abby goes to the door, picking up her shopping bags and taking them with her, and then stops, sizing up the two shrinking men.

'I mean, look at you, Sid. Quite apart from your failed career, your exploitation of my financial and sexual generosity, and your continual and habitual failure to do anything around the flat, you can't even dress yourself.' Sid looks down. A Luther Peyote T-shirt, bought by mail order, machine washed to Turin Shroud texture; grey, crumpled jeans; and one Wile E Coyote sock.

'Abby. You've caught me on a bad day, but . . .'

'They're all bad days with you, Sid,' says Abby, 'and me staying here isn't going to make them any better.' Her hand is on the lock.

Sid hits her with his best shot. 'Don't go. I'll kill myself if you go!' A half blossomed tear, curling on the cusp of Abby's eyelid, sucks itself back into its duct, boils somewhere in the centre of her skull, and turns to black tar.

'No you won't, Sid. You haven't got the guts.' Danny catches her eye and can't help but nod in agreement. 'Goodbye, Sid.' And she goes.

'Bye then, Abs,' says Danny, shutting the door after her. They sit as invisible air escapes from a crack in the ceiling with an inaudible hiss until the whole flat is deflated and falling in on itself. Sid looks at his sock.

'You know what, Danny . . .'

'What?'

'I really don't think she's coming back.'

'No. Nor me. Now we'll have to learn how to use the washing machine.'

Down below in the street Abby is fiddling at the lock of her green Mini. The sound of her sobs is so close to the sound of pure elation as to be indistinguishable. The summer night sky cracks and rumbles. An instant downpour soaks her. Lightning flashes eastwards over Streatham and with a hiss and a flicker the street lights of South London fail as one. Abby stands sodden in the sudden darkness, laughing at the absurd theatricality of it all. Somebody up there is determined to make her see this moment as a vital turning point in the drama of her life. Somebody has staged this. It's too perfect. She's left the scene through her appointed exit and the spotlight on Sid has been switched permanently off. There is a God. And he has a hack screenwriter's sense of drama. Abby opens the car door and slithers in.

Sid watches her through the window, her skirt riding up over her knees in the car's cramped cabin. He wipes at the wet window and presses his forehead against the glass. She is gone.

Never again will he lie alongside her sleeping shape at night and sniff the sweet smell of her. Never again will they fuck like dogs on Sunday mornings. Never again will he evade the question of marriage and a weekend with Mr and Mrs Quinton in their Warwickshire cottage. Never again her hips and arse, her kindness, her cleverness, her chicken soup, and never again the thin curls of black hair that run down from her navel. And never again will they act out all the dialogue from Jeff Wayne's *War of the Worlds* album. Next week, her delighted parents will hear the news by telephone with barely concealed relief, and will dutifully prepare themselves to entertain a new, gratefully received and respectable young professional suitor, some time between Christmas and the New Year, whenever's convenient with the two of you, really. 'I knew it would never last,' her father will say to her mother over cheese and crackers, in confidence, after the *Ten O'Clock News*, an hour before his bedtime.

Danny is still speaking: '. . . bright side, we could always start using the launderette, I suppose. Come on, let's go to Pixies'. Derek will gladly lay on a late-night lock-in for a man in your state. I'll buy you a Budwar.'

'What with?'

'Oh, yeah. Well. Plan B. We'll stay in and I'll make us a cup of tea. Is there any milk?'

'No. Abby said she'd get some . . .' says Sid, and starts to cry. Danny sits watching him for a while and then walks to the window and puts a hand on his shoulder.

'Come on, Sid, I know what will cheer yous up. A brief look at the Balham and Wandsworth Borders Only Free Nightly Live Entertainment.'

It's impossibly black now out in the unlit avenue. Alarm bells are ringing on Balham High Road as desperate opportunists take to the streets in the temporary darkness and attack the off licence. Wrapped against his will in Abby's pink abandoned duffel coat, Sid is being led by the hand up Marius Road towards the junction with Trinity, to the little traffic island by the post box. Propping his sniffling friend up against a traffic barrier, Danny lights him a joint and gestures over the road.

There, in the ochre circle of the lamplight, the usual midnight spectacle. The crazy fat naked woman of Wandsworth Common has commenced her nightly display, jumping and laughing, drinking deep on a can of something, swinging her dry old tits loose from her blouse to terrify passers by, flapping up her ballerina dress to flash her red arse into the headlights of oncoming traffic, and singing the usual song; *'Well would you like to swing on a star . . .'*

'Come on, Sid,' shouts Danny, slapping him vigorously on the back, 'join in if you know the words.' Sid's tears coalesce into hysteria, as Danny pushes him over the speed bumps, across to the old woman, and forces him to take her puffy, scabby hand. And the three of them circle in a wobbly ring, her smiling her two toothless mouths joyfully back at them, as they all sing with one voice: '. . . *carry moonbeams home in a jar, oh would you like to swing on a star, or would you rather be a pig?'*

A haze of mosquitoes follows Deputy Cowdrey and Littwick the police doctor up the steps to the sheriff's office. 'Yeah, but it's been coming for months,' protests Cowdrey. 'I've had it every Friday night since New Year. My kids went round his house trick or treating last Halloween and he sent 'em on their way saying Halloween was the work of the Devil and that the both of 'em were already on a one-way trip to Hell. Doug couldn't sleep with the lights off for a week.'

'That's Sheriff Hopkins, sure 'nuff,' says Littwick. 'Grace said he wouldn't even let their daughter watch the *Wizard of Oz* when she was a kid. Too satanic.'

'The sheriff has a daughter?'

'Yep. But she left him too. You can't help but feel sorry . . .'

'Oh, you can, Don, you can so easily help but feel sorry.'

Littwick pauses a moment, and wipes his glasses, considering Cowdrey's comment. 'Matthew wasn't always quite so bad, Roy. He had a spark once . . . Let's just say, were the sheriff a patient of mine I'd just recommend a long rest.'

'If the sheriff was a patient of yours, he'd be bagged and numbered and put on ice for evidence, and we'd both be a lot happier.' Cowdrey pushes through the door. Littwick sets his little leather bag on a table and opens it. The young policeman seated behind the desk looks up to greet them.

'Sheriff Hopkins not with you, Deputy Cowdrey?'

'No, he isn't with us. He's got better things to do than his job, apparently. Transfer any calls to me in his office. Cocktails at seven, Don. Don't forget, now.'

As Cowdrey enters Hopkins's room he hears the clatter of

Littwick, tangled up in his forensic equipment, struggling to disengage his hand from some rubber tubing. He shuts the door behind him, puts his feet on the desk and looks at the wall. There, hanging above him, is all the accumulated evidence of the sheriff's private project: a map full of pins, and a web of coloured string that connects them, each and every one, waiting for a woman to walk straight into its state correctional cast-iron heart.

The Hopi Boy
and the Sun – ii

On the following morning the boy made a
prayer stick and went out. Many young men
were sitting on the roof of the kiva. They sneered
when they saw him going by, though one of
them remarked, 'Better not make fun of him, I
believe the boy has supernatural power.'

The boy took some sacred meal made of
pounded turquoise, coral, shell, and cornmeal,
and threw it upward. It formed a trail leading
into the sky, and he climbed until the trail gave
out. He threw more of the sacred meal upward,
and a new trail formed. After he had done this
twelve times he came to the sun. But the sun
was too hot to approach, so the boy put new
prayer sticks into the hair at the back of his
head, and the shadow of their plumes protected
him from the heat.

'Who is my father?' he asked the sun.

'All children conceived in the daytime belong
to me,' the sun replied. 'But as for you, who
knows? You are young and have much to learn.'

The boy gave the sun a prayer stick and, falling down from the sky, landed back in his village.

Hopi Indian legend, reported by
Franz Boas in 1922

Five

Mr A.R.Y. Lewis, astronaut, takes a last look around his bedsit. His afternoon was spent packing, making phone calls, changing money, chasing cheap air tickets, and tracing over every casual encounter he'd ever had in a new light of darkest suspicion. 'They closed me down,' he had concluded, 'and wiped my memory to cover their tracks . . .' They'd told bigger lies before, after all. He knew. He'd read all the available literature. The Russians accidentally burned two dogs alive on Sputnik 6 in 1960 and nobody ever found out, and when Valentin Bondarenko went up in flames in an isolation chamber around the same time, the Soviet Space Agency made it a state secret for twenty-five years. Only last week he'd read that NASA had faked photos allowing them to pin any failure in John Glenn's 1962 orbit flight on Fidel Castro. But of course, none of that meant anything. He might just be mad. 'Or maybe they just lost me in action somewhere, and now they're getting nervous because they think I might have figured things out.' Everything fitted the theory. When Laura told him to look at the compass ceiling carvings upstairs in the Masonic pub back room, was she testing him somehow, trying to see if he'd make a connection? And the fat old man on Hampstead Heath, had he been hoping Lewis would let something significant slip, concealing his line of questioning as a fumbled attempt at some sexual assignation? What had he meant by his mumblings of moonbeams and jars? Even Lewis's internet informers might have some sinister hidden agenda, double-bluffing him with skill and subtlety, leading him to his death. He alone held the secret to the destiny of nations. Or else, he had thought, sober suddenly, he could just be . . . imagining everything. How attractive, to be a lone wolf at war with an organisation of global influence. How sad, to be no one anyone could remember. Maybe his entire experience from the point he woke up on the corner of Archer Street and Shaftesbury Avenue that cold January night had been an absurdly detailed hallucination, running at double speed in his head, as a grieving wife mourns by his hospital bedside and wonders whether to turn the life-support machine off. It stands to reason. His situation is like a bad dream, enough people had told him that, struggling sympathetically to find something to say. So maybe it simply *is* a bad dream. Or a waking delusion. Of course, he could have chased up Laura via their landlord then and there on a phone at the café. 'Laura. I'm on to you. You are an agent of the Freemasons and you only had sex with me to see if I remembered anything about stealing the Holy Grail off the Americans from its orbit around the moon. Yes. That's right. You heard correctly.' Either way she'd have denied it. If Lewis was imagining the whole thing then he'd just have become another anecdote, that crazy guy she slept with once in London who had such low self-esteem he invented a conspiracy to justify someone fucking him. And if he was right? Then he'd have given himself away and they'd be obliged to finish him off once and for all. SAS men in black balaclavas, smashing in through the window at 3 a.m., brandishing sharpened compasses and blunt architects' tools. A child would pinch itself awake. But Lewis's anxieties were too deep beneath his skin for such a simple remedy. He had no choice but to see the whole thing through, to follow every blind alley he encountered and see where he wound up, no matter how far from home they led him this time. Only then could he learn to trust his own mind. Or, alternatively, only with the certainty that he was wrong, could he abandon himself to madness with good grace, give up the struggle for sanity and slide into publicly-funded, opiate bliss with a clear conscience. And besides, he'd always wondered what life would be like on Jupiter and Mars.

So, on his way home from Café Cyberama, Lewis had stopped in Henry Pordes' second-hand book shop on Charing Cross Road, surrendering himself happily to circumstance. After successfully locating a map of Arizona, a dusty Middle English edition of Malory's *Morte Darthur* soon offered itself up. Leaning against a stack of unsold paperback pulp, he read the crucial passages again, mentally cross-referencing them with the other ancient texts he'd committed to memory, mouthing the words with increasing excitement. *'Than anone they harde crakynge and cryynge of thundir, that hem thought the palyse sholde all to-dryve.'* Bastardised from the earlier, anonymous *Queste de Saint Graal,* of course, but impressive none the less. *'So in the myddys of the blast entyrde a sonnebeame, more clerer by seven tymys than ever they saw day.'*

'This isn't a public library, sir.'

Woe betide those cunts if I am right, he thought as he left the bookshop. He'd teach them to shoot him into space and then throw him on the scrapheap. He was a skilled space professional! Probably.

A young woman in a duffel coat stopped him to sign a petition against animal testing. 'Can I ask you your name, age and your occupation?'

'My name isn't mine. And nobody knows how old I am exactly, not even me myself,' he said to her, wide-eyed. 'But one thing's for certain. I *am* an astronaut.' And, walking away as she stared after him, he regretted his candid reply immediately. He saw her write something down. What if she was one of them?

And later, back home, lying on his bed, Malory's text offered Lewis the words that finally made explicit his only available course of action: *'Than entird into the halle the Holy Grayle coverde with whyght samyte, but there was none that myght se hit nother whom that bare hit . . . "Now," seyde sir Gawayne, "never shall I re-turne unto the courte agayne tylle I have sene the Grayle more opynly than hit hath bene shewed here."'* Of course. Spreading the map over the bed, he had checked the location of the airbase the Sphincter Boys had mentioned. There, some way to the south-east, north of the Mexican border, nestled between the valleys of San Simon and Sulphur Springs, is the print and paper topographical reality of Coronado. Why shouldn't the Grail be in a deserted American airbase? Lewis had read all the available research, after the image of the floating chalice first invaded his dreams, and still he was none the wiser.

The common consensus was that the Grail resided at Roslin, north-east of Edinburgh, in an underground room beneath a chapel built in 1440 by Sir William St Clair. St Clair had inherited treasure saved by the Knights Templars from the Temple of Jerusalem in 1140, the supposed resting place of the Grail, and transported it to Scotland to the Kilwinning estate of the St Clair family. The building replicates in miniature the floor-plan of the Temple of Jerusalem, and is inscribed with Masonic symbols masquerading as conventional Christian images. Lewis had hitchhiked north last winter, stared at the building's unnecessarily hideous gargoyles, and wandered around its esoterically encrusted interior, but to no avail. There was a presence there, a sense of the supposed evil-doing that had seen the Scottish Church deconsecrate the chapel for nearly 300 years, but why hide something, only to announce it with carvings even an amateur adept like himself could easily decode? He had stood on the spot where self-published paperback archeologists claimed the cup was concealed, and yet he had felt nothing.

And over half a century ago, Lewis discovered, an SS officer called Otto Rahn and the Nazi philosopher Alfred Rosenberg searched the Cathar castles of Southern France to find the Grail for the Führer, who had hoped its powers might turn the tide of the war, but they returned home to Hitler empty-handed. And the Zodiac allegedly spelt out on the landscape by the rivers and trackways of Gorges du Verdon, in Provence, apparently revealed the location of the holy cup, but it too had been proven to hide no secrets. Travelling south-west on an awayday return, Lewis had observed that the people of Glastonbury, with all their incense shops, crystal merchants and tarot readers, had a financial incentive for maintaining that their crumbling abbey had hidden tunnels that concealed the holy blood. But they knew in their tie-dyed, hippie hearts that they were lying to get the tourists in. The Italian castle of del Monte, founded by mystical Teutonic Knights, is built in the shape of a giant cup, but that would be too simple, wouldn't it? And a painting in the church of the Italian village of Torre suggests the holy chalice is hidden there. But it isn't. And Lewis had read of Narta Monga, in the Caucasus mountains, which legendarily boasted a magical cauldron with Grail-like properties, and of how Genova's cathedral at Cesarea had once held a green glass dish, allegedly used to collect the blood of Christ. But the thing was, Lewis had once held the Grail, had held it in his hands, floating before his face as he drifted out from his ship, and he knew it wasn't a cauldron or a dish. It was the Grail. And if it ever had been buried under the floor in Roslin chapel, or walled up in the Cathar castles, or hidden in a natural Zodiac in Provence, or buried in Glastonbury Abbey, or concealed in a cup-shaped palace, or rusting in Russia in another shape, it wasn't any longer. Because Lewis remembers, clearly now, that he himself had taken the holy vessel from its new heavenly resting place and brought it back home to earth, only to lose both it and his identity at some crucial moment. Wherever the Grail had been, it was there no longer. An empty airbase in Arizona was as good a place as any for Lewis to begin his quest, to recover both the Holy

Grail, and himself. Now, if only he had a squire to help him saddle up.

And now Lewis waits at Archway underground station for the last train of the evening. There's a flight to Las Vegas at 4 a.m., the most convenient bucket-hop his savings could buy at such short notice.

'Did you get me my bow and arrows then, Wally?' A voice next to him. It's the bearded freak from the hospital, crouched down by the bench, parting his long hair to look under each seat in turn, and seeing him down here in the striplight Lewis suddenly remembers where he knew him from.

'You. You were at Willesden depot on Sunday night.'

'That's right, Wally. Peter Rugg's my name, and didn't you have a night of it, running around like you had a space rocket up your arse. Calmed down a bit now, have you?' Lewis smiles, and watches Rugg crawl along the deserted platform, checking every inch of floor.

'What are you looking for, Peter?'

'A fag-end, Wally. Bloody thing.'

'You're looking for one cigarette butt in particular?' asks Lewis, curious.

'Oh, yes,' says Peter Rugg, sitting now, uncomfortably close to Lewis. 'The rollie that undid me.' A brief pause, listening to the last northbound Northern Line train rattle past on the other platform.

'And how will you know it when you find it?'

'Oh, by the smell of it. Finest Mexican weed it was, not the homegrown crap the youngsters puff away on. Back then there was weed that could send you to sleep for a thousand years. And would that it had, would that it had. For now I'll never rest until I find it.' Peter Rugg stares fixedly into Lewis's eyes and clutches at his collar. 'Bloody Calvert, yes him, Robert Calvert, from Hawkwind. Silver Machine, remember? You know it from some fuckin' advert or something. But this was back before Captain Lockheed and any of that nonsense, when Calvert was in Hawkwind, the finest acid-rock band this island ever produced, Blighty's own Grateful Dead, still slogging on somewhere they are, the psychedelic warlords that disappear in smoke. Pouff! And Calvert, to see Robert Calvert in full flight, well . . .' The names are meaningless to Lewis, but he nods appreciatively all the same. Rugg continues. '"Come and stay," he said, old Captain fuckin' Calvert, "it's no problem, Peter, my good fellow." And for one languid early 70s summer I was the cock of Portobello Road, Bobby Calvert's left-hand man, with a paisley pad to crash down right comfy in, early every morning after the night before. Bob brought the ladies and I brought the rest, know what I mean. The keys to the kingdom. How do you think old Captain Calvert knew that space was deep? 'Cos I fuckin' showed him. The exact depth, to the nearest inch, give or take a million light years, eh? Then one night I was in alone in Calvert's castle, alone and smoking that powerful Mexican grass. Passed out I did, dead to this world and most of the others. But what fantastic dreams may come, eh, and come they did. Columns of orange energy licking at my heels, my little old cock spitting spunky firebolts, and the heat of a thousand exploding suns warming me from my nuts to my heart, all toasty like. Only, it weren't a dream, was it? Oh, no. I'd let that little number drop down the back of the sofa somewhere and whoosh!, now Captain Calvert's prize pad was aflame in gilded cinders.'

Lewis disentangles himself from Peter Rugg's clawing fingers. 'And what happened?'

'Well, Wally, I'm outside with the fire engines givin' it some of that, when Calvert comes home, off his tits and everybody else's too by the looks of it, shaking like nobody's business, flying helmet, jodhpurs, the usual get-up. "Jesus, Peter," he says, "I leave you for half an hour and . . ." "Lay off, Bobby," says I, "it could have happened to anyone." "No, Peter Rugg," says Calvert, "it could only have happened to you, 'cos you, Peter Rugg, are a fucking dozy scrounging cunt. Now fuck off!" And that was the last I saw of him, apart from on the telly and the like. He died in the end, old Captain Calvert.

Nobody asked me to the fucking funeral either. They think I'm shit, those cunts, shit on their platform shoes. That's why I have to find it, see, the rollie that undone me. Cunts!'

'I'm sorry, I wish there was something I could do to help.'

'Oh, but there is,' says Peter, smiling. 'You just keep your pretty eyes skinned for that fucking pesky joint, and if you see it, make sure it's well and truly stubbed out, eh? Then I won't have to spend all my bloody time looking for the sodding thing. I've got better stuff to do, you know. I used to be an antiques dealer, part-time like, but I was me own boss, and the profits, and the posh snatch, plenty of money, husbands away . . .' Lewis shakes Peter by the hand. 'Lemmy from Motorhead's real name is Ian, you know, not Lemmy at all. Ian? What's all that about?' Lewis hears the rumble of his train, and stands, ready to board. 'It's a pity you're off so sudden,' says Peter, 'there's so much more I had to tell you.'

The empty train squeals in with a hiss of brakes and the doors open. 'Anything in particular?' asks Lewis, stepping off the platform, keen to get away all of a sudden, and a little disconcerted somehow by the way the conversation is developing.

'Oh, a special story just for you, Wally,' Peter reflects. 'All about the white bird that sleeps beneath the sand. It's going to spill its greasy guts, you know, Wally. I met Merlin at Stonehenge in '74 and he told me, straight up, I ain't jokin' ya. I was tripping for England at the time, admittedly, but I'm sure it was him. I recognised him from the films, you know, white beard, four-leaf clover, funny hat . . .'

'Really . . .' says Lewis, and feels a sense of relief as the doors close in front of his face.

'He told me all about the holy blood,' shouts Rugg, 'and the desert. And the voice of the serpent. And the white bird.'

'I'll bear it in mind,' mouths Lewis through the glass. As the train pulls into the tunnel he's sure he can hear Peter Rugg shouting, something about blood, something about a white bird. And how a whore shall lead them.

* * *

A white bird, half crushed by a car that's long since passed, struggles on the sun-baked blacktop, crawling in circles that centre on a crippled wing. As its life drains away, the bird suffers a memory of flight, and wonders how an action once instinctive has suddenly become impossible to achieve. It arches its back, raises its head a little from the road surface, and seems to find its balance somehow, sensing that the cool roadside dust is within its reach, a more dignified place to die. The wheel of Sheriff Hopkins's patrol car squashes it flat in a white flurry.

Hopkins waves away a fluttering squall of dislodged feathers, sucked in through the open window, and gives the bird a cursory backwards glance as he winds up the window. A lone feather bobs miserably on the thermals of the air conditioning, and finally floats to land on the dashboard, next to a six-inch plastic Jesus and a gummed-down photo of a plumpish, cotton dress woman. Hopkins tears the photo off the dash and holds it up to his face. He turns the Holy Saviour face forwards.

'Enjoy the view,' he says, and slowly screws up the photograph. And winding down the window a little once more, he bundles it out into the desert.

At Tuba City Hopkins pulls up and looks at his notebook. Seeing Alice's Breakfast Stop over the street he opens the car door and steps out, stopping only to check his reflection in the shiny metal bodywork. He pulls his belt up over the tiny bulge of his old man's belly, pushes his balls down between his legs, and enters the restaurant.

Alice stands behind the counter cooking, and Little Joe still lurks in the shadows with a cigarette and a coffee. 'Good day, ma'am,' Hopkins steps up to the counter. 'I'm looking for a woman, hair tied back so, about so high, driving a white convertible. Did you ever see her?' Alice looks across nervously at Little Joe. He gets up and leaves. Hopkins notices and presses her. 'Well?' She fakes thinking about it a moment, methodically sucking on a pencil like a schoolgirl actress.

'No. Can I get you a coffee, sheriff? On the house.'

'Sure. Thanks.' She gestures for the sheriff to sit, but he just stays standing. 'You know she's probably a nice enough looking girl,' he elaborates as she pours his cup, 'as normal looking as you or I, maybe a regular customer for whom you might feel a misplaced sense of loyalty, but . . . a person can easily be other than they seem, a person can betray you as easily as look at you. A woman can . . .'

Alice slides the coffee in front of him. 'That'll be two dollars.'

'You said it was on the house.' The old woman points up at a sign above the till and stands impassive. 'The management reserves the right to withdraw special offers without prior notice.' Hopkins grunts and fishes through his pocket. He slams down the change, takes one brief sip of his drink, spits it on to the tiled floor, and turns to go. 'I'll be back, ma'am, back to refresh your memory. You can count on it.'

'Pleasure doing business with you, sheriff,' Alice shouts after him, as he slams the door and the bell rings. She watches him as he crosses the street.

'Fuck, shit, and piss in my eye.' The sheriff stares at his car. All the tyres are slashed, hissing almost inaudibly into the dry air. He puts his hands on his hips, and looks up and down the empty highway. Across the street Alice is hanging a closed sign on the door. Sheriff Hopkins tips his hat to her with grim-faced courtesy, and walks off to find a mechanic.

Not twenty miles south, down on the banks of the Little Colorado, and a few hundred yards off road in a sheltered sandy depression, Tracy settles down to sleep under the stars. Fed fat on potato chips and the better part of a six-pack, she pulls a brown Navajo blanket up over her body and lies down on the back seat. Alice had given it to her, wordlessly and without charge, before she watched her go. She listens to the erratic impulses of the in-car radio as it struggles to find a signal it can trust, finally fixing on the haunted whisper of some distant country-rock station. It could be a bunch of reverential youngsters, or a classic cut from the 70s, she wouldn't know. Her father had banned it from the house.

'The Devil has invaded and distorted country, classical, soul and Christian music,' he had said, snapping a copy of a reluctantly loaned Kiss album over his knee, 'and heavy metal is turning millions into rock-a-holic zombies.' And he had handed her a copy of a pamphlet called *Dancing with Demons – The Music's True Master*, and sent her up to bed. Once he found her, huddled under the covers, tuning a tiny transistor to classic rock radio at mouse volume. He snatched it up, stamped it into the floor before her, and spanked her raw.

Tracy shuts her eyes and submits to the music on the radio, as a hickory-smoked voice fades in over the gentle acoustics and pedal steel arcs. And as the song dissolves into a beer commercial, a coyote howls, and she dreams that she sees Roscoe, floating over the dry river-bed before her, hanging suspended above the barrel cacti, somewhere between the windshield and the sunken sun, making his peace, and wishing her luck.

At Alfredo's Licensed Kebab and Vegetarian House of Delicious Mediterranean Eats and Live Music, 1137a Streatham High Road, Alfredo puts his hands over his ears as his mouth hardens into a frown. Dire Straits never sounded like this. An old lady chokes on her olives and a party of drunken office girls head for the door. Seconds earlier, Sid's broken spirit finally rose up from its shackles, and he stepped forwards on to a primed effects pedal to supply a uniquely distorted re-interpretation of the bass riff of 'Twistin' By The Pool' that Mark Knopfler would have been hard pressed to identify. Elderly diners winced. The barman threw up his hands. Ian had ignored the feedback fuzz for a few bars, mistaking Sid's burst of self-expression for Alfredo's PA picking up local minicab radio messages as usual. But now he turns, catches sight of Sid's determined expression, and pushes him away from his pedals. Danny abandons the rhythm and belts a cymbal, paff!, a silent film fighting sound effect. Ever the professional musician, Andy tries to keep playing the lead part properly, as Sid stands and pushes Ian back towards the lip of the stage. Danny laughs and paffs his cymbal. Sid picks up his bass and holds it above his head.

'Go on,' says Danny, 'do it, you can only regret it for the rest of your life.' And Sid smashes the wailing instrument into the front of his tiny Marshall amplifier.

'Sid, ' says Ian, clenching his hands in his trademark gesture of suppressed rage, 'you fucking . . . twit!' They scuffle, Sid swinging Ian round playground-style by his collar, which tears and rips as the fat man falls to the floor. 'Sid, you wanker,' he shouts, 'that's my Brothers in Arms tour jacket!' Down by Sid's feet there's a belated pop, as the amplifier fizzes and dies.

'Imagine how exciting it would have been if that amp had exploded, though,' says Danny, over the sound of Andy still manfully forging ahead. A tiny puff of smoke trickles out of the amplifier. Fffffft. Sid looks down at it, and down at Ian's prostrate form, and then with a last burst of defiant energy he flicks his Vs into the insignificant crowd, rips off his stone-washed denim shirt and exits stage left. Ian turns from Danny's laughing face and sees Alfredo, standing in front of the empty tables, arms folded, and slowly shaking his fat old head. Andy catches the restaurateur's eye and smiles appealingly, as he finishes the song alone and bows. Danny plays a celebratory circus rimshot, shrugs, and starts to skin up on his snare drum.

'I expect it'll be Shepperton Starship down here next Tuesday and Thursday, then,' he says, to no one in particular.

Hours later, Danny and Sid enter the flat, Sid carrying a broken, twisted bass, with one black eye, his Sultans of Streatham stage clothes shredded. They clutch the back of the sofa for support, wrangle the last of the evening's perfunctory rider from a bag, and collapse. 'I was really on a roll there, Danno. I think, for a moment, on stage tonight, I finally found my own artistic voice.'

Danny starts to skin up. 'I'm very pleased for you, but in

case you'd forgotten, the Sultans of Streatham was our only paying gig.'

'Ah, well, come on, Danny, did you really want to spend the rest of your life playing in a Dire Straits tribute band?'

'It might have been nice to have the option, Sid. What do we do now?'

There's a pause. Sid starts smiling to himself as he recalls a plan that he has previously proposed only in moments of extreme drunkenness. He raises an eyebrow, and points to a poster of Luther Peyote on the wall. Danny looks at the wizened face and winces. 'No, no, Sid, you can't be serious. Not that . . . No.'

'Yes, Danno, that. Let's actually do it. Abby's gone. I honestly don't give a flying fuck. I've finally got nothing to lose. Things can't get any worse. We pack up, fly to Arizona, track down Luther Peyote, and convince him to reconvene the Round Tabyls . . . with us to back him up.'

Danny takes a long, calming drag, and explodes. 'Have you any idea how much it costs to get to America, Sid? We haven't got any money, we're not even sure if Luther Peyote is still actually alive, let alone whether he's in a fit state to play anything! We'll end up a pair of bleach boned skellingtons laid out in the dust of the desert with vultures pecking out our eyes and wolves doing worse things. And, correct me if I'm wrong, but didn't you smash your only bass to bits in a Greek restaurant only a few hours ago? The whole idea is the stupidest, most ill-conceived, ridiculous, hare-brained scheme I have ever heard!'

'So, you're coming with me, then?'

Danny looks at his friend, standing before him in torn Dire Straits pantomime costume. He looks at the decaying flat, at the sofa Sid has let him sleep on for the best part of a decade, at the empty fridge, and at Sid's now empty bed. He remembers the day he talked Sid out of following the Lemon Pies into pop stardom with Timothy Waterhouse, and he feels, in an uncharacteristic moment of charity, that he owes him, if not a few thousand pounds of unpaid rent arrears, then at least this.

'Of course. What else am I going to do?' he says. They laugh at their joke, a rehearsed formula they've used a thousand times before.

'Great. I knew I could count on you, Danno. We're outta this shithole in twenty-four hours flat, before I come to my senses, eh? Now, who are we going to get to pay for our flight?'

In the silence, Danny grins, and it's Sid's turn to feel anxious. 'No, Danno, not Pat, anyone but him.'

Six

Vegas. The night heat rises invisibly from the pavements as Lewis wades the Strip, ankle-deep in discarded pornography. Four-colour pamphlets promoting personal services are thrown at passing pedestrians by skinny leaping boys. Lewis pushes through dollar-eyed waves of the fattest, ugliest, most tragic human beings he has ever imagined. Inside the casinos, the cyclical electronic melodies of the slot machines merge with the clatter of small change and the air-conditioning hum to fashion a formless symphony of futility. At the end of the Strip, where the artificially cooled city scuffles briefly with the desert and then retreats defeated, a cobalt blue pyramid renders even the most absurd excesses of the rest of the Las Vegas landscape utterly irrelevant, bigger than anything Pharaoh ever dreamed of. The pyramid, he remembers, was one of the few manmade structures he had seen from space. Or did he? Or had he just been told that? No, no, the Las Vegas Luxor pyramid and the Great Wall of China, dammit. But even with the curtains drawn, its neon aura could still cast nauseating geometrics on a motel room wall. Above the bar of the Treasure Island Casino, more TV channels than could realistically be useful pulsed eviscerated fractals of local news, some new law for Nevada state, a motel murder by a mystery date, a man last seen near the Hoover Dam, and more news at eleven. And from space, this is what you can see. This and the Great Wall of China. Tomorrow he would drive south-east and seek his answer, but tonight he had been persuaded to linger a little in Las Vegas and take in the sights.

'See, ain't you glad you stayed?' Lewis had got talking to Spike on the flight over. He had shut his eyes to quell the memories that rose within him, as the upsurge of the jet at take-off created secondary echoes of all the landing platform nightmares that woke him nightly. And then he had heard a voice in his ear and felt a hand on his forearm. 'Hey, man, relax. It's safer than crossing the road.'

Spike was nineteen, twenty, a student in Tucson. She'd been in England to see Stonehenge on a research grant. Lank brown hair fell down over a chubby, pretty, sun-browned face, and the seat-belt pulled against her tummy, soft and shapeless behind a white T-shirt. A cartoon alien with curly antennae stared back at him from her bobbing chest. 'Hi, how are you?' said its speech bubble. They fell into conversation, somewhere between peanuts and pasta.

'What are you studying in Tucson anyway?'

'North American Indian peyote rituals,' began the girl, rolling a white tab of gum on to her fat pink tongue. 'There's so much the magically disenfranchised Anglo-Saxon West can learn from Native Americans' respectful relationship with natural hallucinogens. I hope, one day, to be in a position of enough power and influence to provide every living American with a chemical short-cut to a vision of their own faux-objective notion of a reality, one which they can so far only perceive but subjectively. Then I'd like to see the Republicans get re-elected, know what I mean?'

'Oh yes, most definitely,' Lewis agreed, though he had lost the thread half a minute ago. 'I'm terribly sorry, I don't know your name?'

'Spike,' she said, putting out a hand.

'Spike . . . I'm Lewis. A.R.Y. Lewis.'

'Weird name.'

'I forgot mine, so I chose a new one off a war memorial.'

'Uh-huh? Cool!' The fuselage hummed around them as they both struggled for something else to say. 'What are you going to the States for anyway, A.R.Y.?' she had asked at last.

Lewis hadn't been addressed like that before and it caught him unawares, making him suspicious. 'I'm looking . . . looking for . . . something.'

'Oh, yeah,' Spike laughed. 'Let me guess. This is some big self-discovery mid-thirties life crisis trip, and only the wide open spaces of Arizona are big enough to accommodate your problems, huh? The rock stacks and cliff faces will echo your inner torment while our vast landscape can offer you the chance to escape into an emptiness a childhood diet of westerns and bad road movies has imbued with a mythological significance, yep? The original pathetic fallacy! Seen the Grand Canyon yet, A.R.Y.? Bet that put the gaps in *your* life in some kind of perspective, didn't it? You European men are so predictable . . . with your *anxieties*.'

'I beg your pardon?'

'Look, A.R.Y., it's just the place where we live. There's nothing so very special about it. A sense of distance allows you and your tea-drinking buddies to buy into an American dream that doesn't ring true for any of us.' Spike had hit her stride now, and other passengers in the next block of seating looked round as her bellowing voice woke them from semi-slumber, but Lewis couldn't help admiring the young woman's gusto. 'Try asking the guy in the gas station if he's "found himself" lately and you'll just get a smack in the mouth for an answer.'

'Young lady, I really feel you have misjudged me,' Lewis protests.

'Oh, yeah? Well, prove it. If it's your first time out here you really should make a space to, like, submit to a local's idea of the tourist high spots. I'll show you something that'll kill your quest for spirituality stone dead.'

And, indeed, she had done. 'Look at this place. Out of all the sucky casinos, this has to be the super-suckiest.' Lewis stands next to Spike on the sidewalk and looks ahead at a glowing white plastic castle, the turrets topped with red and blue cones, like the palace of Mad King Ludwig of Bavaria rebuilt from scratch in Lego bricks. 'Behold!' she shouts, throwing back her arms and making her bra-less breasts swing. 'Excalibur!'

Spike takes Lewis by the hand and leads him over a white concrete bridge that connects the casino to the road. Beneath them an eight-foot-high robot dragon rises from a dismal moat and does battle with an underpaid actor in chain mail. A woman in a long blue dress stands on a rock and screams appropriately. Pushing into a wall of cool air, they enter the building by a moving walkway, and Lewis laughs at the plastic crests and coats of arms nailed up on the wall.

'Hey, you wanna buy me dinner?' says Spike, bypassing an enormous domed space of rattling slot machines and downcast, dazzled gamblers. 'I know just the place.'

In a huge underground vaulted chamber, they file into lines of benches surrounding a central arena, hung with banners. Mock-medieval music plays as sun-browned wenches in Alpine blouses dole out chicken, brown bread and diet coke in plastic goblets. A dressing-up-box king takes centrestage, singled out in a spotlight. 'I am Arthur,' he shouts into a concealed microphone through a false beard, 'and I welcome you to my Grail Quest!' At the other end of the arena, through a translucent blue sheet, Lewis sees the shadow of a slim maiden raise a shining cup, and suddenly six armoured riders thunder into the ring on strong, sleek black horses. 'Let the games commence!' says the king, and hurries to safety as the knights clash together in minutely choreographed combat.

'Isn't this just too perfect,' says Spike, squeezing his knee. And indeed, thinks Lewis, it is too perfect. This woman has been placed, just like his neighbour before her, to monitor his reactions to this low-rent pantomime of his own personal hopes and fears. He wonders for a moment if the whole event really happens twice nightly, or whether it has been staged solely for his benefit. Even the audience might just be actors. Then he smiles, shakes his head, dismisses his theory as a momentary madness and, somehow, finds himself settling back to enjoy the show. Why not? In an hour or so they'll be out of here. Spike wants a ride. He's hired a car. He can drop her in Tucson, and maybe call her bluff.

Across town, the Hampstead Man has found himself inexplicably drawn to the black pyramid of the Luxor Casino. He has noted the registration of the car Lewis hired, and now he wanders through the building, appalled at its architecture. While the exterior of the Luxor is an imposing structure that the master masons of old could not help but have admired, the interior strikes the Hampstead Man as silly. It's so cluttered. Random stages and raised restaurants rise up into the potentially impressive open spaces of the building, clouding his vision and making it impossible to get any sense of scale. Every inch of Luxor defies logic and makes a mockery of the cosmic sense of order, imposed and expounded by the Great Architect himself, and which great architecture is duty-bound to echo. He feels an urge to knock off all the superfluous knobs and excrescences; to further smooth and prepare the stones; to adjust the rectangular corners of the building; to assist in bringing rude matter into due form; to lay and prove the horizontals; to adjust uprights while fixing them on their proper bases; for thus, by square conduct, level steps, and upright intentions, one might hope to ascend to those immortal mansions whence all goodness emanates.

But the Hampstead Man fights off his disgust, and ascends instead not to an immortal mansion, but to the gaming floor, where the slot machines call to him from beneath the cacophony. 'All work and no play makes Jack a dull boy,' he whispers to himself, and waves over a waitress.

*　　*　　*

A telephone box stands, pointless and alone on a desert highway, miles from the nearest settlement, perhaps some loss-making tax dodge for a unusually profitable local communications company. Back in the 70s the natives hereabouts had complained that their kids learned about telephones in mission schools, but rarely had the opportunity to use them. Maybe this one had been a peace offering, but the shabby shacks it served have long since fallen. As the sun sets, Hopkins's patrol car passes it in the fading orange glow, left to right in widescreen, speeding between Cedar Ridge and Bitter Springs, and it is alone again. A minute later, the car re-enters the frame in reverse, and screeches to a halt. Hopkins gets out. He adjusts his belt, his tie, his balls. He looks over his shoulder, and up and down the empty highway, and approaches the telephone, hunch shouldered and low to the ground, determined. He flips in a coin and dials.

In a pink-wallpaper bedroom in Prescott, a woman sprawls on a bed, popping one chocolate after another into a mouth that chews with relentless bovine symmetry, fat leaking from a green nightdress. Over TV game-show noise a phone next to the bed rings unanswered, as a train rattles south on a railway track outside the window. Downstairs, an old woman calls up. 'Grace? Are you going to answer that, Grace?'

Grace Hopkins looks at the phone. And finally picks it up. 'Grace?' The distant, condensed, insect voice. 'Grace? When are you coming back to me, honey?' Grace Hopkins savours the desperation in her husband's voice. 'When, Grace, honey? People are starting to talk.' She bites her bottom lip.

'They're starting to talk, are they, Matthew? Well, they've talked before, haven't they?'

'Grace, honey . . .'

'No, Matthew,' she continues, 'they talked in public when we married, so young. And they talked in private about your little peccadilloes, but I overheard them. You shamed me, Matthew. Stella saw you with a woman in Winslow when you told me you were just working a shift.'

'Grace . . .'

'They talked to me too, Matthew, the talkers, when you drove our only daughter away . . .'

'For the last time, Grace, I didn't drive her anywhere. She left of her own free will.'

'You drove her away, Matthew. You know it in your heart. She did nothing wrong, save the usual things. She got high a few times. And she made out with older boys at drive-ins. And because she could never remember the name of the main feature when you quizzed her in the kitchen, after you'd waited up till all hours, flicking on the hall light as she came in the door, Lord, did you hate her for it . . .'

A hundred miles away, Hopkins chokes. 'I didn't hate her, Grace. I was her father. She was my daughter.'

'You hated her, Matthew, you hated her because you envied her, because she made you feel old and ugly, because she asked too many difficult questions, because she reminded you of what you had become.' She hears the receiver shaking in his hand and scents victory. 'Twenty years now, Matthew, and we don't know if she's dead or alive, and you drove her away, and now you've lost me too. I hope you die alone, Matthew Hopkins . . .'

'Grace . . .'

'I hope you die alone, in an unmarked grave, shot dead by a stranger's gun, somewhere out in the desert where no one will ever find you. It's more than you deserve. I will not miss you. I will not mourn you. No one will. There's no one left for you, Matthew.' Click. She's finished. Grace Hopkins pops another chocolate in her mouth. The casing cracks, and oozes strawberry.

Elsewhere, the sheriff smashes the handset against the plastic phone box casing, and walks back to his car. He sits a moment, gripping the steering wheel with white knuckles, and drives off to find a motel, somewhere north towards Utah, well shot of Indian lands. Dust particles dance in the fading light around the phone box, pointless and alone on a desert highway.

*   *   *

Pat's grey lips part, and his mouth opens to exhale a cloud of smoke, hanging translucent in the candlelight. Bunsen burners, hydroponic systems, and deflagrating flasks cast scientific shadows on the walls of the garden shed laboratory. Sid can't actually remember ever having seen Pat's face, but he assumes he has one. It is 5 a.m. on a Thursday. He doesn't believe he's let Danny talk him into this. He'd rather strike a deal with Jabba the Hut.

'Export now, is it, Pat? Surely that's an eccentric business proposition, even for you?' ventures Danny through a skunk fug.

'The international web of commerce. The rules of supply and demand, boys. Supply and demand.'

'Yeah, Pat,' says Sid, 'but usually Britain demands and the rest of the world supplies.'

'There are forces at work beyond the scope of your tiny Balham imaginations, boys. I serve a higher interest. A lifetime's work boiled down to pill form. Lead into gold. Lead into gold. Do we have a deal?' Pat's mouth emits another cloud of smoke, this one so enormous that it suggests to Sid that he must have a secret third lung specially evolved for the purpose. A cash advance to buy air tickets is pressed into his trembling hand. 'Los Bros O'Fernandez will pay you a courier fee on delivery, the rest of the details you need know nothing about.' Pat fishes out the plastic-wrapped packages from underneath a blanket. 'Careful with these, now. A lifetime's work, like I said.' He prepares to pop open a bottle of Thunderbird. 'A toast to the pair of you and your new lives, eh?' He pours. 'Now, best leave necking the stash until the very last moment, and remember, lads, if you cross me . . .'

'Yeah, yeah. We better teach our arses to speak.'

'I'm glad we understand each other. Cheers!'

Tracy wakes in her car to the sound of the radio. Something about a suicide and a suspect. She shudders, wipes the sleep from her eyes, swigs at some water and lights a cigarette. She imagines Roscoe's grandmother, or Alice at the café, called in for questioning and cracking under pressure, and suddenly Mexico seems very far away. She straightens up, turns the keys in the ignition and steps on the gas, southwards.

She remembers the last time she went so far south. South of Heaven. Her journey had been an unashamed smorgasbord of previously forbidden pleasures. First she had tasted the obvious ones, buying short skirts in Tucson and smoking cigarettes as she chatted to the border patrol. And she got drunk alone in a bar in Nogales and rode a bus out of town overnight, unsteady and not a little sick. Waking in the big city, work was easy to come by, dancing in clubs where owners were easy on age restrictions. And there were drugs, of course, easily available, and free. At least at first.

But Tracy had no regrets. To be seventeen, dressed like a princess, and standing on the roof of a penthouse in Mexico City out of your mind on somebody else's dope and speed, had seemed to her then to be as close to Heaven as it was possible to be. On her birthday that year, Tracy had balanced her swaying body on the rim of a fiftieth-floor balcony, her bra stuffed with bundles of cash, her heart hammering in her head, as real or imagined fireworks exploded into the purple city sky. Later, things were to turn a little sour, but as she took the applause of her party guests, for the first time in her life she had been truly happy. She knew she had finally escaped the gravitational pull of her parents, but at such an extreme escape velocity that two decades later she's still slowing down, shedding broken people and burned out places into the vapour trail behind her.

Tracy pushes the car out into the fast lane. This is to be her last journey, the final leg of her evacuation. She looks in the rear-view mirror and resists the urge to wave goodbye to the world, as it withers in her wake.

Back home in the early morning light, Sid and Danny have phone calls to make. Andy's mum stirs him from headphone

Metal dreams and he says he'll be glad to flat-sit indefinitely, and that his parents will bung him a top-up loan for the minimal rent just to get him out of the house. Sid and Danny pop a note to Derek under the door at Pixies' with enough cash to settle their outstanding Budwar bill, and Danny leaves flowers on Alicia's doorstep on Boundary Road with a vaguely sentimental note attached. 'You have to keep all your options open, man,' he explains. 'Who knows when we'll be back with our tails between our legs.' At the Bonanza cornershop they buy their morning cigarettes and Danny extravagantly kisses the old Indian lady behind the counter goodbye.

Back upstairs, a politely-spoken ticket agent phones back to confirm standby seats to LA that afternoon, paid for by Pat the night before. 'That's it, then,' says Danny. 'It's goodbye to Blighty, and more importantly, to Balham, and all her secret wonders. I never sampled the local Italian, I never beat Derek at Scrabble, and I never got to shag the divorcee downstairs, for all my transparent desperation.'

'They hate desperation, Danno, you should know that by now. And you're talking as if we're dead men.'

Danny picks up the plastic-wrapped pill packages from the kitchen table and holds them up in a shaft of winter sunlight. 'We may be, Sid, we may be.'

At twelve midday they sit down to swallow, with two pint pots of water and a prayer. 'For what we are about to receive . . .' starts Sid.

'. . . may the Lord turn a blind eye, just this once, and then keep us safe, and then forgive us and forget us both. Amen,' Danny concludes.

Still without having slept, and hopped up on the last handful of a secret stash of speed, they enjoy the dubious luxury of a minicab to Heathrow airport, cutting through the dense midday traffic of the South Circular with suicidal daring. 'My name's Winkle, 'cos I was always the littlest round our manor,' says the scar-faced driver, regaling them with British tales of football violence, racial attacks and petty crime. 'Be sure to ask for me again next time you take a trip.'

'I'll be glad to get out of London,' whispers Sid.

At the doorway to the Departures building, Sid stops Danny for a second, before it's too late to turn back. 'Are you sure this is wise, Danno?'

'What, Sid? Swallowing a plastic bag of Pat's untested class-A drugs and then taking a nine-hour international flight? No, funnily enough, I'm not sure it's "wise". In fact, I'd go so far as to say that I should imagine it is probably unwise in the extreme. Did you have a better idea?'

And a shrug-shouldered, 'No.'

After check-in they anxiously down two beers in a Shakespeare theme bar, having weighed the alcohol's calming properties against the increased volume in their bowels. 'There will be someone there to meet us at the other end, won't there, someone who knows how to get it out safely?'

'Oh, yes, Sid. The O'Fernandez Brothers, remember. I'm sure they'll be very pleased to see us. And they're bound to be charming fellows if they're friends of Pat's.'

'What's the purpose of your trip, gentlemen? Business or pleasure?' says an air hostess, pleasantly enough, handing them two bloody Marys.

'Neither,' says Danny. 'We'd simply run out of options.'

They sit pin-pupilled through nine hours of complimentary drinks and a charming film about a young Canadian girl who adopts an orphan goose. Sid shifts uncomfortably in his seat, feeling the contraband contents of his colon turn to clay. He remembers an urban myth about a page-three model whose silicon implants exploded at high altitude, splattering the neighbouring passengers with fragments of Britain's favourite breasts, and rubs his belly nervously.

If the pack burst now, flooding him with expensive poisons, he'd die screaming in mid-air, with only Danny to offer him a last embrace. Abby's parents would read the story on the fifth page of *The Times*, and nod their heads sagely. 'He always was a bad sort . . .' Police would search his flat, and find a dozen Luther Peyote bootlegs, some mouldy bread, and a video of two nuns having sex with a farm animal. 'Dead Drug Courier in Bestiality and Poor Diet Riddle.' The nice lady at the Bonanza would feel slightly soiled by her daily politeness as she picked up the morning paper, and 'The Mysterious Death of Sid' would become a favourite tale at Pixies' Wine Bar, told late at night during drunken lock-ins, growing more elaborate as the years went by. 'The strange thing is, he always used to love Derek's pork sausages . . .'

Sid shuts his eyes and sees his grave, carved out of the fresh earth already. The mourners gather, breaking valuable Luther Peyote vinyl LPs over their knees, and throwing the cracked fragments in handfuls after him. 'He tore my Knopfler jacket,' says Ian, pointing into the grave, as people offer him their commiserations. Abby is weeping. Serves her right, Sid thinks, and tries to jump out of his grave, to go around the crowd of his farewellwishers one by one, punching them, kissing them and asking them to return the records he loaned them, but his crumbling limbs fuse with the wet muck as the soil falls over his dead face.

Danny watches Sid stir in his sleep and turns to a computer display on the back of his seat, showing the progress of the flight in animated pictorial form. Arching over Greenland he realises he is a long way from Balham. Back there, he had been a king. After nine years, tramps knew his name, and hailed him daily for cigarettes and small change. And at Pixies' he had reached the stage where he had his own stool, and Derek knew what he would be drinking without even asking him. Young boys behind the counters of takeaways were his regular late-night confidants, and the old Irish men that drank cheap beer all afternoon in the Moon Underwater would welcome him to their tables like a long-lost son. But Balham was changing. Their neighbours, once other struggling musicians, mature students and dole-cheque dreamers paying rent on housing benefit, were suddenly suited City types and their power-dressed women, all aloof and untouchable. As he entered the flats at night they regarded him through frosted glass as if he were a burglar, come to relieve them of their laptops. Pubs became wine bars and where once they'd been stocked with friendly alcoholics, now they were stuffed with braying wankers. He realises that if he and Sid are away too long, when they return they will not recognise the place they left behind. There was a half-built block of new luxury apartments opposite their window, rising daily, and soon it would obscure the view over the housetops to Tooting Bec Common, where once Danny had dallied with a whore beneath a dripping canopy of autumn branches. And in other, cheaper parts of London, drummers half his age are making phone calls to would-be Beatles who have pinned their numbers to the noticeboards he himself no longer looks at. He knows Sid is grateful for, and surprised even, by his decision to accompany him west but, really, what was left for him at home? He is losing his rhythm. Even Fat Ian has noticed it.

And then Sid and Danny hear the pilot announce their impending safe arrival and both allow themselves a moment of quiet respite from thought.

'Has the purpose of your visit anything to do with the intended downfall of the US government?' says the Asian official on the gate, chanting monotonously through her list of prepared questions.

'It is the sole purpose of my visit,' says Danny, with an Irish charm that, for once, reduces her to an unprecedented fit of laughter, and smoothes their passage to freedom.

'No further questions, Mr O'Connor.' Sid wheels the trolley out of the double doors into a slab of sunlight.

Outside on the forecourt they stand a moment, blinking into the wall of afternoon heat, and stand around limply, sucking on their first Stateside cigarettes.

'Let's find those O'Fernandez fellers, eh, Sid.'

'Right. I feel like I could shit a house.'

'Yeah, and the sooner we shift Pat's lucky parcel, the sooner we're off, full speed ahead into your ill-considered fantasy future in which I am but a bewildered onlooker. After all, we mustn't keep Luther waiting. It'd be the final irony if the mad old bastard croaked before we got there.'

Croak!

In the echoing, metallic darkness, a clearly distressed toad struggles between dextrous bony fingers, as it is raised to an open mouth. The head bows to meet the amphibian in a cataract of unruly hair, and a tongue emerges between the lips, to slowly lick the wriggling creature's leathery back, right up from the tip of the spine to the base of the neck. The mouth gasps with pleasure. 'I'm sorry, little brother,' rasps a gravel road voice, 'but since I supped on the sacred cactus I'll try just about anything once.' The toad croaks. The old man hurls it at the wall. It splatters like an over-ripe squash and slides down to the floor.

As far as Bob Nequatewa knew, the Sioux medicine man Black Elk had been the first to build a sweat lodge in a hotel room. This, of course, was typical of Sioux humour. Black Elk had been a *Heyhoka*, one of the Sioux clowns whose duty is to do everything in reverse. Once Black Elk had pitched a teepee upside down, and sat inside it with his feet up in the air and his back on the ground, a story which had found its way from the plains to the pueblos. So no one should have been that surprised when, some time in the 1940s, Black Elk built a sweat lodge in a Denver hotel room.

And as far as Bob Nequatewa knew, he himself was only the second man to build a sweat lodge in a hotel room.

Bob had gone out that afternoon, after his meeting with Alan Stapleton, and walked along the freeway out of Phoenix until he found a garage where he could buy some briquettes. These he heated up on the barbecue by the swimming pool, his grandson watching him wide-eyed from the water. While the fuel began to smoulder, Bob had put all the furniture in his room in a circle, and cast all the bedding he could find over the top. Then he put the heated briquettes in a metal bucket, placed them under the covers, stripped off, and crawled inside, to sing, pray and, above all, to sweat.

After a while his grandson peeped through the flaps. 'What's the matter, Grandfather? Why have you done this?'

'To wash the smell of the white men off my skin, boy,' Bob began, beckoning him in. 'And because . . . because last night . . . I dreamed. Like I have not dreamed for thirty years . . . I saw Kóhkang Wuhti, the Spider Woman, moulding men and women from clay, and one day singing her making song too quickly, so a single woman stumbled forth alone, without a partner, with a language of her own and no one to share it with.'

Half a world away, Peter Rugg begins to examine Billy's bin bag of butts. Five hours later, he isn't even halfway through its stinky contents. He looks down at his yellow fingers and wonders if they will ever be clean. At Los Angeles airport two arrivals wait uneasy, punching and kicking at each other as tourists skirt them, playing games to try and avert their anxieties. On a desert highway a woman drives south to safety, smoking her thirtieth cigarette and stubbing it into an overflowing ashtray, hoping she hasn't made the news. North of her, a man heads south-east in a hire car. A woman he's not sure if he can trust sleeps at his side. He has a slight erection. In a little town, nowhere-somewhere, a sheriff asks for a room, and in a tin shed cave near the border, an old man sleeps amidst baked bean tins and broken instruments, unaware that he is looked for. And in a hotel room in Phoenix, Arizona, smoke seeps out of the sweat lodge sheets and sets off the sprinklers. And Bob Nequatewa laughs to see his grandson, dancing indoors in a rotating shower of falling rain, as alarm bells burst into deafening life and, all along the corridor, the shrieking begins.

The Hopi Boy
and the Sun – iii

On the following day the boy left home and went westward, hoping to begin learning. He came to a cottonwood tree and chopped it down. Then he cut a length of the trunk to his own height, hollowed it out, and made a cover for each end. Then he put in some sweet corn-meal and prayer sticks and decided he was ready to go travelling. Climbing into the box he closed the door and rolled himself into the river.

Hopi Indian legend, reported by
Franz Boas in 1922

Seven

A mongrel dog called Laika steered her steel kennel between the stars for seven long days and seven long nights. Soon she grew used to weightlessness, comfortable even with the rubber seal that cramped her hips and sluiced her waste around her hindquarters. She sat and watched the distant lights spin meaningless and wonderful in the black and blue, fluttering silver birds, shining sticks and stones that she was never meant to chase and capture.

And perhaps Laika's long-lost gun dog instincts beckoned her to swim in the shining river that rippled before her, and retrieve fowl undreamed of for her much missed masters. But as she leaned forwards to leap she found herself still secured to her seat. The click of a food dispenser marked out her astral week. The babble of electronics, beaming invisible ECG readings back to earth, twittered a permanent and distant dawn chorus. Maybe she had a sense of mortality and, like the dog that drags itself under the stairs to die, thought that this was it, time up. Death was just a resolution of revolutions, turning her eternally in the shimmering hemispheres of night and day, never again to nestle in blanket or breast, never again to feel fear or hunger, weariness or thirst. And then a pin pricked out from the wall and punctured her, and she grew slow and drowsy, and God sped Sputnik 2's sealed cylindrical capsule to earth, burning our canine pioneer to ashes in a series of ever-decreasing orbits.

And four years later, Sputnik 5 carried skywards a tiny zoo, diverse enough not to disgrace a small seaside holiday resort in summer. They called the pair of dogs Strelka and Belka, but were less sentimental towards the two anonymous rats, the forty nameless mice, and the fifteen flasks of fruit-flies, realistically too many insects to christen individually. History records only that Belka vomited once in her fourth orbit, and that the modest menagerie 'made a heavy parachute landing at a speed of 18 mph, only six miles from the target zone', Strelka and Belka, two rats, forty mice, and fifteen flasks of fruit-flies and all.

'Why couldn't they just have sent another dog instead, something better equipped to seek and retrieve than I?' Lewis is parked in a cool darkness some miles south of the Grand Canyon, watching shooting stars scar the rapid healing skein of the heavens, and mulling on the liquid crystal vapour trails of satellites, their orbits easily visible in the smokeless desert sky. Spike leans on the car, softly singing a song she doesn't know the words to. After an evening in the dazzling neon of Las Vegas this is bliss. Out here in the desert, tonight there are no lights. This is the purest darkness he has ever seen, the most perfect silence he has known since . . .

It would have been safer with dogs, of course, with their dumb loyalty, not sophisticated enough to crack under the weight of the intellectual implications of breaking through mankind's imaginary fourth wall. Perhaps that's why Americans won the space race, strapping fat-headed football players, flat-footed military personnel, and egg-headed scientists into the Apollos. Giants within their fields, of course, but saddled with the knee-level vision of circus midgets. Had the Russians made the moon first, that historic footfall would have been accompanied by a debilitating epic poem, inviting the world to contemplate man's place in a godless universe, that grew ever less mystical as Science drew and quartered it. As it was, Neil Armstrong reduced its impact to a tautologous epigram. A hooligan loosed in an orchard, America had catapulted its missiles towards the fruit of infinity with a blind faith in God and technology, unencumbered by fears of philosophy, a toddler relieving itself exuberantly into the fountain of knowledge, curious to see if the water would change colour. Lewis, in turn, had fallen to earth at high speed, an amnesiac asteroid, accelerated to escape velocity by the weight of experience.

Of course, the idiot Apollo 13 astronauts had found their way home safely in '70, when their fuel cells started to falter and fade. Americans to a man, raised on Disney, cheese whizz and chocolate milk, they were expressly ill equipped to grasp the full hopelessness of their situation. Americans have no choice but to survive, Lewis thought, creatures of instinct and habit. A command module Odyssey full of Celtic poets or effete English intellectuals, beset with the same ill fortune, would soon have given up hope, crippled by meditations on mortality or a sudden shocking sense of scale. But even with one wheel on his wagon and flaming spears around his ears, commander James Lovell of the Apollo 13 just kept rolling along, singing a happy song, the clodhopping, God-fearing, resourceful American fuckwit.

Lewis stares at the sky, smoking cigarettes from an exotic soft pack in the silence, while Spike kicks at stones around the roadside. Here there are a million stars, scattered like silver dust with careless abandon, while in English nights they are sprinkled with a cautious meanness of spirit. He stubs out his cigarette on his sole, opens the car door for his supposed hitchhiker, and starts to head south again, the hire car engine humming intrusively in the measureless emptiness. The moon is bright and the cacti cast long pale ghosts over the desert road. 'Turn off the headlights,' she says, 'go on, turn them off for a second. Drive the darkness. Trust it.' Taking his life in his trembling hands, Lewis flips the switch and drives half-blind and happy into the iridescent night, singing a song he'd last heard at Willesden depot to himself to keep awake: *'Fly me to the moon, and let me play among the stars . . .'*

There seems to be a phosphorescence in the air, a fine shining trail that guides him, and he is unafraid. This is a freedom Hampstead Heath had never offered, and there are two days of road before he has to think again, before he has to act, two days of road to Coronado, and whatever secrets she may or may not shelter. The moon hangs pregnant and milky in the stratosphere. *'Let me see what spring is like on Jupiter and Mars . . .'*

And a hundred miles beneath his eyelids a white gloved hand reaches for the spinning chalice once more, reaches and grasps a moment, and then the smooth metal slides loose, skimming the lunar surface. *'In other words, please be true . . .'*

Jet-lagged and heavy lidded, he realises he is sliding in and out of consciousness, veering from hard shoulder to hard shoulder in the night. Under the wheels, a sudden soft thud. Spike screams and he wakes and brakes.

Headlights on again, Lewis curses and gets out of the car. Spike jumps out and follows him. Under the back axle, a stray farm dog, a well-cared-for German Shepherd, as like a working animal and a loved family pet also, now spine snapped and bloody, but struggling for life. Spike steps back and covers her face. Lewis takes a soft paw pad in hand, and thinks of Laika. Supposing she had grasped the immensity of her achievement, even for a moment. At least they had the grace to let her die. The dog looks up, confused, a lifetime's blind faith betrayed in an instant, the moonlight turning its rolling eyes to empty white shells. Lewis raises a rock above his head, and brings it down, like pulping fruit, and down, and down, to drown out the whimpers. Spike turns and walks away. And he stands back, shaking, and wipes his bloody hands on his coat. And they both drive on unsmiling.

In a car parked a mile or so back up the road leather-gloved fingers pour sweet tea from a tartan Thermos flask, as Lewis's intermittently visible headlights once again light up the horizon. 'Ah, there's a good fellow!' says a sonorous, oh-so English voice. *'May our labours, thus begun in order, be conducted in peace, and closed in harmony.* Star-gazing again were we, brother "Lewis", you ninny?' A slurp of the fat lips, and the warm liquid glugs down an overinsulated neck. Lab rat eyes flex and focus on the distant, departing vehicle, and the keys are turned in the ignition. 'Lead on, Macduff, says I! *So mote it be!'*

'I've loved many men in the last fifteen years, all of them better men than you, and every single one of them is lying somewhere between here and Mexico City, throats slit, wrists slashed, necks broken, arms and legs separated from their bodies by speeding locomotives, heads crushed by passing trucks, guts contorted by deadly poisons, hearts broken and dead, all dead, every one of them dead.'

The man's eyes widen a little under the brim of his hat as he considers this information. 'Ma'am?'

'Now,' Tracy continues, 'do you really think you still want me to come with you?'

'There's no need to go overboard, ma'am,' says the thin man, scratching at his stubble and knocking back the remains of a cloudy local brew. 'I understand when I'm not wanted. Goodnight.' It always gets results.

She watches him walk back to his stool at the bar, boots clattering on the wooden floor over the background noise of some reconstructed country singer crooning out ballads to a small but appreciative crowd by the stage. Flagstaff on a Thursday night, in the downstairs bar of the Hotel Monte Vista, and she hasn't even got enough money to get drunk.

As she drove into town at sunset, a Chinese man in a 4-wheel drive had pulled up alongside her at a red light. He had wound down his window. 'Lady? You want room? Good room. Cheap room. You name price I go cheaper.'

'No.'

'Yes. You follow me, yes.'

'No. I'm not interested.'

'Yes. Good. Is left after light. You follow me, yes?' She had smiled at him as the lights turned, waited for him to get ahead, and then arched right away from him, off towards a clustered huddle of motels that hugged the railway line for safety, and down into town.

In the bar she looks at a map, tracing again a route south down to Mexico, via Tucson and out to Nogales. She nervously counts her money once more. Fourteen dollars. Pitiful. In a lull between live entertainments, a TV above the bar flickers into life. She looks up. It's the motel where Roscoe died. '. . . a suicide in suspicious circumstances. Police are anxious to talk to a woman seen leaving the motel in a white convertible in the early hours of last Wednesday . . .' Scattering cigarettes and a handful of change, Tracy gets up and leaves, her drink unfinished and a butt still burning in the ashtray. The thin man clocks her exit, throws twenty dollars over the bar, and follows her out into the lot behind the building, lit red in the light of the hotel name, spelt out in square six-foot letters on the roof above.

A cab across town, through Westwood and skirting the southern end of Beverly Hills, and Sid and Danny wait in a Hollywood Boulevard bar. Night is falling and the famous thoroughfare is sweetly turning from tourist trap to no-go area. On a star-spangled stage, a husband and wife duo perform old Porter Wagoner songs with live guitar and programmed percussion. *'I got back in town a day before I planned to, I smiled and thought, "I'll sure surprise my wife."'* Young hipsters who have archly adopted them as an ironic apogee of bad taste whoop and holler for more. 'They filmed a scene from *Swingers* here,' someone says. *'I don't think I'll phone, I'll just head on home, For I didn't know the cold hard facts of life.'* An over-friendly waitress serves Sid and Danny at their table, thrilled by Danny's accent. 'Hey,

I'm Irish too! My great-great-great-grandmother was Irish, from . . . is it Cardiff?' she shrieks, from behind teeth whiter and straighter than any Danny had ever seen in the Emerald Isle.

'Cork, maybe?' Danny offers.

'Yeah, Cork. My folks are out in New York now. I'm really an actress. I only do this shit between jobs.'

'We're musicians,' says Sid, before remembering that it was nothing special. Everybody in LA, they had realised already, was really something else. Even the cab driver was pitching a movie. Sid had wanted to see the famous Sunset Boulevard billboard of the Marlboro Man. He had looked up as they passed Tower Records in the cab, turning away from the view over the hill and into the city. The Marlboro Man had been replaced by anti-smoking lobbyists with a twenty-storey image of a smoking skeleton, still somehow herding cows and riding the range. 'Anyhow, what can I get you guys?'

'Lord you should have seen their frantic faces, they screamed and cried "Please put away that knife!".' Now they're on their second packet of cigarettes and their sixth beer each. *'I guess I'll go to hell, or I'll rot here in this cell, but who taught who the cold hard facts of life?'* Sid's nerves are getting the better of him at last and he really needs shot of his colon-couriered parcel. But he feels that every move he makes looks suspicious, every minor gesture triggering an invisible illuminated sign above his head that says: 'Arrest Me Now. I Am Evil And My Small Intestine Is Full Of Drugs.'

'What now, Danno? I'm fit to burst, man.'

'Dunno. Pat said we were to wait here and they'd find us.' A hand on the shoulder, and two early twenties Hispanic hustlers in fake designer short-sleeve polo shirts slip into the boys' booth. They wobble with the ugly energy of muscle run to fat and glare up through bushy brows, green bows tied through their pigtails.

'You Steve and Danny?'

* * *

A hand clamps on to Tracy's wrist as she reaches to open her car door. She turns. 'Care to set a price on silence, lady?' says the same would-be suitor from the bar, still having not quite given up hope, and seeing a new opening. Attempting unsuccessfully to shake her hand free, she stiffens.

'What's the going rate?'

'That's negotiable,' he answers, coyly looking her up and down, and twirling her around by her hand like they're waltzing. 'So start negotiating. But I warn you, lady, it's a buyer's market. And I'm the only man around here interested in buying.'

Tracy considers her options. She looks her assailant in his dead blue eyes, follows the square line of his jaw, his pitted skin, like somebody exfoliated him with a rock. She's had worse, and she's done worse. Twenty years ago the chance of a tussle with a stranger in a car lot would have thrilled her, fled free from her father's house, going south, gobbling up experiences, greedy and hungry. She knows, in a dozen households from San Francisco to New Mexico, there are men, middle-aged now and married, who blush at her memory, behind newspapers, over breakfast. Since the day she reached her own elastic limit, Tracy remembers such things less fondly, but she is still familiar with the lexicon of stupid little gestures, guaranteed to titillate and excite.

Tracy unbuttons her shirt and lets it slip back off her shoulders. 'You're buying huh? See anything you like.' The man looks as if he's actually weighing up the decision, whether to stake a claim on her or not, she who once sold for a single night in Las Vegas for more than his week's wages.

'Reckon I do,' he says, and reaches up to take her, as her knee makes contact with his groin. 'Fuck!' She kicks him again and he goes down, clawing his way down the wing of her car as he falls. 'Bitch!' The keys jangle as she opens her car door. The man rolls over once on the tarmac, cupping his aching balls and moaning. A mouthful of exhaust smoke and

he splutters black phlegm as she reverses the car, and then
pulls back to twenty feet from him, lighting up his prostrate
body in the glare of her headlights. She revs the engine and
he looks up, shielding his eyes from the beam. 'No . . .' She
fixes him in the sights of her lights, and moves the gear-shift
into first. Her feet juggle the clutch and the accelerator. She
could crush him flat now, and quieten him for ever. Raising
himself on his elbows he tries to crawl away, dragging his
body over the grit, a raised hand clenching and unclenching.
He hears the gravel lurch of the engine and the cold crunch
of tyres, and bows his head to die. And then the moments
pass, the point of impact ebbs away as his heart reaches
bursting point, and he looks up. The car park is empty now,
save for the moonlight, and him, a thin man lying ashamed
in a pool of his own piss.

'Ah! Los Bros O'Fernandez?' says Sid.

'That's right, man. Los Bros O'Fernandez, the chemical kings
of Beverly Hills!' announces the bigger brother, in an accent
that somehow mixes blarney sing-song with Spanish to entirely
unattractive effect. 'Your friend Pat, he's been pitching us his
new pill for two years now, and there ain't nothing of that
nature enters our orbit without our say so.'

'Yeah. If Pat's new pill has half the neural acceleration he
says it'll spread through the rich and famous in this town like
a fuckin' virus.'

'Yeah, like the fuckin' Aids virus, I'm tellin' ya.'

'Better than that, man. Like herpes through Hollywood circa
1982 in the era of unprotected sex! Bam!'

A stunned pause. 'Very pleased to meet you,' says Danny,
putting out his hand. 'Thanks for coming to find us.'

'Hey! You're Irish, man! Our great-great-great-grandfather
was Irish,' announces the shorter gangster, suddenly smiling
and affable.

'Really?'

'Yeah, from Ballyporeen. Near Cork, in the west. You know it?'

'Funnily enough . . .' The older brother cuts Danny off, upbraiding his sibling.

'Cork ain't in the fuckin' west of Ireland, Hector.'

'You sayin' I don't know my fuckin' geography, Cathal? My ancestral fuckin' heritage?'

'You don't know ancestral shit, faggot!'

'Gentlemen, we really should . . .'

The older brother continues: 'Cork ain't in the fuckin' west of fuckin' Ireland, fuckhead!'

'It is,' says the younger, snatching up a napkin to demonstrate. 'There's Ireland there. And it's fuckin' there. In the fuckin' west.'

'You don't know shit. It's there. Down there. In the fuckin' south!'

'Danny. I really think . . .'

'South fuckin' west then, you gay fuck?'

'No fuckin' way!'

'That's fuckin' south, that's fuckin' south where you's pointing with your big fat gay fuckin' finger!'

'You sayin' I don't know my roots? By Jaysus! That's west Ireland! The fuckin' west of fuckin' Ireland! Fuckin' Maria mother of fuckin' God!'

'Hey! For fuck's sake, fellers! Aren't you forgetting something here?'

The brothers look at Danny, as if ready to turn on him together instead. 'Uh?'

'No offence, guys, but I and my colleague have brought you some presents we're anxious to off-load.'

'Yeah, sure . . .' The O'Fernandez scuffle a little longer, the older one pinching his brother's forearm in closure, before finally taking out a tube of pills and tapping two out on the table. 'OK. The usual procedure. Welcome to America, boys. Here's your complimentary, fast-action laxatives. Aloha!'

In the men's room, the boys sit in adjacent cubicles, breathing in decades of prime Californian stench, pants around their pasty pink ankles, and pushing like mothers in labour. 'How are you getting on there, Sid?'

'Oh, any minute now I think, Dan. I'm just nervous, you know.'

'I'm sorry for the delay, gentlemen,' Danny calls out to their contacts, stooging suspiciously around the urinals. 'I assure you my associate and I really are doing our very best.'

There is the sound of a splash. Then another. The weight is gone. Sid feels like he's shit out a ball and chain leading all the way back to Balham. 'Hey – were any of you lads expecting a package? There's two express deliveries here for you.'

The older brother bursts into the cubicle with tweezers and a plastic bag at the ready, then steps back, covering his mouth. 'Jesus fuck man! What do you guys eat back there in England?'

'I'm Alan Stapleton. Good Morning Arizona!'

'Good morning Al!' the cue-card mass response.

'Today we're going to be talking about clowns and clowning.' A studio audience of elderly women and tiny children surveys the scene. Lined up along the stage, behind a barricade of cameras and melting under the lights, more clowns than any of them had ever seen assembled in one place. A fat clown, white-cheeked, stuffed into a too tight red shirt, bowler-hatted and big-lipped; a smudge-faced child clown, aping his elders, with curly yellow shoes and a pointed felt hat; a French Pierrot, in a one-piece pom-pommed pale jumpsuit, with down-turned blue lips; a Charlie Chaplin impersonator, twiddling his cane and smiling tombstone teeth; an eco-clown, adorned with dolphins, teaching care for Mother Earth through slapstick and tumbling; a feminist clown, dressed in dungarees with arcane power symbols drawn on them in marker pen; a Ku Klux Klan clown, his white robe topped with a red fur bobble, sporting a squirty flower – 'I provide comic relief at most of the big race hate rallies in the South,' he had explained backstage; a rodeo clown, stetsoned and leathered in a ripped flannel shirt like some gay fantasy; a police clown, with ten-league boots and an impossibly broad peaked cap; and, at the end of the line, Bob Nequatewa, sat unsmiling and half naked, his elderly body painted in black and white stripes, his hair tied up in bunches, gold tassels hanging at his knees. A *Tsuku*, the sacred shaman clown of the Hopi people, lured here under now transparently false pretences. Claudia the researcher watches nervously from the wings, her hand placed reassuringly on the shoulder of Bob's grandson.

Al introduces each clown in turn, and each does a quick party piece to the delighted crowd, falling over, squirting their neighbours with water from plastic flowers, or emptying confetti over the audience from pantomime pails. The Klan clown explains how he hopes humour can help people to hate niggers, and Al Stapleton feels obliged, briefly, to make a dubious face and look despairingly to camera. And then it's Bob Nequatewa's turn. 'Al . . . there's nothing I can do for you here . . .'

'Oh, come on, Bob, surely there's something you can show us . . .' pleads the host.

'Not really. The Hopi clown is not so much an entertainer, as a priest. We don't have "routines" or tricks, we don't tumble as such, or juggle, and we only perform once or twice a year.'

'Leave 'em wanting more, eh?' the host doggedly persists.

'No. That's not it at all. We spend the year studying the dynamics of our pueblo, seeing what is required, seeing where the pressure points are, and then, after a period of prayer and fasting, the community allows us the licence to diffuse its tensions however we see fit.'

The crowd is losing interest, and the other clowns look bored and embarrassed, visibly wilting even underneath their carnival greasepaint. 'And what kind of form would this diffusing of tension take, Bob Nequatewa,' the host determinedly continues, 'zany dances, crazy songs, what kind of stuff?'

'You really want to know, eh, Alan?'

'Yeah, come on, tell us, unless it's some special Indian secret.'

And then Bob Nequatewa cracks. 'Well, Alan, once, for example, when I was a younger man, I sexually assaulted a bad-tempered old woman, and rolled her in animal dung, and then climbed up a ladder and pissed over a group of young boys who had been misbehaving all summer.'

The child clown laughs. The Chaplin covers his mouth and giggles. The rest hang their multicoloured wigs in shame. And the audience is suddenly stirred to vocal disapproval. And Alan Stapleton, every inch the consummate professional, moves swiftly into a commercial break. 'We'll be back, right after these messages! Don't go changin'!'

As the lights dim, the feminist clown moves swiftly over to Bob, poking at his bare chest. 'What the fuck are you saying, man? You think sexual assault's funny? There's a virtual genocide of women going on worldwide and . . .'

The Klan clown interposes himself in front of Bob and steps in. 'Listen here, you bull dyke bitch, that Indian freak might be talkin' a load of disgustin' red-nigger shit, but we have a constitution in this country that ensures his right to say it,' he raises his fist, 'and I ain't gonna see no lesbian pervert say it ain't so!'

The police clown moves in to restore order. 'Ladies and gentlemen please. Can't we sort this out in a civilized way? Move along now.' He puts his hand on the Klan clown's shoulder. The Klan clown turns round and punches him in the face. The police clown topples back on to the rodeo clown, and the line of chairs falls, taking the clowns with it one by one, greasepaint dominoes. The lesbian clown pulls the recovering policeman back from setting about the Klan clown. 'Don't do it, he ain't worth it, redneck scum.'

The eco-clown appeals for peace, waving a stuffed toy whale. The police clown pushes him aside, and lunges for the Klan clown's throat. The two of them fall into the front row of the audience, and old women set about them with bags and rolled-up newspapers. Bob Nequatewa realises he will not be invited back for the second half of the discussion.

At the side of the stage he sees Claudia cheering, and his grandson laughing. With hindsight, he knows, they'll see this little act of rebellion as pathetic, but as the security guards escort him from the stage and Al Stapleton glares at him red-faced, he swells a little with a feeling he'd long forgotten. A feeling something like pride.

'Thank God that's over, Danno,' says Sid, as Danny furtively counts their fee under the bar. 'I'm never doing anything like that again.'

'Ah, look at it this way, Sid. We just got paid five thousand dollars for taking a dump, something we're both happy to do at home everyday for free.'

'Five thousand dollars, for that! We were done. Pat saw us coming.'

'Ah well, Sid. It's better than Streatham.'

Sid laughs, and drains a glass of whisky. 'Oh yeah, it's better than Streatham. Come on. Drink up. I don't think our relationship with Los Angeles has got off to a great start exactly.'

Danny slams back his short and pockets the cash. 'We'll find a place to stay. You will allow me one night in a decent hotel, as a reward for our sins. Then you'll start making this trip worth our while.'

Sid stands and heads towards the exit. Outside sirens splinter the city as he waits on the kerb for Danny to pay and follow him out. As he feels the hot night air settle on his skin and stick, he realises they have arrived. Their immediate business settled, now the world stretches out before them beyond the boundaries of Sunset Boulevard. Whatever Danny's motives – indifference, boredom, curiosity, or a twisted sense of loyalty – he is here alongside Sid none the less, awaiting his instructions and expecting him to have at least half an idea of how to proceed. Somehow, for the first time in his life, he feels almost responsible.

Eight

When Abby finally rings Sid, 'just to see if he's OK', it is Andy, one of his useless loser musician mates, who answers the phone. 'He's gone to America with Danny, love. They're going to form a band with some old geezer and come back millionaires.' And then he asks her if she can sell him any Temazepam, 'purely for recreational use, obviously'.

She hangs up, hoping Sid hasn't done anything stupid, more than a little relieved that he's out of the picture for a while, and turns back to the case notes spread out over the desk. Mr Lewis was puzzling her. She knew the would-be astronaut's story couldn't possibly be true, but it was still proving difficult to diagnose exactly what delusion he was suffering from. 'Call his bluff,' a senior colleague had suggested. 'Put him in touch with some space expert types down at the Science Museum. See if they think he knows what he's talking about.'

It wasn't such a bad idea. Once someone in an official capacity had shown Mr Lewis that he didn't know one end of a spacecraft from the other, maybe they could set about sorting out exactly what it was that had made him fabricate the whole fiction. She'd sound him out, see how he felt about the idea. Apart from his insistence that he'd walked in space, she had always found Mr A.R.Y Lewis to be a very intelligent man.

But there's no answer at Lewis's bedsit. The landlord doesn't know where he's gone, but says his clothes are packed and someone reported him leaving late at night. She hangs up. A young nurse enters the room.

'Dr Quinton, it's Mr Rugg. He doesn't have an appointment today but he wants to know if it's OK for him to go through the bins in the staff smoking room.'

Abby laughs. 'Yes. That's fine. Let him in.'

Sheriff Hopkins kicks off his shoes and settles back on to a bed. He's in a Days Inn in Page, just north of the border of Navajo territory, a little south of the Utah state line, an island of sanity in between Native madness and crazy Mormon shit. He flicks through the TV channels, briefly tempted by the adult movie, but switching over after fifteen seconds of subtly filmed lesbian licking, before a moment's indiscretion can show up on his bill. His mobile phone rings in the pocket of his jacket and he rolls over the bed, like a beach-bound seal, to answer it. 'Deputy Cowdrey, what time do you call this?'

'I just thought you'd like to know, sir. A guy in Flagstaff says he tried to make a citizen's arrest on the motel suspect. Says she tried to run him down. Anyhow, he got a licence number.' Hopkins takes out a pen and writes the number down on the back of a cardboard coaster. Cowdrey says the car belonged to the deceased and that they can't trace the woman directly through it. 'Don't do anything stupid now, Sheriff,' he adds. 'Remember, she's not a suspect for anything as such. She's innocent until proven guilty. Any idea when you'll be back?' Hopkins hangs up. Retirement is closing in on him daily, just as he is closing in on the case of a lifetime.

As she pulled out of Flagstaff, Tracy had seen patrol cars overtake her on the freeway. She heads east, back onto the 180, back into Indian lands, hoping to pull over somewhere secluded to sleep, aware that she may have attracted a little too much attention to herself. She should head straight south for the border at Nogales, but they'll be expecting that, so she thinks it might be more sensible to stick to the less direct route, working her way back to Tucson via Winslow, and down through Payson and the Tonto National Forest. Hell, she'd always wanted to see Lake Roosevelt. A little west of Two Guns she sees a roadside space and pulls into it. There are two empty Navajo jewellery stands at the rear of the lot, closed for the evening, until their owners return next morning to set up shop once more. She looks at the hand-painted sign: 'Genuine Indian Crafts.' Funny how the Navajo still use the word Indian when there's a commercial imperative at stake, while the liberals try and convince everybody else to abandon it in favour of the less loaded 'Native American'.

She pulls in behind the shadow of the stands and switches off the engine. She and Roscoe had travelled the length and breadth of the state in their two years together, doing odd jobs and the occasional petty crime. Once or twice they'd found a town they both felt happy in, but she always felt the urge to move on. 'Why are you so restless?' he would ask her. 'Why can't you ever settle on anywhere?' She had resisted the urge to tell him. And when she finally did, he was gone, like all the others.

She lies down again on the back seat, and flips open the comic book case on her chest. The stars are so bright she can read the titles clearly. There are 143 publications in the Bible Messenger League series. As a kid her father had helped her collect the set, and he had read them to her at bedtime since before she'd been able to speak. In the twenty years of her travels she'd almost reassembled her collection, from copies found lying in restrooms and bus stations, where distributors were encouraged to leave them once they'd written the usual message on any available cover space: 'Please pass this on to a friend when you have finished with it.' Sometimes she wondered if she recognised the handwriting.

Even now there was something comforting about mouthing over the words she had known by heart as a girl, even though they were filled with hatred and rang hollow. She almost enjoyed the simple dramas: *Bad Bob*, the story of an unrepentant criminal burned alive in jail by the fire of Hell; *Boo*, the tale of innocent children lured into unwitting damnation by their participation in an innocent Halloween night of trick or treating; *Holocaust*, the story of a skinny concentration camp survivor who turned to Christ; *Angels*, in which a rock star abandoned his flirtation with Satan to embrace the one true faith. They all had happy endings, of a sort. Even the damned realised their mistakes. Tracy longed for resolutions that were so simple. But the clear black and white lines of the Christian comic books did not reflect the grey areas she so often experienced in her life. She closes the case and props it under her head as a pillow. On the road behind the empty craft stands, the gentle hum of passing trucks slowly lulls her to sleep.

Early the next day, Bob Nequatewa and his grandson got off the bus in Payson, 150 miles south of their home on the Hopi Indian reservation. Bob had left the studio immediately, without changing, and they hadn't had transport available. He had stayed a final night at the motel, in a new, less damp room, and signed a form making Channel 8 liable for the water damage. For some reason, known only to himself, he stayed in his clown clothes all night – they suddenly felt comfortable somehow – and he was still dressed in them the next morning while he waited in the Payson truck-stop for a connection. The diners turned and stared anyhow, at the half-naked old man, painted with concentric stripes, his ankles bound with beads, his wrists braided with metal. Normally a Native American could travel around Arizona without attracting comment, but not looking like this.

'What kind of a life for an old man is this?' he wheezes to himself in the washroom, as he finally scrubs off the make-up, after one wolf whistle too many, and changes back into jeans and work shirt. He watches kaolin and charcoal swirl down the sink and folds his clothes away into his case, while outside his grandson zaps Viet Cong on an arcade game machine, or glances furtively at the front cover of *Big Butt* magazine, racked high on a shelf above him.

Bob asks for coffee and a table he can smoke at and sits down, remembering the events of the previous morning. Of course it wasn't the first time he'd made a fool of himself. In the late 60s he'd sold those peyote cacti buttons to the college kids who befriended him. And even though he and his Navajo friends had sat them down in a desert hogan, around a crescent earthen altar, and invited them to enter the spirit world with him as equals, soon they had cracked open beers and turned on a tape recorder, drowning out his drum and rattle with the cod-mysticism of a Doors album, and transforming the sublime ceremonial into a chemically buzzing off-campus fraternity keg party. And maybe, he'd admit when pressed, maybe he'd enjoyed their company just a little too much. Maybe, he'd admit when pressed, he'd been lucky to get through the whole thing without a paternity suit. The police harassment, well, he'd paid for it in pleasure.

In contrast, the one of Bob Nequatewa's new white friends who had shown some real sensitivity to the experience had soon become lost to it. A local rock star up from Tucson, that wiry white boy had never really come home again, drifting out of reach in a dead-eyed, waking sleep. Then they locked the boy away somewhere, and broke him. The two were still friends, nearly thirty years later, linked across the cultures by the occasional call, and by the memory of their vivid nights in the desert, chasing dream eagles out into the starlit empty night. But Luther wasn't the same, and Bob Nequatewa never shared peyote with anyone, white or brown, again. And his subsequent six-month prison sentence hadn't helped.

The 1978 American Indian Religious Freedom Act and the 1994 American Indian Religious Freedom Amendment now protected Native people's right to perform their rituals, but Bob Nequatewa had come to feel that such things belonged in the past, and venerating the spirits had arguably done little to preserve the Hopi, cramped into a corner of the state of Arizona, and surrounded on all sides by Navajo lands. The world had changed. He had a seat on the administration committee for the Second Mesa Cultural Center, and at the start of every season he helped review the exhibits at the museum, to tell tourists something of Hopi history. Though he despised being asked about the demise of the buffalo by thin white men in Save the Dolphin sweatshirts, he had to admit, it did bring in the dollars. The doorway to the spirit world, it had seemed, was closed.

But yesterday morning, at the TV studio, briefly he had shone once more. And last night, turning uneasily in the nylon sheets of a motel bed in Phoenix, the old stories he learned by heart in childhood had come back to him again, just like the night before, the tale of Kóhkang Wuhti the Spider Woman, and of how she fashioned the first people, and the legend of the Hopi boy whose father was the Sun. As he slept, Bob Nequatewa saw the Hopi boy set out across the world to find his father, throwing cornmeal skywards to climb. And Bob Nequatewa had seen the Spider Woman more vividly than ever before, a beautiful ugly monster, whose legs touched on all corners of the world at once, crouching as she moulded men and women from clay, in rebellious mimicry of the goddesses. From out under her *möchápu* cloth they crawled in pairs, each with their own language and customs, and Bob Nequatewa watched as Kóhkang Wuhti grew careless in delight at her ability. And one night she put too small a piece of clay under her *möchápu*, and sang her making song too quickly, and a single woman stumbled forth alone un-partnered, all her thoughts echoing back to her unanswered. And the Spider Woman blessed her, and told her to be patient and watchful. And Bob Nequatewa fixed the woman's face in his memory, with her black hair tied back, and eyes that spoke of suffering, of wisdom, and of an indefatigable strength of spirit.

And eight hours later, he looks up from his coffee, and a car pulls up outside, and suddenly that same woman is before him, walking into a diner in Payson, 150 miles south of his homeland, 100 miles north of where he first dreamed her into life.

Disembarking from the Greyhound at lunchtime, Danny and Sid stink of four-star hotel shampoo and soap, and sweat from a celebratory first night that finished with drinking the minibar dry and laughing themselves sick at Public Access Television. Now, that had been an *Evening*. Danny had played the professional Irishman at the hotel bar until morning, regaling gullible Americans with fifth-hand blarney, keeping himself in free Guinness until 4 a.m., while Sid had fallen into conversation with a couple in their late forties. They'd come west into the city for a night to celebrate a legal victory they were reluctant to elaborate upon. The man, it was revealed under Sid's dogmatic interrogation, had seen Luther Peyote play at the Fillmore in San Francisco in 1969, two and a half years before incarceration on a narcotics charge all but ended his career for good, and he delighted in the young Englishman's rapt attention. And even if Travis could ever have satisfied Sid with the finer details of a set list, then tonight's heavy drinking, coupled with nearly thirty years of chemical dalliances, had taken the edge off his memory. 'Let me tell you Luther . . . Luther just rocked, that's all,' was the best he could offer.

Besides, Angie and Travis, it had soon transpired, were seeking alcoholic oblivion, rather than a euphoric release. Whatever court case they had won, their success somehow rang hollow to them. Ordering three-pint pitcher after three-pint pitcher, and ordering Sid to drink deep in tribute, their celebrations smacked of desperation. When Travis got up to go to the bathroom some time after one, Angie looked up at Sid, sweating through a ton of make-up and bleached blonde locks, and confessed: 'They said he shot a Hispanic guy that he found on our land, but he says it was self-defence.'

'I'm sure it was, Angie,' Sid offered, politely.

'Maybe. But it got me thinking – how well can any woman ever really know her husband?'

Sid wondered if this was a come-on, and wondered how drunk Travis would have to be for Angie to slip away unnoticed, and wondered how drunk he would have to be to allow himself to accompany her. But the only point of a cheap fuck like that would have been to think of Abby, and to imagine her anguish had she been able to see Sid in the throes of . . . well, if not passion, then at least an erotic entanglement of sorts. But Abby would hardly have envied her ex-lover such a battle-worn trophy, seized so sordidly in the depths of despair. 'Yes, Abby, I am shagging a drunk old woman who fears that her husband may be a murderer. That's right. Look impressed.' Still, he could have done worse. And then, as he finally stiffened his resolve to initiate negotiations, Travis emerged from the men's room to watch his drunk wife slide, slowly and beautifully to the floor, taking a jug of beer, a dish of peanuts and a tablecloth with her, and effectively closing down Sid's options.

Morning saw Sid and Danny feed on the heaviest breakfast they've ever eaten, and board a bus east, and now it's afternoon in Kingman city, on the fringes of the desert, and they sling their rucksacks over their sweat-soaked shoulders as the sun reaches its zenith, and wander off through the little town. The simplest billboards and fast-food advertisements fascinate by their unfamiliarity. *Buy. Eat. Sell. Save.* It goes without saying. They feel as if they are in a film, or at the very least a cheap TV movie, seen late at night on Channel 5. At the Highway 40 East exit they stop, next to a sign reminding nostalgic travellers to drive historic Route 66, to hitchhike on into Arizona.

Sid stands at the roadside a moment, relishing his first opportunity to contemplate the enormous landscape, brown scrub stretching unremittingly to a distant range of hills, telegraph wires mathematically measuring an immensity which would otherwise be unimaginable to a mind cloistered too long in South London's grimy thoroughfares. He feels exhilarated, on the verge of something, the bright empty space suggesting a future of limitless possibilities. He sniffs the air. The gasoline is long gone and the traffic hum a distant buffalo stampede. He theatrically sucks in the deep breaths of a satisfied pioneer, christening the rivers with the names of dead childhood pets and naming the hills after ex-girlfriends. 'Christ, look at it, Danny, would you look at the sky. I never knew skies could be so big.'

'Fuck me man, those pancakes . . .' moans his travelling companion, doubled up and ignoring him. 'I think I just put on a stone.'

'Ah, well, try and look healthy, Danno. No one's gonna give us a ride the state you're in.'

'Oh, we're hitchhiking now, are we? What the fuck's all that about then?'

Sid sticks out his thumb. 'Trust me, Danno. It's all part of the plan.'

Tracy weighs the last of her change in her hand, and sits down. Bob Nequatewa watches as her coffee is poured, waits for her to settle back comfortably, sipping and smoking, and then shuffles over and sits himself opposite her. 'Miss,' he says, as she looks up, 'I know you.'

'Uh-huh,' says Tracy. 'In your dreams, grand-pa!'

Bob laughs. 'Yes. That's right. In my dreams. I have spent many nights, it seems, looking into your eyes.' Tracy wonders if the old man has recognised her from the news, and is trying to hold her here so he can be a hero. But suddenly he's sitting next to her. 'I'm Bob Nequatewa.' And he puts out his hand, which she takes and shakes. Even if her face has finally hit the small screen, Bob doesn't look like the type to turn her in. All the same, she needs to know.

Tracy offers the old man her cigarettes. He fumbles with the packet, puts one in his mouth, one behind his left ear, and slips three into a flap in his denim overalls. 'Thanks. Reparations.'

'So, Bob, have I made the news yet?'

'The news? No,' he says, lighting up. 'Like I said. I know you from my dreams. I say dreams,' he elaborates, 'but they are more like visions. There is a difference, you know.'

If he's playing for time, she thinks, he's very good. 'Oh, I know. Then tell me Bob, will I be healthy and wealthy or will I die alone in poverty?'

'You won't die alone. Even if you think you might.'

'Oh, really? And how do you know this?'

'Your story isn't in the future. It's in the past.'

Tracy breathes out a cloud of smoke and folds her arms, as Bob leans forward conspiratorially and begins to tell her. Of how the Spider Woman grew envious of the skills of the goddesses, and placed some clay beneath her *möchápu* cloth to begin fashioning her own pairs of people. Of how she grew careless, and left one of her pairs unfinished, making a woman without a partner, with no one to speak her language. 'Kóhkang Wuhti, the Spider Woman, forgot to fashion a partner for you . . .' he concludes, as Tracy eyes him sternly. 'But be assured, she has made you one now, and all you have to do is find him. I know. I saw it in my vision.' Tracy looks unimpressed. 'Look,' he continues, 'do you think I'm enjoying this "wise Indian shit". It's as much of a surprise to me as it is to you.'

'Yeah. Yeah. Listen, Bob,' she answers. 'I've loved many men in the last fifteen years, and every single one of them is lying somewhere between here and Mexico City, throats slit, wrists slashed, necks broken . . .' And Bob takes over her story, '. . . arms and legs separated from their bodies by speeding locomotives, heads crushed by passing trucks, guts contorted by deadly poisons, hearts broken and dead, all dead, every one of them dead. I know.' Tracy narrows her eyes. 'They were the wrong men. But, somewhere, the Spider Woman has made a partner just for you. And she is watching your search even now, and she admires your courage, and your determination, and she will reward you.'

'I don't need this,' she says, jabbing at him with her cigarette.

'You're so nearly there, I can sense it. And you will know him when you find him. He is searching for his father, whom he does not know. Seek him out, and make him yours, and you will give birth to a happy brood of rattlesnake children.'

Finally Tracy has to laugh. 'Rattlesnake children, huh? Will this be a hospital birth? I mean, will the cameras be there? Do I get the rights to the story? Hey, we'll both be rich. We'll tour the state fairs for ever with our rattlesnake children, packing them in from Chicago to San Francisco. Roll up for the wriggling lizard kids!'

But Bob Nequatewa is still smiling back at her. 'I don't know if you are trying to humour me or insult me, but every time you open your mouth . . .' and he pauses, 'it makes me even more certain that my dream spoke truly.' She shakes her head, and smiles. 'Look,' he elaborates, 'since a few misunderstandings in the late 60s it is not my personal policy to share my thoughts with strangers, especially white strangers, but something special has happened here. I have no choice.' Tracy remains unmoved. 'I assure you, I am not trying to trick you, or to seduce you. I gave up on women soon after they gave up on me.' She sniggers back at him. 'Here,' he offers, looking at her little pile of change, 'let me buy *you* something to eat. You may not believe me yet, but you have a very important journey ahead of you.'

'OK, Bob,' she relents. 'I'll accept your kind offer, but only out of necessity. I'm in desperate straits, see. And since you're paying, I'll have the biggest steak they've got, with fries. Oh, yes, Bob Nequatewa, I'll make you regret telling me I'll give birth to rattlesnakes.' And she hisses at him, like a snake, as he waves for the waitress.

'White woman speak with fork tongue,' says Bob, making a cigar shop Indian expression as he takes the cigarette from behind his ear, lights it, and blows the smoke full on into her face.

Half an hour later Tracy's pushed her empty plate away and is rocking back in her chair with her hands behind her head. Bob Nequatewa has finished all her cigarettes, smoking one after another as he watched her eat and listened to her speak. 'The well has run dry for me, Bob,' she had explained, 'and I've made such a mess of things there's nowhere to go now but south.'

'You shouldn't regret it.'

'I don't,' she had continued, adopting a French accent which meant nothing to the old man. 'I regret nothing. But . . .'

'You are not as others are. The Spider Woman set you out on a difficult path, and only when you have explored every one of its twists and turns will you find what you are looking for.'

She shrugs, and drains the last of her coffee.

A truck pulls up alongside Sid and Danny, coughing black diesel smoke into their pasty faces. The driver leans over and winds down the window to regard them, pushing a baseball cap back up over his forehead. Sid nudges Danny and calls up. 'Hello.'

'Well, "hello" to you too,' the driver shouts down, flicking his own tousled locks in a flamboyant parody of Sid's sweat-wilted quiff, 'and by the way, I love your hair – faggot!' The black smoke belches again, and a dust storm blinds them as the truck accelerates on to the road.

'Cunt!' mutters Danny under his breath.

'Ah lay off, Danno. The cry of "faggot" is traditional in this region, and is to be expected when any primitive culture comes into contact with a sophisticated foreign exploratory force. Indeed, the journals of the early pioneers Lewis and Clark record how they themselves got called faggots by the Indians back in the 1800s as well. You could have done a bit of background reading.' They laugh. It's OK.

An hour passes. Danny and Sid still stand alone at the edge

of the highway, watching the afternoon shadows slowly circling the cacti stalks that sprout weakly from the stony ground. 'This is shit, Sid,' says Danny, lighting the first of his third packet of duty-free cigarettes. 'If I'd wanted to waste hours at the roadside I could go home and try and catch a bus in South London.' He takes stock of the situation and resorts to desperate measures. 'OK, Sid, I spy with my little eye, something beginning with D.'

'Denny's diner, desert, dust – you did them all an hour ago.'

'OK, OK. C, then.'

'Cactus, you've done that. And you've done highway, horizon, sun, sky, sand, and The Copper Kettle inn.'

'Ah, well, that's it then, Sid, the sum total of our known universe, catalogued and correlated, letter by letter. If you fancy another round you'd better dredge up your O-Level French, then we can have another game in a foreign language.'

'No need, Dan,' says Sid, visibly relieved. 'I got another one. R.'

'Ride?' says Danny, as a truck slows down to glide in to rest noisily beside them. Danny spits on his hand and cautiously flattens and scrapes Sid's floppy hair back up over his balding scalp. 'Best be on the safe side, eh?' he says, as the driver winds down the window and leans out.

'Going east?' he says, with a smile. And Sid breathes a sign of relief.

'*We're* Lewis and Clark now, Danny,' he shouts into the wind, over the deafening engine throb. 'Lewis and Clark, ready to remap America's long-lost musical geography. We're unstoppable.'

Seeing the driver start to look doubtful, Danny seizes Sid under the armpit and propels him bodily towards the truck.

Bob Nequatewa and his grandson follow Tracy out to her car. 'Good luck.'

'Thanks,' she says, getting in, 'and don't worry. I'll keep an eye out for them rattlesnakes.'

'Take this. A phone number for me. Just in case . . .' He scribbles on a napkin scrap.

'Thanks.'

'We'll meet again.' Bob watches her, speeding south out of Payson on Highway 87, until he can no longer make out the shape of her car as it dissolves into the hazy distance. And then he waits, pondering his dream, and this chance meeting, before scooping up the boy and hurrying to the bus-stop.

Nine

Sheriff Matthew Hopkins is sat on the edge of a motel bed in shorts and a white vest. Crumpled white tissues pile up on the table, amidst beer bottles and hamburger wrappers. He looks at the clock and rubs his face. He gulps black coffee and furiously dials a phone number. 'Cowdrey? Hopkins.'

In Hopkins's office, Cowdrey wipes away a blob of cream from his mouth and drops a spoon into his bowl with a clatter. Over a mound of candy papers and coke bottles, Dr Littwick laughs behind his hand as the pair struggle to regain their composure. Cowdrey points at the phone and silently mouths to Littwick. 'It's the boss man.' They snigger.

'I'm out in the field here, Cowdrey, tracking the fugitive, with no visible support from you at base I might add. And I was wondering, just what in Hell's name is going on back there? Did you find anybody who knows anything about the woman the deceased was with?'

Cowdrey swallows a mouthful of chocolate cake and answers, 'Sheriff Hopkins. I was just about to contact you. Seems we got a lead. After the TV news spots somebody reckons they saw the woman. They recognised the car.'

'Uh? Where? Where?'

'In a diner in Payson. Acting kinda suspicious. Got some Indian guy to buy her dinner. She's long gone now, Sheriff, but here's the strange thing. The guy she was talking to, somebody else recognised *him* from the TV too. Seems he was on a chat show 2 days back talking about some Indian cultural issues. Sounds like he caused quite a stir. We tracked him down via Channel 8. Name's Bob Nequatewa.' Hopkins stiffens. 'He should be home about now and you can find him at . . .'

'Bob Nequatewa. I know where I can find him.' Up the winding road towards Walpi, high on the second Mesa, a journey Hopkins hasn't made for years and hoped he could forget. 'I'd better get going. And Cowdrey . . .'

'Sheriff?'

'Get your boots off my desk, boy! It ain't yours yet!'

Hopkins hangs up. Cowdrey shrugs and lowers his feet to the floor.

'How does he do that, Littwick?'

Hopkins had nailed Bob Nequatewa more than a few times, back in the good old days before the 1978 American Indian Religious Freedom Act took the teeth out of the 1965 Drug Abuse Control Act. Matthew Hopkins never had been one for procedure, but back then he hadn't needed to be. It had been open season. Those nights when he and his men would pour kerosene over piles of newly harvested peyote cacti buttons, seized by stealth, and clink their beers as they watched them burn are long gone.

Bob Nequatewa was always the worst of the local savages. So proud, and pleased with himself, standing tall and contemptuous, as if he owned all of Arizona. And Hopkins would bust into some desert hogan and find the bastard sprawled out there with half a dozen half-naked hippie chicks down from Berkeley, hoping to 'find themselves' through the cult of Bob, bare legs and arms spread slack on the blankets. Glassy-eyed sluts, Hopkins had kicked them out into the cold night in their cotton panties without so much as an authentic Native

American craft shop shawl to shield them against the wind. 'Hitchhike home, little whores, out of my jurisdiction!'

In 1971 he had caught Nequatewa *in flagrante delicto*, passing a little parcel to some long-haired faggot singer in a car park in Tucson, and they both went down. Nequatewa emerged from doing time stronger if anything, with a silent resentment that's burned Hopkins black whenever he's seen him since. The long-haired faggot, meanwhile, was fucked over inside after he pleaded insanity and got fried with shock therapy in an institute somewhere, so they said, and Hopkins never saw him around again.

But now the bastards had a get-out clause. All they had to do was flash a Native American Church membership card, or invoke some liberal statute, and they could stand in front of him gobbling down as much of that green shit as they could stomach, or doing whatever fucked-up dances passed for religion among their kind, and he couldn't raise a trigger finger to stop them. A quarter blood was enough to get you clear. A quarter Indian blood! Bob Nequatewa alone had probably polluted the water supply enough to ensure that half of Arizona was entitled to thumb their nose at the law, so long as they were carrying the correct paperwork.

Times had changed. Maybe he was glad to be giving it all up. Too many rules and regulations, too many rights to respect. In the meantime, Bob Nequatewa was back on the scene, buying breakfast for fugitives, and Hopkins smelt his last big bust, calling to him from among the cacti and stinking out the whole state.

A.R.Y. Lewis and his hitchhiker rumble to a halt in the car lot, on a road south of Two Guns off Highway 180. They overlook the scrubby plateau of a formless landscape, the cracked earth rising up towards the towering rim of Meteor Crater. Spike had forced him to make one further tourist stop on the way to Tucson, and when she had told him the site included an Astronauts' Hall of Fame, he could hardly have let the opportunity pass. Again, she seemed to be taunting him with her choice of attractions. As they had passed in the early hours through Flagstaff, Spike had pointed up at Mars Hill, where since 1894 Percival Lowell had studied the surface of Mars, seeing canals that never were, and predicting the existence of Pluto, or Planet X as he himself called it, thirty years before it was finally found. The local natives had named him 'the man with long eyes'. Lowell's eight-year search had ended in disappointment, as the American Academy of Arts and Sciences passed up his paper on his efforts to confirm the position of 'the ninth planet', and Lowell soon ceased to speak of Planet X. In 1916 he died of a stroke while working at the observatory. Clyde Tombaugh inherited Lowell's position, and in February 1930, seeing a star shifting position, he realised he had finally found Lowell's phantom world. The existence of the ninth planet was confirmed on 13 March 1930, the date of Lowell's birthday.

Spike knew her local history well. In 1540, she had explained, Francisco Vasquez de Coronado, for whom the mountains to the east were named, had pushed north this way from Mexico. He'd journeyed as far as Kansas, in a silver helmet and striped pantaloons, to claim the legendary Seven Cities of Gold for Spain. But he found only the poor Indian pueblos of the south-west, where souls unwon were unwillingly substituted for the slave church's anticipated bounty. Lowell and Coronado, Lewis noted, both had hilltops and craters and rivers named for them, but nowhere would ever take his name. But then his name wasn't his name anyway. And he wasn't in the game just to try and take his place on maps.

Spike enjoyed telling Lewis the stories of these futile local quests so much. He wondered again if she was trying to force him to confess his own search for something just as insubstantial and unknowable as a planet revealed only by the shadows of its gravitational effects. But she seemed somehow too open and honest and innocent to have any hidden agenda.

Above her head here in the car park of the crater, he watches birds whirl distantly on invisible thermals and the silence is a thousand miles wide. Spike slams her door, and circles the car, gesticulating wildly up towards the crater, a student tour guide holding court to anyone who'll listen. Lewis looks on entranced.

'Forty-nine thousand years ago, A.R.Y., now it sure would have been something to have been sitting around here then, don't you think? Picture if you will, whatever mutant pre-evolutionaries were walking the Arizona desert at the time, running in terror as a meteorite one hundred feet across came blazing down into this godforsaken patch of dirt. Voooom! And all that's left, a five-hundred-foot hole a mile wide, oh, and a roadside signpost calling it "planet earth's most *penetrative* attraction". Those copywriting boys must have taken the rest of the fuckin' week off when they thought of that one, eh, Mr Lewis?' An elderly couple tut at her as they pack away their cameras. Lewis hands a twenty-dollar note over the counter as Spike flashes student ID to the cashier, and she leads him through a corridor out into the bright sunlight once more, to stand on a viewing platform overlooking the scene.

Lewis stares out into the mighty hole, the afternoon sun painting the crater with a dozen different pink-orange-purple highlights. At the centre of the depression, twenty football fields across, a telescope view reveals a little huddle of abandoned, rusting drilling equipment. In 1902, a Philadelphia mining engineer called Daniel Moreau Barringer decided that a large iron meteorite had caused the crater to form, and spent the next twenty-six years drilling to find it. Initially he assumed his mineral treasure would have buried itself dead centre, but subsequent experiments observing the final resting places of bullets fired into soft mud led him to excavate numerous other sites around the crater. In 1929 Barringer's drill bit jammed itself permanently into debris at a depth of 1,376 feet. The cable snapped. His money ran out. Barringer abandoned his search for the meteor and died a year later. Subsequently, scientists decided the meteor would have shattered on arrival, and that Daniel Moreau Barringer, though his work on angles of impact was later vindicated, had essentially wasted his life.

The obvious parallels here are not lost on Lewis. But even as he feels himself doubting his dreams, something about the desolation of the shock-wave-shattered land surrounding the rim of the crater draws him back towards his own buried belief. Running his hand through his hair, he sighs, and remembers. He has seen a landscape like this before, of course, but discoloured and wrung dry into monochrome white. It's the same world he visits every night, and its familiarity makes him sick. 'It looks like . . . the surface of the moon,' he murmurs.

'Egg-zackly!' says Spike, sparking up a cigarette and slapping him hard on the shoulder. 'Which is why they trained the Apollo astronauts here, on America's own private little patch of moondust.'

For Sid and Danny, the afternoon in the truck cab is a glorious haze. 'Hey, you Irish?' the driver had said to Danny as he hoisted him up. 'My great-great-grandfather was Irish. From Cork, I think.' And so it began, them passing cigarettes and soft drinks between them as they reached over to honk the horn at female drivers and sang as much as they could remember of the theme song from a 70s American TV show about a truck driver and his pet monkey. Danny had always identified with the driver, smashing his way into sealed storage units to save grateful ice cream parlour waitresses. But Sid had always felt a certain kinship with the chimp, powerless in the passenger seat, the cabin controls a mystery to him, the only primate in the haulage industry, waiting to be swung up on to a shoulder and carried on into the next incomprehensible human drama.

They watched the scenery roll by like a continuous provincial cinema support film travelogue, time marked out by road-signs and tiny trailer trash townships. The truck driver took the old Route 66 east out of Kingman, shadowing the main highway, but avoiding speed-traps. Fifties-style diners and fuel station forecourts, artificially preserved to snag stray nostalgia seekers, just seemed like the real thing to Sid and Danny. They were more impressed by the retro-futurist launderette somewhere between Nelson and Yampai, looking like the sort of building in which Flash Gordon would have strutted around in his body stocking, than they were by distant glimpses of the southern rim of the Grand Canyon, an artificial horizon, intermittently threatening to suck away the land that swept towards it out of the driver's side window. There was only one sticky moment, when Sid excitedly broached the subject of his and Danny's mission to search out Luther Peyote.

'Jesus! Let him rot! Peyote was a college boy pantywaist,' asserted the driver, his stubbled face suddenly glaring mean under the peak of a baseball cap. 'He was so lame he was virtually gay. Did you boys ever hear his last album, *Satellite Dog*, from '74? I mean, hey, what the fuck was going on there?'

'He was experimenting with random noise and radio interference,' Sid countered, defensively.

'Bullshit. Worst five bucks I ever spent.'

Sid is stunned. 'You . . . you bought a copy of *Satellite Dog* when it was released. I've only got a Greek vinyl reissue. I've never seen the real thing. Do you . . .'

'Threw it out with the trash. Piece of shit. What you have to understand about Luther Peyote is he was never really that good. Believe me. I saw him twenty, maybe thirty times, playing Tucson and Phoenix at the end of the 60s.'

'You saw the Round Tabyls?' Sid was aghast, like a cryptozoologist suddenly finding another villager keeping a mythical creature as a family pet.

'Too many times. Now, the Tabyls were a great band, but there was always this fuckin' clown Peyote bellowing his meaningless, gay shit over the top of everything they did. His whole rep is built on the fact that he talked a load of mystical college-boy bullshit, fried his brain on Native drugs, got himself locked away, and then disappeared into the desert. If he was still around he couldn't get arrested. You seek him out, see if I ain't wrong and tell him I said so.'

'I think there's more to it than that . . .' began Sid.

'No. There ain't more to it than that,' the driver said, in a tone that suggested the matter was well and truly closed.

'Y'man's probably right, Sid,' says Danny, sensing danger. 'He was there, after all.'

'Yep. I was there. Now, Ted Nugent and the Amboy Dukes, they are the unsung heroes of acid rock,' the driver asserted, 'and Peyote never recorded anything that kicked ass like *Journey to the Center of Your Mind*.'

'I'm afraid I can't agree,' Sid announced. 'For all his early hippie posturing, Nugent later revealed himself as a redneck bigot with no . . .' Danny managed to cough loudly and diplomatically into Sid's tirade.

'Nah, y'man's right. Luther was not without his merits, Sid, but Ted Nugent, Ted Nugent rocked!'

'That's right! Nugent rocked! And he fired a mean crossbow! You wanna listen to this Irish guy, man. He knows his shit. He's from a musical people. Hey, did I tell you my great-great-grandfather was Irish?'

And now Sid sits, watching the scrub swallow itself mile after mile, struggling to smother his doubts, as they rejoin the main route west of Williams and head towards Flagstaff. They might never find Luther, of course. But suppose they do. Suppose they do and he's a useless husk, a wicker legend built of flimsy strands. For most of his life, Sid's finest moments have been soundtracked by the buzz and yowl of Luther Peyote and the Round Tabyls. He remembers being thirteen, owning his first Walkman, a Christmas present from his estranged father, and walking out into the snow at night, while Luther sang the drifts into the shape of ancient monoliths and angry monsters, conjured the flakes into falling stars, and made street lights into melting suns with a sudden flourish of his fuzz pedal. At that moment, he was as close to heaven as he ever got, and Luther was there in spirit, holding his hand and pointing the way ahead.

Then he had gone home and played Trivial Pursuit with his Gran. She had said 007's real name was 'John Bond'.

If he finds him, and he is hollow, his world will fold in on itself and fall.

Spike and Lewis wander away from the crater, towards the entrance to a low brick building, the Astronauts' Hall of Fame. In a small glass cabinet near the doorway, the local Hopi people have offered the goodwill gesture of a meteor *katsina*, a standard spirit carving customised with appropriate symbols to indicate its abiding interest in Barringer's folly. Lewis follows Spike in, looking around in awe. 'Of course, those sceptics among us know that NASA didn't only rehearse the Apollo moonwalks here in picturesque Meteor Crater,' Spike continues, taking him by the hand, 'they actually filmed them all here as well, without having to set foot off terra firma.'

'NASA faked the moon landings?'

'Some people say so. When you think about it, doesn't the idea of men in space does seem kind of . . . unlikely.'

'Ha! Yes. But so does the idea of faking the whole thing.'

'Sure,' says Spike, stopping to look at some photographs of various astronauts and heroes of the republic lining the entrance corridor, 'but the history of the Western world is a secret history, a history of powerful elites controlling man's destiny over and above comparatively petty and insignificant international squabbles.' She's good, he thinks, very good, again pre-empting his own paranoia as if to put him to the test. 'There's no such thing as truth, Mr Lewis. The only real question is who controls the means of communication. Take a look at this if you don't believe me.' Spike points out a picture. Seven men in silver, Buck Rogers style space suits line up in front of a dark blue background, smiles of military dignity shining from behind flimsy-looking plexi-glass visors. Lewis reads the caption aloud: 'The Mercury Seven, 1959.'

'That's right, Mr Lewis. The Magnificent Mercury Seven. The forefathers of the space race. Seven good men and true chosen by NASA as the first astronauts. And here's their publicity shot, taken to let the American public know that their hard-won astro-cash wasn't being wasted. Or was it?'

Lewis fixes John Glenn's face, a skeletal grin, his eyes a little too close together, and his gaze wanders down to the astronaut's gloved hands, hanging limply at his side, almost apologetically. 'I don't follow you.'

'Use your head, man. In 1959 our boys were army airforce guinea pigs, training for the rocket ships in flight suits and combat fatigues. But line up a bunch of guys in natural fibres for the camera and Joe Public is gonna think you're pissing away his tax dollars. Back then the average guy's idea of space was a 50s' vision of sparkly silver and futuristic consumer-friendly electrical gizmos. Buck Rogers in silver and spandex! Flash Gordon socking it to the Mole-men in a tin helmet! But this was the golden age of advertising and NASA's publicists knew their market. So they gave people what they wanted to keep the cash flowing in. They gave them a photo shoot that said 'Space – here we come!'

And it was true. Lewis casts a critical eye over the photograph. Suddenly the astronauts' sophisticated headgear just looks like so many motorcycle helmets, sprayed white by schoolchildren in a secret class project. Clumsy suckers connect discarded washing machines' intestinal plumbing from the sides of the seven helmets to random points on the body suits, simple silver foil cut and paste numbers, unflatteringly fashioned by costume-makers hot from the latest B-movie.

Walter M. Schirra Junior holds an obvious silver-sprayed hot water bottle under his right arm, in a hollow gesture of scientific advancement, while the buckle of M. Scott Carpenter's left space glove, clearly a bastardised oven mitt of some sort, flaps casually undone, as if to tip off the sharp-eyed observer, and an old kitchen plunger hangs between his legs at an oddly obscene angle, perhaps indicating the ghost of a sense of humour at work within the public relations machine. Donald K. 'Deke' Slayton looks as if he can barely contain his mirth, while, on the back row, Virgil I 'Gus' Grissom has had to duck down into his crash helmet to conceal a sheepish grin. And, just above their left hips, each man is proudly wearing a small cheese-grater, clearly a state-of-the-art item. How could anyone have fallen for this? 'You're right, Spike,' says Lewis at last. 'This photograph is rubbish.'

'It did the job, A.R.Y.,' she says, taking him by the hand again and leading him into the main chamber of the museum. 'It got us . . . this.' She leads him out of a doorway, into a suntrap courtyard.

Glowing in a harsh desert light that does its ageing skin few favours, is a spacecraft, an actual Apollo capsule, here rescued from meaningless, mythological iconography by its simple symmetrical beauty. Only the red and blue of the Stars and Stripes painted on its side, the ugly block capital lettering of the words UNITED STATES and PLEASE KEEP OFF, stencilled on the entry hatch, break the flow of the capsule's smooth, utilitarian contours, a pure white cone, aching towards the sky, an unaero-dynamic bumblebee bulk of impossible weightlessness. Boiler-plate 29a had been manufactured in 1965, from aluminium and fibreglass, for the first series of water-tank and at-sea upbringing tests. How fortuitous, that functional design imper-atives unwittingly gave way to such graceful form. How appro-priate that they should surrender to us a miniature Christopher Wren cathedral dome, to fall intact from the sky, and bring home the architectural blueprints of Heaven. This is no fake. 'It's so beautiful . . .' Lewis inhales. He can smell space, the smell of emptiness, the absence of any of the trace elements of the everyday, the heady stench of nothing at all, a direct chem-ical highway straight to buried memories. Or else, he knows, a yellow brick road taking him directly to his most deranged delusions. *Fly me to the moooon . . .* He shuts his eyes to savour the scent, remembered or imagined, and staggers for support, a lovelorn boy struck once more by a lost one's perfume, as he sees again the shape of the ceremonial chalice, drifting over the face of the moon, only inches from his grasp. As it tumbles away from him his hand opens and closes uselessly in the vacuum, thrashing wildly to no avail, and he opens his eyes, feints and stumbles forwards, his head greeting the metal surface of the space capsule with a clang that resounds through the museum courtyard like a bronze church bell.

'Sir,' comes an amplified official voice as Spike breaks into giggles and helps him to his feet, 'please, step away from the exhibit.' Lewis stands and rubs the ache on his forehead. Spike hoists his arm around her neck to keep him upright.

'See this, Spike,' he says, pointing at the rapidly reddening bump. 'This isn't faked. It just met real metal, head on.'

'What did you expect, Lewis?' she laughs, dragging him towards the exit, past postcards of Richard Nixon. 'Plywood? Give them some credit.'

'Bob,' calls out Sheriff Hopkins, as Bob Nequatewa clambers out of the community transit van that had picked him up at the nearest bus-stop. 'You trying to pass yourself off as a TV star, I hear? The Hopi nation's answer to Jerry Springer, huh?'

'Sheriff Hopkins,' says Bob Nequatewa wearily, staring at the sheriff in the setting sun at the gates of the little Shungopavi settlement. 'It's been a long while.' A little Hopi boy in a Bon Jovi sweatshirt bounces a ball past them, heading to a basketball hoop mounted at the edge of the plaza.

'Times have changed, Bob,' Hopkins reflects. 'I couldn't bust you for dealing your Native drugs these days. You're a protected species now. I couldn't hunt you even if I had a licence with the President his-self's little signature on it.'

'What do you want, Sheriff Hopkins?' says Bob, his hand on the door of his house.

'I'm looking for a woman, Bob.'

'You don't change.' The old man pushes open the door, but

the sheriff's hand on his shoulder gently restrains him.

'Funny. I like what you did there, Bob, you sure made me look foolish, very funny,' Hopkins shouts over the roar of the departing minibus. He sits down on a low wall beside the doorway and beckons Bob Nequatewa to join him. 'Listen in, Bob, and listen good if you wanna stay outta trouble. She drives a white convertible, black hair, tied back so, and she was last seen this morning in Payson talking to a TV celebrity Indian. Well, we put the word out, Bob, and soon found out it must have been you. If you're gonna consort with the criminal fraternity Bobby-o, it can't hurt to be a little more inconspicuous. First law of crime: don't fraternise with felons when you've just been on state-wide TV. Blend in with your surroundings. It's no surprise we wiped you fellers out really, is it? Didn't they teach you about camouflage at the Braves' Academy?'

'I don't know anything, Sheriff Hopkins.' Hopkins regards the old man, and spits out a gob of chewing tobacco. 'Please, Sheriff, this is sacred land.'

'The fuck it is. And don't shit me about knowing nothing, Bob. There was a time you used to tell all those little California honeys you knew everything.'

'Times have changed, Sheriff, like you say.'

Hopkins loses his patience. 'Look, Bob, it's going to be a cold night and you're an old man, we're both old men now, goddammit. I don't want to have to keep either of us out here any longer than is strictly necessary, so why don't you just tell me what dirty little pagan pact you were cooking up with that murdering whore in Payson this afternoon, then you and I can both go home.'

'Murdering whore, Sheriff?' asks Bob, still calm.

'Yeah. Don't tell me you didn't know. Even if she didn't tell you, you can smell death on a killer, Bob, especially on a female one. It sticks to 'em like sweat.'

'Sheriff Hopkins,' says Bob, 'the woman I ate lunch with seemed as honest as you yourself.' The sheriff drags the old man up by his shirt collar and presses him up against the front of his house.

'Fuck you, Bob, fuck you! Now I want some answers, I want a name and I want a direction of travel. Now!'

A smile creeps over Bob Nequatewa's lips as he speaks. 'OK, Sheriff, I'll tell you everything. Get your notebook ready.' Hopkins releases his grip, pats Bob on the back and gets out a paper and pencil. 'The woman you are seeking has no name, Sheriff. She is the unwanted, nameless daughter of Kóhkang Wuhti, the Spider Woman, conceived in error, and doomed to wander alone.'

Hopkins draws in close to Bob's face, hissing into his ear. 'I can make life very difficult for you, Bob, protected species or not . . . tell me, in God's plain English, her name?'

'She never told me, Sheriff,' splutters the old man.

'OK, where's she headed, then? You must have some idea. You bought her a steak for Christ sakes! You've fathered children by women you've never even bought a bag of Doritos. Where's she headed?'

Bob slithers out from Hopkins' grasp, and stands once more at his door. 'That I will tell you, Sheriff, without betraying either her or my conscience. She's a frightened, lonely woman, Sheriff, accused of murder, pursued by a crazy man, a man full of hatred for the world. Under such circumstances, Sheriff Hopkins, where would you go?'

'Mexico?' says Hopkins, breathlessly, as if he'd worked it out all by himself. 'She's heading for the border at last.'

'That's right, Sheriff,' says Bob Nequatewa, gathering his belongings and heading home, 'and with barely more than ten dollars to her name. I would fear for her. But she need not be afraid of you.'

'Oh yeah,' Hopkins calls after him. 'Why?'

'Because the Boy whose father is the Sun is waiting for her, and rattlesnake children as yet unborn already clamour for her milk. And you, for all your hatred, cannot change that now. You are a million years too late.'

And Bob Nequatewa disappears into his home. Hopkins hears the bolts slide shut, and spits – 'Fuck you, Bob, with your rattlesnake shit!' – and walks to his patrol car. He touches the plastic Jesus on the dash, a heavenly protection against all this devilry, and drives off into the gathering darkness.

On the eastern side of Phoenix, rising from the desert into the green forests of the Superstition Mountains, Sid and Danny's chauffeur slows into a lay-by just west of Globe, and bids them farewell. 'It's been a real pleasure, Danny, to meet another son of the soil of Ireland.' They climb out of the cabin. The sun is all but set, and the first flurry of a cold evening wind flutters around them. Danny waves the truck off and shoulders his bag. South on the 77 or east on the 70, all routes it seems will lead them eventually to Coronado. Sid points into the distance, and they begin to walk east along the roadside, miniature explorers shambling along between the tarmac and telegraph wires, in the fading shadows of the cottonwood trees.

It grows dark. Danny grows angry. 'I can't see a fucking thing. This is the darkest place I have ever seen in my life. There's more darkness here than in the darkest dark dark Irish moor. And I thought foreign countries were supposed to be sunny.' Hours pass. Cars and trucks whip the two travellers with their tailwinds, unmoved by their pleas, and splattering them with grit and dust by way of response. 'Fuck it, Sid. Why didn't we just buy ours-selves a car with all Pat's dirty drug money? It's burning a hole in my pocket.'

Sid stops, leans up against a tree, and starts to explain. 'We need to save our money, Danno. We don't know how long we're going to be here, and we can't expect Luther to subsidise us. Once the New Round Tabyls start getting paying gigs, we'll be fine.'

Danny drops his pack heavily on to the gravel. 'Oh, the *New* Round Tabyls, is it? You're talking like you actually know the guy.' He slaps his forehead with his hand and starts to walk in tight, agitated circles. 'We might not even find him, y'know, and then what gives you the idea he'll be anything other than baffled by us? You heard what our friend in the cab back there said!' Sid looks anxious for a moment. Danny rages on. 'What's he gonna say to us, Sidney, y'man Peyote? "Great! Two pasty-faced foreign fellers I've never heard of before who haven't even got a car. And, wow, they used to play in a Dire Straits covers band. Heavens, my prayers are answered! Now I'm ready to start recording again. Oh, I'm fucking mad by the way."' Sid drops his bag, and sits down on it. Depressurised by his rant, Danny softens a little, but continues, 'Man, you're living in dreamland. We're wasting our time here.'

Sid stands, stares straight ahead, and begins to strap his rucksack back on. 'It's your fucking fault anyway, Danny. If we'd stuck with Timothy Waterhouse and the Lemon Pies we'd never have had to work another day in our lives. Understand?' Danny stiffens. They never talk about this. Never. 'Even Fat Ian would never have us back in the Sultans now, and that's my fault, OK. That's my fault and I'm sorry. But you owe me! And just once in your life, don't you want to do something that matters?'

Danny turns and squares up to him. 'Yeah. Maybe I do. But looking for some useless old hippie isn't it. This is your trip, Sid, not mine. And I've had enough.' And he pokes Sid in the chest, all but pushing him back towards Los Angeles.

'You didn't have to come, Danny. I didn't make you,' Sid shouts, rolling up his sleeves and assuming a stick-armed, floppy-fisted pugilistic stance.

'Oh, fuck off, you little cunt!' Danny spits into his hands and rubs them together. 'Without me Los Bros O'Fernandez would have cut Pat's package out of your arse without so much as a "by your leave" and left you bleeding to death in the bogs.' And he gives Sid another shove westwards.

'Look, will you just fuck off. Just fuck off.'

'First I'm going to fuck you up, and then I'm going to fuck off. Good luck. On your own!' And then a car behind them. Sid turns towards the road and raises his thumb into the beam of the headlights. Danny grits his teeth, straightens his clothes, and signals too. The car pulls up suddenly, a white convertible with the hood drawn up. The driver had slammed on the brakes the moment Sid's thumb came into view, but still overshoots them by some distance. The two men hoist their burdens and hasten towards it. A woman reaches over and opens the door, her face hidden by a cascade of displaced black hair as she bends down to the handle, her features half lit by the dashboard glow. 'Where you going?'

'Coronado?' says Sid.

'I'm Tracy.' Muffled introductions are made. 'I can take you all the way,' she mutters in the darkness, 'but here's the deal. I'm trying to get to Mexico on fourteen dollars. You two buy all the gas and any food and drink we need and I'll drive, OK? And don't try anything funny.'

Danny sees some of Tracy's Christian comic books scattered on the back seat – *This Was Your Life*, *Somebody Loves Me*, *The Word Became Flesh* – and desperately makes discouraging gestures out of the woman's sight, but it's too late. Sid is already manhandling his pack into the car and gesturing for him to follow. For a moment, Danny considers leaving Sid to get in the car alone. Then he looks around him, and the thought of standing there at the roadside alone somehow seems a less appealing alternative. 'That's great,' he says, as Tracy directs both of them into the back seat. 'Thank you very much, ma'am.'

'Hey, are you Irish?' the woman starts as the car lurches forwards and back on to the road. 'Well, don't think you'll be able to get anywhere with me by acting all cute and Celtic.'

They proceed on into the night in silence. Sid and Danny struggle to sit apart in a space too small to make this petty gesture effective. The engine hums beneath a crackly AM country-rock station and the night offers up glimpses of the shining surfaces of great lakes and rivers, glittering through the trees.

Half an hour into the trip and Tracy's driving is unsettling her passengers. She overtakes trucks on the narrow, winding two-lane passes without looking, her foot to the floor, her head craned forwards over the steering wheel as if she's stretching herself out for a photo-finish. Sid and Danny look at her eyes in the rear-view mirror, searching for signs. 'You drive very fast,' offers Sid, at last.

'Yes. Got a problem with that?'

'No, no, he's fine. The faster the better,' says Danny, silently kicking his companion in the shin, as he sees the driver's eyes narrow, and is struck . . . by their familiarity.

The forest gives way to flatlands, black, featureless and quiet. The woman is uncommunicative, choosing unmarked roads south-east with little or no traffic. Sid finally sleeps, drooling a little on to Danny's shoulder. But Danny keeps looking at those eyes, the one point of light in the vast, enormous darkness. He knows those eyes. He runs mental photofits in his mind. Ah! So many women! Maybe she recognises him, too. That might explain her unfriendly attitude at least. Settling back to trawl his memory for any possible meeting, Danny revisits every party he ever gatecrashed, every gig he ever went to, every shop he ever served in, every class he took in school, every magazine advert he ever looked at, every woman he ever lusted after, on various modes of public transport, every blu-tacked to the fridge photo he ever lingered on in every friend he ever had's flat, and every film he ever saw. And then, a tiny bell rings somewhere deep in his brain, as a match is made. And he feels his cheeks flush and his stomach turn and his heart race as he silently nudges Sid awake and whispers, 'It's her.'

Sid wakens and mumbles, 'Who is?'

'She is, Sid, she is . . . her.'

'Who?' And Danny puts his finger to his mouth to silence Sid.

'Everything OK there, guys?' comes the voice from the front.

'Yes, fine thanks,' says Sid, before softening his voice again to speak to Danny. 'What are you talking about?'

'It's *her*, Sid. I stake my life on it. Different hair, though, and she's lost a bit of weight, but it's her.' Tracy looks behind her briefly in the blackness, silencing their debate momentarily. When she turns back, Sid launches into Danny, pleading for sense, and finally losing his patience with an audible 'Look, Dan, just tell me . . .'

The woman turns again. 'OK, boys, what's going on?' She sounds desperate, frightened even.

'Nothing,' says Danny. 'Nothing, nothing, nothing . . . it's just . . .'

Sid interrupts, assuming that in such an absurd situation, a moment of honesty really can't hurt. 'It's just that Danny thinks he knows who you are, but for some reason he doesn't think it's appropriate to share the information . . . Ow!'

The car lurches off the highway, Danny and Sid banging their heads on the headrests and clinging to each other for support. The woman brakes in the dust and rounds on them, angry and afraid. 'Yes, yes, it's me, OK, is that what you wanted to hear?'

There's a long embarrassed pause. Sid breaks it. 'If my Irish friend has offended you in any way then . . .'

'Listen,' Tracy says, beginning her usual soliloquy again, her voice breathless and shaking slightly. 'I've loved many men in the last fifteen years, all of them better men than you, and every single one of them is lying somewhere between here and Mexico City, throats slit, wrists slashed, necks broken, arms and legs separated from their bodies by speeding locomotives, heads crushed by passing trucks, guts contorted by deadly poisons, hearts broken and dead, all dead, every one of them dead.'

'Eh,' Danny splutters, 'we don't know anything about any of that. It's just that you're the spitting image of a woman we once saw shagging a pig.'

Tracy turns back to the wheel. She sighs. Sid puts a hand over his mouth as the blood begins to drain from his face.

Tracy runs a hand through her hair. She lights a cigarette. And then she starts to laugh, finally doubling up into an infectious hysteria. Danny laughs too, not really knowing why, as Sid scrambles out of the car. Finally the laughter stops. Over the sound of Sid throwing up at the roadside, Danny breaks the silence and asks . . .

'So. What was it like?'

The Hopi Boy
and the Sun – iv

After he had climbed into the box and rolled into the river, the boy drifted for four days and four nights, until finally he felt it strike the shore where two rivers join. He took the plug out of a peephole he had made and saw morning light. But when he tried to get out he couldn't open the door, no matter how hard he pushed.

He soon resigned himself to his situation. He thought he would have to die alone inside the drifting box.

Hopi Indian legend, reported by
Franz Boas in 1922

Ten

'So, A.R.Y., you really believe that, in the 1960s, a secret conspiracy of high-ranking American Freemasons arranged for Neil Armstrong to put the Holy Grail into orbit around the moon . . .' Lewis is relieved that the other drinkers in the art deco bar of the Hotel Congress, Tucson, Arizona, are all too distracted to bother to try and tune in, and takes some comfort in the sound of the live band next door that drowns out even Spike's breathless and excited tones. Tonight, he isn't afraid of spies and plotters, not in this comforting Western-styled building, with its creaking wooden staircase, and timbered safety. 'Where Summer spends the Winter', boasted the letter-head in his room, with a poetic economy of phrase that didn't seem in the least bit dishonest. Dillinger was captured here, so he feels probability is stacked in his favour and lightning never strikes twice. Initially he'd intended to put Spike to the test, just as she was clearly testing him, by telling her his story and watching her reactions. But, over the course of the last hour, he has finally become convinced he's got her wrong, and reproachfully blames himself for his own unforgiving suspicions. She seems to want to help, and she's just the kind of trash culture teen who'd take someone to the Excalibur Casino and the Astronauts' Hall of Fame, whether she suspected them of being a Grail-seeking astronaut or not. Now he sees Spike is merely fascinated by him and, unlike his doctors back home, is under no professional obligation to be sceptical. She continues her summation of his case: '. . . and that in the late 80s, a secret conspiracy of disaffected European Freemasons sent you to recover it.' Lewis nods, pouring himself another drink from their pitcher of beer. 'OK. And then, mission accomplished, your shuttle was shot down over American airspace, the Grail reclaimed by the United States Air Force and you were brainwashed, albeit partially unsuccessfully, into forgetting the whole story.' Even Spike seems a little incredulous. Her neat encapsulation of his story only emphasises its absurdity.

'Yes. Do you think that could be true?'

'True?' says Spike, knocking back the last of another beer in the glow of a soft green light. 'There's no such thing as objective truth, A.R.Y., like I said. That's what the psychedelic experience teaches us. But if the story works for you, if it helps you to make sense of your life, then by all means believe it. No single mythology can be objectively superior to another, be it Christian, Muslim or . . . paranoid conspiracy theory.'

She's pleased. Lewis senses her thesis writing itself in her head even as she speaks. She pours another drink and clinks her glass to his, sealing the veracity of her argument. 'What do you mean?' Lewis asks, lost.

Spike takes a deep breath, and begins. 'Well, A.R.Y., I'll give you an example. My mother had a friend, yeah, in the 70s, Treat. Now Treat went off on the hippie trail to India, as was the fashion of the day, and fell in with some weird transcendental Tantric sex and levitation cult. He stayed with them a few years, but when he left, their guru warned him that he had spies everywhere, and if Treat ever revealed any of their secrets he would be punished. Now, ten years later, Treat was bumming round the south-west coast of Turkey. One night, at a party in a tent on the beach, he started telling anyone who would listen the secrets of the guru, whatever they were, I dunno, yogic flying, astral travel and staying hard all night. While Treat was speaking, he remembers seeing a little squirrel coming in under the tent flap and watching him. He remembered thinking it was odd because he hadn't seen many squirrels in that area, particularly on the beaches. Anyhow, while he slept that night, Treat awoke suddenly in enormous physical discomfort to find that his balls had swollen to ten times their normal size. They were the size of watermelons, A.R.Y., and aching like they were on fire. Then he realised – the squirrel had been one of the guru's spies and now he was being punished for his betrayal of the great flying and fucking secret. So, Treat prayed for forgiveness, and in a vision, the guru's mother appeared to him, and forgave him. And when Treat awoke, his balls were back to normal.'

Spike smiles. Lewis realises she feels the meaning and relevance of this peculiar parable should be immediately apparent. 'An amazing tale, Spike,' he says.

'It sure is. But that isn't why I told it you, Lewis. You see, once I asked Treat if he really, really, really and truly believed he had been spied on by a squirrel, and then punished from afar by the guru. Did he really think it had all happened? And he said, it didn't matter whether it really happened or not. What mattered, get this, was that he *believed* it had happened, and it worked for him.' And she makes the face again, before continuing. 'But, A.R.Y., what if you get to Coronado and the Grail isn't there? What new myth will *you* adopt to help you explain away your experience?'

Lewis pauses, and swirls the liquid around the bottom of his glass, as her intention finally sinks in. 'I don't know, Spike. I just don't know.'

She reaches over and squeezes his hand, letting her fingers entangle with his for a minute or more. Then she looks up at a clock, catching herself.

'I have to go. I hope you find what you're looking for, I really do.'

She stands, and kisses him lightly on the forehead. 'Thanks,' he says. 'It was nice meeting you.' And he watches her hitch her bag over her shoulder, and walk towards the door. In another time, in another life, in another place, then maybe. He orders another pitcher and settles into the corner of the bar, alone, preparing for an evening of oblivion.

But later on, Lewis folds back the shutters of his window and lies awake on the bed, staring out at the moon. No matter how drunk he gets, it just won't let him sleep. And the clarity of the cloudless desert sky beyond the buildings only makes it seem clearer, crisper, nearer. The room spins. He shut his eyes. And then the chalice spins instead, still out of reach, and drifting ever onwards.

In a roadside country music bar somewhere between Globe and Wilcox, Sid's mouth falls open. Danny smiles in admiration as Tracy finishes telling her life story, or as much of it as she was prepared to let slip. She has skirted around the finer details of the incident with which they were already more familiar, in Sid's opinion, than they would wish to be. Behind them, a quartet of local musicians strike up an uneasy, slurred version of Charlene's 'I've Never Been To Me', that seems to threaten to stagger to a halt almost as soon as it has started, an inappropriately deep-voiced male vocalist struggling to find the spaces between the unwieldy instrumental meeting of cello, keyboards and drums.

Tracy concludes her story through the haze of her seventh tequila. 'So, I'm a hard woman to impress now. Somebody buys me some flowers? I just think, "Big deal, buddy. It'll take more than a few flowers to ring my bell."'

'I thought you'd feel like that,' says Danny, studiously maintaining eye contact. 'So it'd take a very special sort of a man to satisfy you, then?' Sid remains silent. Danny always turns conversations with women into a competition, even if he has no real interest in them, and Sid senses the accent strengthening. Gratifyingly, she ignores him.

'But what is it with guys! Jesus! Every time we talk about settling down and raising chickens I feel duty bound to unburden myself and pow!, the lily-livered piece of shit has fallen apart on me and checked himself into the nearest morgue.' She picks up Danny's Guinness and drains it. 'No way am I gonna try explaining that to the police. It'd be funny if it wasn't so . . .'

'Inconvenient?' offers Danny.

'No. Inconvenient isn't the word I was thinking of. Try utterly, unbearably tragic . . .'

The music swells to fill the uncomfortable silence. Then Danny speaks. 'Maybe you just haven't met the right feller yet. I for one found your performance in the film very impressive.'

Tracy looks incredulous. 'Danny, have you been listening to a word I've said?'

'No,' says Danny, smiling. 'I haven't.'

Sid has to admit, Danny timed that little turnaround perfectly. It's almost as if he's finding his rhythm again. Emboldened, Sid watches him blossom further. 'Right! Who's for another, then? My round.'

'I'll help,' says Sid.

As they push through the crowd, the vocalist enters the spoken word section of Charlene's long-forgotten hit, reciting the lyrics over drums and piano embellishments. *'You know what paradise is? It's a lie. A fantasy we create about people and places as we'd like them to be. But you know what truth is? It's that little baby you're holding, and it's that man you fought with this morning, the one you're going to make love to tonight. That's love. That's truth.'* The song surges back into full bloom. Some check-shirted men at the front seem genuinely moved, dabbing at the first flowers of tiny tears with their fingers, and there is a surge of applause.

Sid and Danny arrive at the bar. 'A pint of Guinness, a beer and a tequila. What a fantastic woman, eh, Sid. I must have her.' A six-foot six, mustachioed man, as round as he is high, interrupts them.

'Hey! You Irish? My great-great-grandfather was Irish!'

'Cheers! From Cork, was he?'

'Up the Irish! Let me to buy you a drink.'

The big man turns, smiling, to Sid. 'You Irish too?'

'No,' says Sid, emphatically, and a little drunk. 'I'm English.'

The man makes a disapproving face. 'English, huh? When are you Brits gonna get your troops out of Dublin? Right, guy?'

'Quite so,' says Danny, eyeing Sid anxiously.

'There's no British troops in Dublin, mate. It's in the Irish Republic. There haven't been any British troops there since after the First World War.' Sid lurches forward. 'If you can't find somewhere on a map, don't send it free weapons.'

Danny pushes him away from the bristling man. 'Leave it, Sid. I'm going to keep us in free drinks all night.' And contorting his face, Danny assumes the Brad Pitt accent that had made the two of them laugh a whole afternoon away when they saw a trailer for *The Devil's Own* some years back. *'Oi need dat morney, Tom!'*

But Sid doesn't crack. 'You fucking hypocrite, Danny. You left Ireland when you were fourteen.'

'You're splitting hairs, Sid,' he shouts, handing him two drinks. 'Take this to Tracy. Tell her I won't be long.' Danny turns back to the big man. 'Up the Irish! Here's to a free Dublin!'

In the lobby of the Hotel Congress, just as the porter is closing up for the night, a wooden cane raps at the glass of the front door. 'You're a little late for check in, sir,' says the porter, to the elderly, rotund man in the heavy brown coat.

'I do apologise,' says the man, 'but I didn't wish to check in. I merely wanted to ask if you had a particular gentleman staying with you, a colleague of mine from home. A number of us are here on business and we were planning a surprise night out tomorrow in honour of his birthday.'

The porter leads him over the mosaic floor to the check-in

desk, and begins to turn the pages of the ledger. 'What was your friend's name sir?'

'Lewis. A.R.Y. Lewis.'

'He checked in tonight, room thirty-three, but you may have to move fast. He said he was only staying a night.'

'Room thirty-three, you say! How deliciously appropriate.' And the fat man hands the porter five dollars. 'Remember, don't tell him I was asking after him or you'll spoil everything.'

'You can count on my discretion, sir,' answers the porter, showing the Englishman to the exit.

'Mum's the word, eh, my good man, or we shall have to cut out your tongue!'

Outside the fat man stands alone in the empty street, illuminated by the lobby light, and sniffs the night air. Junkies drift up from downtown under the railway tracks and nestle into nooks at the bus station opposite the hotel, and across the street some student revellers vainly seek out a bar that's still open. The porter turns off the lights and the Hampstead Man is in darkness. He discreetly swigs one deep draught from a silver hip flask, puffs out his chest, and sets off on foot for his hotel, swinging his cane, and singing as he walks, in a rich, proud baritone;

> *The world is in pain our secrets to gain,*
> *And still let them wonder and gaze on;*
> *They ne'er can divine the Word or the Sign*
> *Of a free and an Accepted Mason.*

'Here,' says Sid, sitting down heavily next to Tracy. 'Danny's just reacquainting himself with his lost heritage.'

A pause. 'I didn't kill anyone.'

Sid hands her the tequila. 'I believe you.'

She swallows the whole glass. 'Thanks. You don't know how much that means.'

At the bar, Danny is amid adoring drinkers. The stories

come thick and fast as rekindled race memories stir within the skulls of his audience. 'To wake in Dublin, overlooking the Liffey, after a night spent chasing the craic, why, to be sure, there can be no finer thing . . .' More Guinness! And 'Ah, the Liffey!' they chant as one, as if they had any idea. 'And I remember, riding east out of Cork by moonlight, my little brother asleep in the back of the cart, wrapped up in the flag of the Republic, amidst whatever possessions we could carry with us, and my father on foot, leading the donkey, and my mother singing softly under her breath, *"The Broad Majestic Shannon"* . . . while behind us the fading sounds of English cannons rang in our ears.' And one moment it's 'Down with the English!' and then it's 'Down with the Brits!' The precise geographical boundaries of these faceless enemies shifting every second shout. The Americans' sinews stiffen as they listen, and, as Danny's stories work their magic, each in turn imagines himself semi-naked and painted green, facing an imagined oppressor across a heavy metal album cover land-scape of crimson mist and blackened bodies, burning British flags underneath blood-red skies of wheeling carrion, avenging the rape of their milk-white maidens, and meting out gory payment for the murder, in their beds, naturally, where else, of their red-faced infants. Tell us more . . . 'Yes, I knew Bobby Sands. He was a great friend of mine, a giant of a man he was, he'd eat his own weight in potatoes at a sitting.' Sid catches some of Danny's story across the room, and, despite himself, smirks a little. 'A great fat feller, you could hide a whole IRA unit down the front of his trousers and still have room for the Sinn Fein leadership. But, of course, that was before the glorious days of the H Block hunger strike protest.'

'Yeah,' interjects the moustache man. 'When the boys got the Brits pissed at them by smearing their own shit up the walls!'

'That's right. But it was more than just a simple dirty protest. It was a cover for the prisoners to make explosives out of their own faeces. Here in America, that's not possible, because you have a more protein-rich diet. But back in the old country all them carbohydrates can pack a powerful methane punch.' The men make impressed noises and nod. 'In fact, it's a wonderful irony of the republican struggle that the bomb that blew Thatcher out of the window of the Grand Hotel in Brighton was probably manufactured from Bobby Sands' own shit! That stuck it to the Brits!' A cheer. And Danny's back is slapped so hard he is winded. Someone hands him another Guinness. He winks across the room to Sid and puts up his thumbs.

Tracy turns to Sid. 'So, this is your big new start?'

'Well, it's not quite how I'd imagined it, but we may as well finally grind to a halt here as anywhere. At least the weather's nice. And we've got to meet a celebrity, I suppose.'

Tracy blushes. 'Yeah. Right. I'm a good omen. Now, tell me again, when's your rock and roll friend expecting you?'

Sid would have answered, but as he opens his mouth to speak, he realises he doesn't really have a reply to Tracy's question. To hear the subject of their arrival at Luther's put so bluntly seems for a moment to render his ambitions absurd, so Sid simply leans in, cupping his ear over the music, and pretends he hasn't heard her.

Abby wakes alone at 7 a.m. to the sound of her pager beeping. She checks the number and calls it. 'I'm not due in today, Julie, what is it?'

Outside the flat she teases the Mini into life in the drizzle and starts to drive across town to Ladbroke Grove. Peter Rugg has been hauled in for housebreaking, somewhere just off the Portobello Road. The police know him from their files, and hope she can save them some paperwork. So much for a day off. She fumbles around the floor for a cassette to play. It seems like every one she picks up is some shitty compilation tape Sid made her, with some stupid title that's supposed to sum up the depth of his feelings. 'I Love You Tape', 'Songs For Swinging Lovers i.e. You and Me', 'Doctor Love's Musical Prescription'. She'd have preferred flowers. She puts a random tape in the deck. The familiar sound of the Flan Man's irritating mewl fills the tiny cabin of the car. At Wandsworth Bridge she pulls over in the car park of the drive-in McDonald's, gathers all Sid's lovingly crafted cassettes up in her arms, and hurls them into the Thames. As they fall and sink one by one, she wonders for a moment if she ought to have done her ex-boyfriend the honour of listening to all of them at least once. Ah, well, fuck him. At a petrol station south of Fulham she stops and buys a cheap compilation of songs from Rodgers and Hammerstein musicals, shoves it into the machine, and once and finally washes that man right out of her hair.

In the country music bar, the band strike up a faster song. Its hillbilly guitar licks sound a resonating note echoing through a musical family tree of convoluted cross-fertilised connections, out across the prairies and onwards back to the luminescent green fields of the Old Country, a substitute Valhalla for a displaced white race too young to have a hall for heroes of its own. And Danny's new-found friends raise him upon their shoulders and parade him around the room, as cowboy-booted men dance in and out of their progress, their arms folded across their chests, their feet kicking like mules, Riverdance reborn by way of the Texas Playboys. Danny beckons to Sid and Tracy from beneath a swinging wagon-wheel chandelier, but Sid just shakes his head. As the music spirals to a close, the men lift Danny on to the stage. Danny beckons Sid again, and he shrinks into his seat. The vocalist stands back, kisses Danny on the cheek, and hands him the microphone, as the men below call out for him to speak. Danny coughs, and straightens his clothes. 'Ladies and gentlemen, on behalf of all the people of the Old Country, I'd like to thank you all for the hospitality you have shown us here tonight. I feel I could be at home. And there can be no higher compliment than that.' The cheers rings out. Stout slops into sawdust. 'But, despite all the memories, and all the proud glories of yesterday, perhaps it's time for us to stop living in the past,' Danny continues, as the crowd quietens. 'Sitting over there is Sid Parker, a member of Her Majesty's Glorious Paratroop Regiment, who faced me more than once, rifle in hand, across the Belfast barricades. As part of an American-sponsored bridge-building initiative, he and I have been forced to spend a month together driving across America, learning to communicate, learning to respect one another's cultures, in the company of Tracy there, a UN peacekeeping force officer from this very state.'

Sid's jaw hangs loose, as bristling brows are raised towards him. 'Danny . . . you bastard.'

'For three weeks now, all I have been doing is trying, just once, to make Sid forget the past, forget our differences, and shake me by the hand. But he won't have it.' There are jeers, and shaking fists. 'But maybe tonight, in this atmosphere of forgiveness, well, if he could just find it in himself to come up here, on this stage, in front of you good people, and embrace me, then we could all start to build towards a bright new future.'

'Go on, man!' someone calls out. 'Bite the fucking bullet!' Tattooed arms pull Sid up from his seat and hustle him towards the stage. Bewildered and breaking into a sweat he finds himself forced towards the waiting Danny, who seizes him and presses him to him. 'C'mon, Sid, don't let me down now.' Sid hugs him back and the pair turn and face the jubilant crowd, Sid shaken, Danny wiping away a perfectly timed tear.

'Ladies and gentlemen,' comes an announcement from the bar. 'In view of the momentous historical occurrence that we have all been privileged to witness here tonight, all drinks are free.' A cheer goes up. Danny and Sid are carried aloft from the stage. The band leap to their feet and break into a countrified assault on 'The Irish Rover'. Tracy falls back into her seat laughing. And the moustache man pulls Sid down to the floor and hugs him, soaking his face with hot tears. The evening has begun.

*　　*　　*

'Many Happy Returns, Mr Lewis,' calls the porter as A.R.Y. Lewis closes the door of the hotel. He thinks little of it, throws a bag in the back of the car parked under the trees, and squints in the morning sun. There's a sickness in his stomach as he sits behind the wheel and checks the map. Coronado is so near now, and, with it, the dreadful sense of an ending.

In a breakfast place by the bus station across the street, Spike watches Lewis through a smoked plate-glass window. As he accelerates out of the car lot, she hesitates for a moment, snatching up her sunglasses, but then settles back into her seat as he heads east out of the city. You can't feel bad about betraying a man you hardly know, she reasons.

Suddenly her view is obscured by a bulky form sliding in behind the table opposite her, eclipsing the Wild West façade of the Hotel Congress and blocking out the sun. 'Tea, please,' the fat man calls to the waitress as he sits down. The girl looks up at him and he leans in towards her. 'Well?'

'OK. Get this,' Spike begins, hurriedly, instantly dismissing her anxieties of a moment ago. 'Your Mr Lewis thinks he may have been an astronaut. He thinks Freemasons sent him into space to retrieve the Holy Grail after Neil Armstrong apparently put it into orbit in 1969. He also thinks he may be crazy. Which is why he's headed to a deserted airbase over in Coronado, to see if the Grail's been stashed there since he lost it.'

'Hmm. Why Coronado?' says the Hampstead Man, consulting a map.

'Some net-head freaks told him that was where it was. But that doesn't prove anything.'

'You're not going with him?'

'Things looked like they might get heavy. Besides, I think he wanted to be on his own.' The tea arrives. The fat man sips it and winces.

'Ugh! Ghastly! Still, I trust you used every means at your

disposal to try and convince him to take you along?' And he raises an eyebrow.

'No, I didn't,' spits the girl. 'And I told you when you contacted me, I'm a Private Investigator, that's all. No information is so important it's worth letting someone get into my pants. Talking of which, am I finished now? I really want to get into some clothes more suited to someone of my age.'

The fat man pauses and toys with his spoon. 'Yes. You're finished now. Apart from the small matter of payment. My car is out back.' The fat man leaves an appropriate amount of change on the table and stands. Spike follows him out into the street.

'So tell me, I'm kinda curious,' she says, following him down the alley to the back of the bus station, 'is Lewis really out of his mind or is he on to something?'

'I'm afraid the five thousand dollars cash we agreed on alone is going to have to satisfy you, miss,' says the fat man, arriving in a deserted yard, and flipping up the trunk of the car. 'I couldn't possibly say.' He reaches in and pulls out a gun. 'At my initiation I was taught to be cautious.' The dull thud of a silencer. 'Conceal and never reveal.' He pushes the girl's body into the trunk, locks it, tosses his keys up into the air, and catches them. This is a regrettable turn of events, admittedly, but the superfluous knobs and excrescences must be knocked off, the stone smoothed and prepared, the rectangular corners adjusted, rude matter brought into due form, the horizontals laid and approved, the uprights fixed. He drives away, singing softly under his breath.

> We're true and sincere, and just to the fair;
> They'll trust us on any occasion;
> No mortal can more, the ladies adore,
> Than a free and an Accepted Mason.

Eleven

In the shade of an awning outside the bar, Tracy slams the car trunk shut, and Danny and Sid shudder at the sound, still unsteady the morning after the night before, dry-mouthed with ashtray breath, nursing Guinness bellies. A yellow school bus grinds past them, too brightly coloured for this hour, and noisy kids point at Danny's bald head and wave. He flicks his V's and then staggers to the car for support. Tracy looks up as she suddenly grasps what they've just told her. 'This Luther guy doesn't even know you're coming? You're not serious?'

'Yes. Sid believes if we just turn up uninvited, the great Luther Peyote will be so delighted to see us that he will instantly revive the musical career that he abandoned some twenty-five years ago.' Sid glowers, but Danny continues. 'I for one am not convinced, and would be open to any change of plan, such as following a beautiful woman down to Mexico to start a new life with her, irrespective of her shady past.'

Tracy opens the car door and fixes him. 'All my ex-lovers are dead.'

'Lightweights.'

Through the northern section of the Coronado National Forest and the final slopes of the Pinaleno Mountains, and Highway 10 opens up before them. Tracy drives as Sid and

Danny sweat and shake under their sunglasses. The radio hums alternative rock at ambient volume and tumbleweeds large enough to threaten their vehicle blow in from the flatlands between boulders and over the road. Tracy wants the windows closed to maximise the benefits of the air conditioning, but last night's excess is working a gaseous revenge on her passengers, who lie in the back seat sampling and resampling endlessly circulating imprints of their own breaches of in-car etiquette. 'Aaaah, the Guinness fart,' waxes Danny, 'so thick and creamy you could scratch a shamrock into its surface.' What is it that always compels him to stay in character, Sid wonders once more.

Somewhere west of the junction with Highway 10, a patrol car slips out of the scrub and slides into a discreet pursuit. Hopkins had been riding the reluctant Cowdrey hard for leads and sightings. After talking to Bob he'd have expected the killer to head straight south, but the woman's circuitous route through the little travelled triangle between Highways 10 and 70 suggested an evasive criminal intelligence at work. Back at the office Cowdrey exercised an authority he didn't really have, telling the sheriff he'd issued directions to units in all regions to be on the look-out for the vehicle, but Hopkins knew he hadn't. Instead he drove backwards and forwards along the highway between Tucson and the New Mexico border, knowing that sooner or later the woman would have to cross it. And now he'd finally found her, passing him unwares as he waited at the roadside.

Tracy taps at the fuel gauge. 'If we're running out of gas,' says Danny, 'strap me on the roof and I'll get you over the border under me own steam.' It never ends, Sid notes.

Replacing the fuel pump, Danny stands still a moment, looking out over the desert from the isolated forecourt, greener now than further west, awash with cacti and grubby shrubs, the mountains of Coronado rising in the south-east through the highway haze, unconvincing and overstated like a 60s' TV set backdrop. He hopes the space will make things stop spinning. It doesn't. He follows Tracy and Sid into the store.

Behind the counter, the clerk looks up from under the peak of a blue baseball cap. He knocks out a pipe on the bar and wipes burger mayonnaise off his chin. 'Hey, come on in everybody to the greatest gas stop between Silver City and Tucson. Today's specials are canned soda drinks and cigarettes so, hey, you're in luck. Feel free to look around with no obligation to buy. But remember, a gift is lovely to touch and hold, but if you break it, consider it sold.'

Tracy carefully replaces a Marge Simpson air freshener that she'd been considering. 'Thanks. You're very kind.'

As she puts her sunglasses back on, the clerk suddenly seems animated. 'Hey! Do I know you from somewhere, ma'am?' Tracy says she doubts it and asks to use the restroom. The clerk tells her it's out back. She snatches up an *Enquirer* from the rack, takes the keys from a hook by the cash register, and leaves by a white wooden door at the rear of the room.

Lewis pulls off Highway 10 into the town of Wilcox. He parks outside a row of empty storefronts and stands looking south to the mountains of the Coronado National Forest, the land's last geographical flourish before the road concedes to the atomic plains of southern New Mexico. Airbases should be in large flat spaces, not hidden hills. Everything seems appropriately suspect.

Behind him a family of four load a pick-up truck with the last boxes of stock, as they prepare to lock up their grocery store one last time, to set up on the highway in hope of passing trade. A kid with a pink ice-cream smeared face stares silently up at him. Lewis smiles and the boy runs away, to stand and tug at his mother's sleeve, pointing. Lewis gets back in his car and turns right towards Coronado, as he feels some abstract notion of precedent embrace him and coerce him onwards. Percival Lowell, Daniel Moreau Barringer and Francisco Vasquez de Coronado had all searched this same landscape before him. But suddenly he no longer interprets the evidence of these failures as an indication that his is a vain quest. As he surveys the scene, he stiffens underneath an imaginary standard, shoulders a shield, and mentally takes up arms. When Sir Galahad knelt at last before the Holy Vessel in the court of King Pellés, cleansed and free from stain, he left behind him the fears of his fellows who had fallen. Galahad found the Grail, and tasted its grace first-hand. And then Lewis laughs and looks down at his travel-worn clothes. He's been in the sun too long, literally too long.

Beyond Dos Cabezas the road south is a dirt track, and as it narrows and grows more unstable Lewis shields his eyes from the sun and slows to read a broken-down, weather-beaten sign, rising uneven out of the dirt. 'No Entry. Government Property.' But the barbed-wire fence that ought to block the road has fallen. The wind flails it weakly out over the scrub like a faulty mechanical arm and Lewis drives forwards over its fluttering remnants. He rounds the crest of a hill and stops before descending, turning off the engine and stepping out to take in the view. Breathing in he can feel altitude thinning the atmosphere, and his chest burns as he inhales largely useless lungfuls of scorched, airless air. Below him, trash and tumbleweed blow through the deserted pathways of a scrappy collection of abandoned tarpaulin buildings and hangars, the airstrip cracked and punctured by patches of pasture, scarred by jagged tarmac, its last proud flights a long-forgotten memory. There isn't even a hint of security. Perhaps it's a clever double bluff. But then Lewis would think that. He knows this has become necessary.

For a moment he almost hopes he's wrong, and that the airbase is empty. The journey has given him a sense of purpose he's never known before, in all his brief few years of consciousness. Without the Grail quest all those Arthurian romances he'd spent months arched over would be nothing but stories of men in historically inaccurate armour, sitting around eating venison and trying to knock each other off horses, passing the time playfully until they died content and untested. But crisis had made holy heroes of Malory's feudal parasites. And likewise, Spike had been right, he now realised. Lewis's search had defined him. And given his precarious mental state, though it was unlikely he had really been sent to space to reclaim the blood of Christ from its endless orbit, there was a chance that trying to verify the story had saved him from an even greater insanity. He wondered what Dr Quinton would think of his quest now it had taken him so far. 'A displacement activity', she would call it. So what if it was? It had its purpose. And it worked better than Prozac.

But what will become of him when it ends? Lewis considers turning round and driving away, heading back to Tucson, looking up Spike for another night of drinking, and spinning out the comforting uncertainties of his cloud of unknowing for another day or so. A bustle of birds billows up into the sky from behind a lopsided hangar, their sudden squawks skewering the silence, and Lewis turns at the sound of something scrabbling in the dust behind him. A dry and displaced-looking cane toad, fully the size of his fist, stares up from behind the rear wheel of the car. He lights the last of a packet of cigarettes and waits for divine inspiration. Nothing is forthcoming. The birds spiral over the sun and settle on the crumbling runway, spreading out and pecking at insects surfacing into the sunlight from slivers of soil between the fractured plates of rock. The toad croaks and hops away. Lewis draws a final heavy drag and flicks the dying butt over the hill, towards the empty airbase. He jangles the car keys.

Danny picks up two doughnuts and puts them round his eyes like glasses, and begins to attempt to read a sign on the wall of the gas station about the refusal of credit, eye-test style. Sid sees him and laughs. The clerk starts gesturing to them, openmouthed.

'C'mon, man, they're only doughnuts. I'm gonna buy them anyhow.' The clerk jerks his finger towards the door. Backlit by the sun, a pot-bellied man stands in the doorway, pointing at them with a pistol. He is wearing a sheriff's uniform. Danny raises his hands, a doughnut in each. 'Like I said, I was gonna pay . . .'

'Shut-it, boy! You are all wanted for questioning in relation to a homicide and . . .' The sheriff lowers his gun, takes off his sunglasses. His tiny turtle eyes squint around the dimly lit room. 'Where's the woman?'

'She's in the little girls' room,' volunteers the clerk, shaking.

Danny interrupts, 'Officer, you're making a mistake,' but as the sheriff raises his gun towards him he pauses.

'Hey! Are you Irish?'

'Yeah,' says Danny, relieved, and sensing a way to turn the situation to his advantage. 'Yeah, I am actually.'

'Hmm. Then you're probably armed.' The sheriff scowls and pushes the pistol into Danny's neck. The radio plays an advert for legal advice in the event of an automobile accident. A fly lands on Sid's face. Frozen, he lets it crawl up into his nose, scared even to sniff.

Out back, in a wooden shack, Tracy sits and considers. The boys aren't so bad. Somehow she feels she can trust them. And last night's party in the bar was kind of fun, if a little conspicuous for her liking. For now, they serve her purposes. And Danny's constant banter, even though it grates sometimes, at least stops her having to think too hard. To her left, she sees one of the Christian comic books hanging from a nail by a string. She's already got two copies of *Why No Revival?*, which explains how America is under threat from Catholic immigrants pouring in over her southern borders, but she pockets it none the less. As usual, the scrawled message: 'Please pass this on to a friend when you have finished with it.' She opens the *Enquirer*. A page 4 story about scientists growing human heads on pigs, and creaky photo-montage of possible imagined consequences. A woman in white, walking down an aisle, ready to make her vows with an uncomfortably upright pig body, and its smiling human head. She throws down the paper.

'You, behind the counter, what's your name?' Hopkins' pistol bores deeper into Danny's neck, as he points at the clerk.

'George.'

'OK, George,' says Hopkins. 'Call 911. Tell them Sheriff Hopkins has the motel homicide suspect detained here but I will need immediate back-up as she has two accomplices, OK?'

George begins to dial, but Sid suddenly interjects, 'Don't do it, George. This is all wrong.' Hopkins shakes Danny vigorously and waves the gun. He struggles and shouts. 'Yeah! She hasn't killed anyone. Its just that all her boyfriends commit suicide when she tells them that she had sex with a pig in a Mexican porn film.'

George puts down the phone and looks excited. 'I knew I recognized her from somewhere. I've watched that movie a million times. She's the queen of the Barnyard Babes!'

Hopkins lets Danny go and lowers his gun. 'The barnyard what?'

'The Barnyard Babes, officer,' says Danny, as the sheriff turns to him, 'clearly some kind of Busby Berkeley/bestiality dance troupe. Wow!' There is a rattle from the counter. Hopkins switches back to the clerk who cocks a hunting rifle and trains it square on the sheriff's head.

'George! What are you doing? You could be in serious trouble here, boy.'

'Sheriff,' says the man, suddenly grave and serious, 'once in every man's life there comes perhaps his one opportunity to stand up and be counted, to show what he really believes in. I love that movie. And I love the Barnyard Babes. You ain't taking that woman anywhere. Now put down your weapon and move back.'

'Fuck you!' Hopkins shouts. Time slows, clocks stop, the breeze hangs dead, the air conditioning is silenced and the highway rumble dissipates into the ether. Two shots, simultaneously. Danny covers his ears. Sid ducks behind a snack food rack and worries, for a moment, that the last word he'll ever read is Cheetos. George bounces on to the back wall, clutching at a wound in his arm. Hopkins falls, his gun skating across the floor towards the door, as a bullet shatters the glass of the canned drinks refrigerator unit behind him and the hands of the clock over the counter surge back to normal speed.

Outside, Tracy looks up, pulls up her pants, and kicks open the door of the washroom. The sudden sunlight dazzles her and she runs back to the store. She pauses a moment to listen to the sound of a struggle, then rushes in. Danny is bundling the body of a vacuum-cleaner-flex-bound policeman into a store cupboard by the side of the counter, as Sid pulls a paper bag over the captive's head. She takes stock of the situation and shouts, 'Who the hell do you think you are? Bonnie and Clyde?'

'You should be more grateful, love. This feller was after you. Chuck us them keys.' Danny locks the struggling man into the cupboard as Tracy rushes to the clerk, now bent over the counter and bleeding. George opens his eyes, gargles blood through his teeth, beckons her down towards his mouth and mumbles. 'Gee. I never thought I'd get to meet a real movie star.'

Tracy takes his head in her hands. 'A movie star? That's very sweet of you. But Barnyard Babes was a long time ago, and it's not something I'm proud of.'

George draws her down to him again. 'Oh, but you should be. It was a wonderful performance.'

'Thank you. That means a lot to me.' George's eyes close again. Then he splutters, shakes and is still.

Tracy steps away from the counter. 'He'll live. Danny. Dial 911.' He does so. Sid puts some money for the gas into the unconscious clerk's hand, curling his fingers around the coins, and they head out to the car as the banging in the cupboard behind them begins once more.

At the entrance to the airbase, in between fallen sections of ten-foot wire fencing, a red and white striped barrier lies snapped and ineffectual on the ground. Lewis parks up in front of it, and steps over the ill-defined threshold. The broken windows of a paint-peeling office on his right reveal nothing but crumpled newspapers, a toothless typewriter, and furniture reduced to firewood fossil remnants. He heads towards a flaking administration and accommodation building, two cracked glass storeys rising ashamed out of the tarmac. He walks along the lifeless corridors. Every room is the same. Empty Coca-Cola cans, punctured at the bottom to make bongs by bored kids. Torn up pornography, smeared with human shit. *Barely Legal. Vixens. Hot Tail.* Used condoms, betraying the building's more recent non-military applications. Snack food packaging. Underwear. Pentangles drawn on the wall in spray paint. Accusations as to the sexual worthlessness of the local trailer teens. Phone numbers to call if you are a gay queer faggot and want your cock sucked good. A headless doll. A tiny shoe. No Grail. Nothing holy. But this means nothing. All the holy places and historical sites had proved barren. One might as well look in a twentieth-century ruin. Lewis had done the research.

He walks out of the building into the sun again. There are three hangars over by the abandoned airstrip. He walks across the tarmac towards them, casting a long shadow over the empty airbase, his footsteps bouncing back to him off the corrugated metal. The first hangar gapes open and empty, the metal doors at the front drooping loose and limp from their hinges, scrap metal and burned-out consoles twisting around each other like a petrified forest of cottonwoods. Persistent weeds somehow trail from inaccessible points in the arches of the roof, fed by shafts of light that filter down through cracks and slits in the sheets of metal. The second hangar is the same, apart from the remnants of an abandoned camp fire in the centre, and a few discarded bottles and plastic bags that suggest a daring overnight stay.

Lewis turns to walk to the third hangar. Unlike the others, the doors are intact and closed. Lewis hears something as he approaches, an electronic hissing sound, the babble of voices,

as if dozens of people are within, working feverishly on something secret. He stands at the foot of the doors. There is a
smaller door cut into them at ground level, with footprints in
the dust around it. He presses his ear to the metal and listens.
Music. Chatter. Radio noise. He wraps his fingers around the
handle and tries the lock.

'*Suddenly the hall was lit by a sunbeam which shed a radiance through the palace seven times brighter than had been
before.*' But no. At the far end of the hangar, 500 yards away,
beyond a restless sea of rubble and rubbish, a bank of television sets are piled high on top of one another. Each is tuned
to a different station, broadcasting simultaneous incomprehensible images at excessive volume, creating a cacophony of shapeless sounds. Beer adverts. News of a kidnapping. Shootings.
Weather. Dancing pink puppets. Naked women. A mosque of
murmuring Muslims. A cartoon alien. A couple fighting in a
TV studio. A rap group pointing at a woman's wobbling arse.
Heart surgery. A mountain. Baseball. Lions leaping on to ante-
lope. Lizards. A hamburger. And the noise . . .

'Buy . . . I couldn't make him understand . . . all the children dance . . . over 400 dead . . . the freshest, the tastiest . . .
do, do, do the dinosaur . . . you never told me the truth . . .
press zero now . . . beyond evil . . . oi need dat morney tom
. . . sure to see an upturn in the fortunes with . . . only $9.99
. . . you can't handle the truth . . . . get out of my face!'

In front of the flickering screens an old man sits in silhou-
ette on a wooden crate, bent over the shining steel body of a
stringed instrument of some sort, picking out all but inaudible
notes as if oblivious to the sounds behind him. Lewis sees his
eyes glimmer out of the shadows as he looks up. He clears his
throat and struggles for something to say, shouting over the
pervasive noise of the sound collage. 'Is this the Coronado
airbase?'

'Yes,' replies the seated figure.

'But it's entirely derelict . . .'

'So? I need a new maid. FUCK YOU!' The man looks back

down towards his instrument and carries on his silent playing, unperturbed by his visitor.

Lewis speaks again. 'I'm looking for the Holy Grail.' Without warning the man's mood softens and calms.

'Ha. Ain't we all, son? Come up here so as we can get acquainted.' Lewis picks his way through the wreckage into an illuminated circle formed by spillage from the TVs. Leaning into the light in front of him is a portly, bearded, beautiful-looking, fifty-year-old man, with fingers almost half as long as his forearms and a smile that instantly sets Lewis at ease, despite the earlier outburst. 'I'm Luther Peyote,' he says. 'And who might you be?'

The Hopi Boy
and the Sun – v

In the middle of the afternoon a rattlesnake girl
came down to the river. When she discovered
the boy's box, she took off her mask and looked
down into the peephole. 'What are you doing
here?' she asked the boy.

'Open the door! I can't get out,' he said.

The rattlesnake girl asked, 'How can I open
it?'

'Take a stone and break it.'

So the girl broke the door, and when the Hopi
boy came out, she took him to her house. Inside
he saw many people – young and old, men and
women – and they were all rattlesnakes.

'Where are you going?' they asked him.

'I want to find my father,' the boy replied.

The girl said, 'You can't go alone. I'll go with
you.'

She made a small tent of rattlesnake skins and
carried it to the river. There they crawled into
the tent and floated for four days and four
nights. Finally they reached the ocean, and there
they saw a meteor fall into the sea on its way

to the house of the Sun. And so they offered the meteor a bowl of corn if he would take them with him. The meteor agreed, and in this manner they continued towards the Sun's house.

Hopi Indian legend, reported by
Franz Boas in 1922

Twelve

Sheriff Matthew Hopkins shuffles in the darkness, and retches a little behind his gag, as the stench of cleaning fluids and detergents crawls up his nostrils once more. Two days short of retirement and it's come to this, trussed up like a Sunday spit-roast hog in a broom cupboard by the clearly incompetent accomplices of . . . that woman. For nearly a decade now Hopkins has tracked her movements in the periphery of his vision, looking for a pattern. He admired her, as the hunter learns respect for the bear, before blowing its brains out and making a hat out of its head. All he wanted was to see her, once, before they stripped him of his badge and gave him the gold watch, and the means to track her were no longer at his disposal. Back home, Hopkins had a hammock and a fridge full of beer lined up ready for the day of his retirement, and the number of a girl south of Tucson with reasonable rates if Grace never made it back, or maybe even if she did, but he knew he'd never be able to settle back and swing until he'd finally confronted the woman face to face.

He's heard Cowdrey tell Littwick that he was chasing a killer that didn't exist, a ghost dog he'd conjured from incidences in between co-incidences. But there she had been today, ripe and for the taking, and then slipping past him in a flurry of feathers like a fox fleeing from the chicken coop.

He's heard Littwick tell Cowdrey it was because nothing much ever happened in their jurisdiction that he needed to force random crimes into meaningful statistics, to imagine he was on to something big. Years of solving petty disputes, and domestic beatings, and punching out teenage vandals while no one was looking, well, that wasn't the kind of monument Matthew Hopkins wanted to leave behind him.

And he's heard Littwick saying that his religious faith was a form of obsessive compulsive disorder. That there was some book about monkeys that proved it. And that adding the sheriff's natural misogyny to a mind steeped in fire and brimstone rhetoric was a recipe for disaster. But Hopkins wasn't rightly sure what obsessive compulsive disorder was, so he let it go. But he left a few relevant pamphlets on Littwick's desk when he wasn't looking.

Of course, they'd all told the Lord Jesus he was wrong too, Hopkins reasons, as he sits in the black chemical darkness, the tightly wound vacuum flex biting into his arms and ankles, snuffling through the brown bag as the cleaning fluid makes his eyes sting and his head spin. And he too had been stopped up in a tomb, only to emerge and prove the doubters wrong. But Jesus had been soft on the whores. 'She who has sinned much is forgiven much,' or some such shit. Hopkins was gonna hunt the woman down and bring her in. The Saviour wasn't always right. Giving all your money to the poor? Well, how'd he feel about that if he'd seen them daily coming over the border hidden under the boards in delivery trucks, or fished out of the Rio Grande half drowned by the border patrol boys, to be thrown back south like undersized fish. Shit, no one was right all the time.

As the two men had shoved him into the store cupboard he almost had a sense of her, a scent of her even, in the room behind him, but even as he had tried to crane his neck round to look, they bound him and gagged him and plunged him into the blackness, and he was left with only a nagging feeling of knowing. But he will find her. Assuming, that is, that he ever gets out of this cupboard. Hopkins assures himself that these things have to be taken step by step.

There's a noise outside the door, a bang and a clatter as the lock is shot off and falls away, and light spills into Hopkins' makeshift cell.

Abby stands in the drizzle on a side street off Portobello Road, looking up at a multicoloured mural showing highlights of the local carnival. She had attended it once, as a younger woman. Sid, though, had never liked dancing. Oddly for a musician, he had seemed to have no sense of internal rhythm, and many family weddings had been enlivened by his drunken attempts to keep her from the clutches of leering long-lost cousins by joining her, however unhappily, on the dance floor of various marquees in grandiose Home Counties' gardens. Six years with Sid had made her all but forget who she was, and what she actually liked. Last night she had recognised a song he had once played her, being used as the soundtrack to an insurance commercial, and she had instinctively imagined she would wait and ask him what it was. Sid had always enjoyed the satisfaction of knowing. But that's all over. Next week she will phone up forgotten gay friends from medical school, and they will go dancing. Behind her, a policeman helps Peter Rugg out of the back seat of a squad car. Opposite her, the owners of the house Peter had tried to break into earlier stand looking agitated, a pregnant woman of thirty or so and a man some years older, dressed for the office in suit and tie.

'It was here, you see, Doc,' says Peter behind her. 'This is where I dropped the fucking thing. They've painted the place up, see, since it was gutted, so I never spotted it before.'

Abby goes inside and sits down with the couple in a pastel-hued living room. The woman makes her a weak cup of tea while the man stares out of the window at Rugg, who is trying to explain himself to the policemen. 'The strange thing is,' says the woman, handing Abby a cup and saucer, 'that we only managed to get the house so cheap because it had more or less been left abandoned since the 70s.'

'People had squatted here,' says her husband, still with his back to them, 'but the walls were still black from the fire and the staircase down to the cellar was entirely burned away.'

Abby balances the cup on her knees and leans forwards. 'Yes. Well, my patient, Mr Rugg, feels that he was in some way responsible for the fire. I know it's rather an unusual situation, but perhaps if you would let him in to have a poke about, to see how different everything is here now, he might at least not bother you again.'

The man turns and looks doubtful. The woman thinks for a moment. 'To be honest, doctor, I really rather regret calling the police. We found Mr Rugg down in the cellar entirely empty-handed, crawling about in amongst a load of old cardboard boxes. He said he had no intention of stealing anything, and simply wanted us to let him have a look around.'

'My wife was rather startled, that's all,' says the man. 'But if you think it will help . . .'

Abby sits on the steps of the cellar, watching Peter Rugg sift through a layer of discarded packaging and paper. 'This is where we sat,' he says, 'me and Captain Calvert. There were two big speakers on that wall there, and a load of old cushions down where that freezer is, normally with a few young ladies writhing and wriggling on 'em.' Abby can't help but laugh. Behind Peter's beard you can see he might once have been quite a handsome young man. He scratches a fingernail along the whitewashed wall. Abby winces. Underneath the paint, a thin line of red brickwork shows through. 'It's not here, Doc,' he says, standing. 'It was here, but it's not here now.'

Abby leads him back up through the house. She explains the situation to the couple. They decline to press charges and out in the street the police ask Abby to help Peter fill in a few forms. 'Can I give you a lift anywhere, Peter,' she asks him, as the police car pulls away.

'No thanks, Doc,' he says, sounding disheartened. 'I don't come over this way often. Best have a look through the gutters.' Abby gets into her car and pushes the Rodgers and Hammerstein tape into the deck. Then, just as she's about to pull away, Peter raps on the window. She winds it down. 'I tell you, Doc,' he murmurs, 'just between you and me, I am getting heartily sick of all this.'

Hopkins untangles himself as Cowdrey and Littwick survey the devastation. 'The suspect resisted arrest. Took out the clerk and shoved me in the store cupboard. She's armed and has two accomplices.'

'They say he'll survive,' offers the deputy, 'but he won't recover consciousness for a while. He was an old guy.'

'I told you she was dangerous, boy.'

Cowdrey considers, wipes his brow, and stands and crosses to the sheriff who is stepping clumsily out of the last loop of flex. 'Sheriff Hopkins . . . Having gunned down the clerk . . . why do you think the suspect didn't just shoot you as well?'

Hopkins meets his gaze, eye to eye. 'Who can fathom them, Deputy Cowdrey? Who can say what goes through their minds . . . If we . . .'

Cowdrey ignores him. He walks across the room, his feet crunching on fallen snack food packages. He stops, takes off his hat, runs a hand through his hair, turns his back on the sheriff and speaks. 'Hopkins! . . . Get outta here.'

The sheriff stands back, as if squaring up to take him on. 'Uh? May I remind you, Deputy . . .'

'Go. Go now, or I take you in.'

'I'm the law in this . . .' Hopkins tails off. He sees Littwick looking at him.

'Matthew. You'd best do as he says.'

Cowdrey turns. He walks away. 'Go now, Sheriff Hopkins. Go and do whatever you think you have to do. Or I'm taking you in. Understand?'

Silently, Hopkins stares, rips off his badge, hands it to

Cowdrey, steps back, and spits full in the deputy's face. Littwick passes him a tissue. Hopkins walks out into the sun. Cowdrey wipes himself clean, and steps out on to the forecourt to watch as the sheriff gets into his car and accelerates out on to the highway.

Littwick stands and runs out after him. 'Matthew! Matthew!'

The deputy follows the forensic scientist to the road, and puts a hand on his shoulder. 'No, Don. Let him go.'

The dust settles. Littwick watches the patrol car disappear. Cowdrey turns to him. 'Don . . . whatever report you feel is necessary, I'll sign it, understand? Then we close the files. Whatever it is, this has gone far enough.' Littwick takes out a notebook and goes back inside. Cowdrey follows him. Neither of them expects ever to call Matthew Hopkins 'Sheriff' again.

'Well, if he's down there, he sure ain't houseproud.' Tracy takes in the view and lights a cigarette.

'I dunno. With a bit of work you could really make a go of the place.' Danny looks back from the sprawling, ruined runways, to Sid, shaking and a little afraid.

'You saw the sign,' he says. 'This is it.'

'Don't get your hopes up, Sid. All we're likely to find is a smelly old corpse clutching the neck of an out-of-tune Fender, a copy of the Round Tabyls' first LP, and the fattest joint you've ever seen.'

Quietly, Sid steels himself for disappointment. Experience has taught him that it doesn't always do to meet your heroes. In one of the Lemon Pies' two near brushes with success, a major-label-funded indie had offered them a whole full day of studio time and the producer of their choice to record a single. Sid persuaded the Pies to ask for a certain legendary late 60s Notting Hill session man whom he'd always wanted to meet, whose own band had played alongside Hawkwind, Amon Düül II, the Groundhogs and the infant Pink Floyd, but who had somehow always managed to board the passing bandwagons at precisely the wrong point. The legend had turned up in a state of all too real disarray, crashed out at the mixing desk, said Sid 'looked gay', threw up in the waste-bin, and told the singer's seventeen-year-old girlfriend he could 'smell her sweet cunt from the other end of the room'. And instead of signing the album sleeves Sid brought in with him, the full-time cult figure just wrote swearwords over the pictures of his ex-band members and then drew erect penises shooting off into their sunglasses. The session was scrapped, the single forgotten, and Sid didn't have much influence over band policy from that point onwards. Two years later, the non-producer wrote an article in a fanzine about the worst band he'd ever worked with. It was the Lemon Pies, most of whom were now Timothy Waterhouse's backing group, apart from the bassist, 'who seemed to have only invited me in to the session so he could show off his knowledge of shitty early 70s' B-sides I don't even fucking remember recording'.

But Luther wouldn't be like that, Sid assured himself; Luther, who had sung Sid's world into shape for the best part of two decades now. He could feel it in every groove of the vinyl. And he could see it in the smile that played around the corners of Luther's mouth, creeping out even from behind the pirate beard he'd sported since everything started to crash, even in photos taken in his darkest hours. He was benign, touched, a positive force in a fucked-up world. Put bluntly, Luther was obviously going to be a good bloke.

'Maybe so, Sid, but he lives in a shithole.'

'C'mon, boys,' Tracy encourages them. 'Let's get down there and get this over with. I'm a fugitive from justice, remember. I can't hang around.'

They scramble down the incline. Close up, things aren't any better. Sid had expected a temple. He'd expected Luther to have transformed the empty airbase, to have slung the crumbling walls with multicoloured frescoes, pictures of knights in shining psychedelic armour and hallucinogenic cacti bursting into streams of cosmic light. But instead, Danny was right. It really is a shithole.

Danny and Tracy slouch around together in the shadows of one of the hangars while Sid walks on alone. 'Poor guy. This isn't what he'd hoped for, is it?'

'Not really. I don't know why I allowed him to entertain the idea. I suppose I owe him one.'

'You're a good friend,' she says, kindly.

'Not really,' Danny contradicts her. 'But I'm the only one he's got. Which isn't to say I wouldn't just drop him like a hot potato if somebody made me a better offer. Know what I mean?'

Tracy ignores him, brushes her black hair out of her eyes, exhales a cloud of cigarette smoke and stubs the butt under her boot. 'Sometimes one good friend is all you need.'

Then, stepping out of the deserted hangar into the sun and seeing something, Sid calls back to them. 'Hey! Over here.' Sid is standing by a small door, cut into the lower section of the corrugated steel frontage of the only building they haven't yet explored. As the others arrive he gestures to them to be silent, and listen. There's sounds inside the hangar. Music. Conversation. Noise. 'What do we do now?'

Danny shrugs, takes a deep breath, pushes past him and rushes at the door. It gives immediately and he falls through the flimsy portal on to the dusty floor of the hangar.

A hundred yards ahead, the bank of flickering televisions, and two shadowed laughing figures sit on a raised platform, backlit by the shimmering screens, and apparently sharing a hookah. Amid stray, uncleared debris there're wicker chairs, a paisley rug, some mattresses, a camping stove, a wall piled high with hundreds of tins of baked beans, like some survivalist Andy Warhol installation. A mule is tethered by a pile of straw, left of the televisions. Three ancient guitar amps and a drum-kit half shrouded in dust sheets stand neglected. An enormous, off-white, early 80s' computer is mounted on some empty crates. This isn't a home. It's a rats' nest. If Luther ever was here, he wasn't now. Oh, well. Danny looks back to his companions for suggestions. Sid steps in over the prostrate Irishman and shouts. 'Excuse me. Sorry to disturb you. We've obviously made a mistake. But does the name Luther Peyote mean anything to you?'

'Nope,' calls back the older of the two men, 'but I suppose it ought to, seeing as how I am Luther Peyote.' Sid feels the full force of twenty years of fantasising evaporate and explode. The television noise expands to fill the silence. Danny rises to his knees.

'Well,' whispers Tracy to the dumbstruck men, 'introduce us.'

Sid steps unsteadily forwards. 'Yes. Sorry. Mr Peyote . . . I'm Sid, and this is Danny . . . and Tracy. Danny and I are great fans of yours.' Even as he says them, the words sound absurd. Luther steps down off the platform, leaving the other man alone. He is dressed in faded, ripped blue jeans and a brown T-shirt advertising a farming machinery manufacturer. His beard could house a small family of swallows, but his eyes shine a deep sea blue, and white teeth flash that smile, the smile that Sid had dreamed of, and, behind nearly three decades of surface soil erosion, Sid still recognises the old man as his childhood hero, grown old but no less noble. Luther stares at Sid, Danny and Tracy in turn.

'What do you want?' he asks.

'We've come from England . . . to persuade you to re-form the Round Tabyls . . . with us as your rhythm section.'

'Uh-huh,' says the old man. His voice is dog rough, but resonant, like something heavy scraping over a wooden floor. 'And do you have any previous musical experience?'

Sid suddenly feels a little bolder. 'Well, we've been working musicians for some time and have an encyclopedic knowledge of the Tabyls' back-catalogue.' Luther nods and ponders this information, pulling on his beard with pencil fingers. Sid elaborates. 'With practice we're confident of re-creating the high-points of your old sound while acknowledging contemporary shifts . . .'

'I see.' Then the old man's face takes on a terrifying aspect as, in an instant, his mood switches. 'ARE YOU OUT OF YOUR FUCKING MINDS?' he bellows, before falling silent again as if nothing has happened.

Sid is dumbstruck. It wasn't meant to be like this. 'I'm sorry,' he says. He wants to cry.

'Yes,' says Danny, standing and taking centrestage. 'Yes, we are out of our minds. Him in particular. And so we've come to find you. We thought you might be able to help.'

Luther Peyote puts his hands behind his back and walks around the rubble in a small circle. Sid sees that he is wearing no shoes, only red socks which flop around, half off, amid the dust, recalling the curly boots of a medieval jester. He smiles, and makes an expansive, inclusive gesture. 'Well, we'll manage somehow, I suppose. We'll start rehearsing as soon as I've rustled us all up some supper. Make yourselves at home. I'm very excited about our future.' Sid's eyes widen. Danny laughs out loud. 'Have you met Mr Lewis, by the way?' says their host, pointing up to his other guest. 'Suddenly it seems everybody wants to visit old Luther.'

Mr Lewis smiles and waves. Danny whispers to Sid. 'He hired us. Which settles one thing. He is mad.' The mule snorts. Luther turns around and notices the opening titles of an old Top Cat cartoon on one of the televisions. 'Hey!' he says, immediately forgetting the new arrivals. 'Have you seen this guy? I love him! He lives in a trash can! WHAT AN ASSHOLE!'

It's early evening. Outside, the swift desert darkness has descended, but heat still hangs trapped in the air, unable to dissipate. The cathedral cavern of the hangar is lit by salvaged rewired runway lights, arranged at random from roof and floor and casting pools of blue and red over Luther's minimal domestic comforts. He's cooked, after a fashion, and his guests eat just warm beans out of ill-matched receptacles, a saucepan, a tin plate, a US Army helmet, and an old hospital bedpan, scooping them up with teaspoons and jam-jar lids. 'I don't stand on ceremony here,' he had explained, as he smashed a plate he felt was too dirty to wash. Danny had persuaded Luther at least to turn the volume down on some of the televisions, which he did, reluctantly, though the old man's attention is still systematically distracted by sudden flashes of colour or shifts in sound. Lewis's explanation of his arrival in Coronado is the first piece of information all evening that really seems to have captured Luther, though he reacts to Lewis's story with a polite interest that contrasts with the unconcealed incredulity of at least one of the other diners.

'Wait a second there!' Tracy nearly spits out her beans. 'Freemasons sent you to recover the blood of Christ from space?'

'I think so. Yes.'

Danny tries to catch Sid's eye, but he is staring intently at his idol.

'Makes sense to me, Mr Lewis,' says Luther. 'People have been chasin' that Grail high and low nigh on two thousand years now, and the Templars was always at the front of the queue. Templars filtered into the Freemasons and passed their secrets on, everybody knows that's the case, so you might be right. And there's nowhere on earth safer to hide something than nowhere on earth.'

'You seem to know a lot about the subject,' says Tracy with a raised eyebrow.

'Oh, he does,' interjects Sid, and explains, at greater length than is necessary, about Luther's mid-60s attempt to cross the European myths of King Arthur and the Holy Grail, the ancient stories of the American colonists, with the lore of her Native peoples, so as to create a lyrical canon which would reflect modern America as a receptacle for the subconscious hopes and dreams of modern and so-called primitive cultures. Hence Luther *Peyote* and the *Round Tabyls*. Everyone shifts uncomfortably. Danny hides his face in his hands. Luther smiles. 'Yeah, that's right, son. It was supposed to be *Uther* Peyote.'

'Yes. But there was a mistake at the pressing plant in Phoenix.'

'Probably for the best, anyhow. Basically, I read *The Sword in the Stone* when I was kid, and then I started hanging out with the local Native folks to try and score peyote off 'em, and it all kind of came together from there. Thing is, I didn't mean anything by it, do you understand? NOTHING! WHAT DO YOU WANT FROM ME?' Suddenly Luther is scowling again, pointing an accusatory finger into Sid's face. Then he is calm again, and continues. 'In the early days we went on stage in armour, buckskins and Indian head-dresses. It was a good visual gimmick, but we used to get kinda hot under the spotlights.' The spoons and lids clatter in the hiatus. 'But you're right about the Grail being gotten by the military, I expect, Mr Lewis. People know I had a hankering and so they still keep me up to date on all that shit, like I give a rat's ass these days. Those FUCKERS! WHY CAN'T I GET ANY PEACE?' He throws down his spoon, and the mule at the rear of the room twitches nervously. Then he leans back, hands behind his head and sighs contentedly. 'Why should I care, anyhow? I live like a king! Look at this place!' Luther gestures around his hangar. The mule strains at its tether, brays, and suddenly lets fall a bucketful of urine. Luther laughs and begins again. 'Now Roslin Chapel, Glastonbury, and the Cathar castles sure have a nice ring to them, but one finds that the mystical is usually entwined with the mundane.' He points to a pile of pamphlets and self-published tracts, mixed in with a hummock of unanswered fan-mail and the occasional pair of panties. Behind them, a map of the world showed possible Grail locations marked by red marker-pen stars. In Luther's universe, Germany is yet to be unified and Eastern Europe is still a much simpler shape. It is clearly some time since he has taken his studies seriously. Luther picks some fallen beans out of his beard, drops them into his pan, grinds them into pulp with his finger and thumb, puts them back into his mouth, and continues. 'And I tell you this, Mr Lewis, and I'll tell you it for free. That Holy Grail sure ain't to be found anywhere hereabouts. Fact, there ain't nothin' here but me and them toads. They like to watch me eat.' Luther laughs a wheezy laugh. The others look around. No one can see any toads. 'Now, Holbrook airbase, up north of here between the I 40 and the Navajo lands, well, there's some secret shit going on up there, I tell you. Always was, and still is I should reckon. Me and some local punk kids tried playing a show at the fence back in '77, just to freak the local Nazis, and them soldiers came out and bust our heads wide open. BASTARDS! THOSE BASTARDS! Still, they were only doing their jobs. You have to admire that in people.'

Sid had read of the event. Luther Peyote's last comeback. The short-lived Phoenix Arizona proto-punks the United Steaks had strong-armed the shell-shocked veteran into performing his old songs, with them backing him, at a variety of unsuitable locations, as some kind of situationist art gesture. Sid had the bootlegs, obviously, bad as they were.

'Holbrook! That's where they put stuff, see?' Luther continues. 'Roswell's a smokescreen. So's Area 51. Everything's a smokescreen. There's smokescreens for the smokescreens and there's no smoke without fire. Anybody with even a passin' interest in those subjects that cannot be named knows that Holbrook base is where the real weird shit goes down. They got aliens crossed with humans, flying cars, food that cooks itself, disposable cutlery, TVs that pick up game-shows from Mars, water that ain't wet and fire that ain't hot, and people walking around with pigs' heads on their shoulders. JESUS FUCK! Ten years back now, the geeks that run the appropriate websites say, they built a huge underground hangar, Hangar 18, for containing something secret and powerful, round about the time you say you lost your mind. Called it Project Arimathea, so they say, and that sure ought to set the alarm bells ringing. Brrring! If your Grail is in an airbase in Arizona, Mr Lewis, well, that'd be the place to start looking. Trust the international underground freak network!'

Lewis silently considers Luther's advice. 'Perhaps your internet informers just got their airbases kinda mixed up,'

Tracy suggests, straight-faced. 'It's easily done, I believe.'

Sid turns to Danny as the shock sinks slowly in. With all the excitement of listening to Luther he had failed to make the connection. But Danny already knows, and sits, head bowed, hoping no one will notice him. They continue to eat in silence, until the metal clatter ends, and the final freezing bean is reluctantly eaten. Sid sighs, and pokes Danny in the ribs. 'You have to tell him.'

Danny looks up. 'Er, Mr Lewis? Moonhead?'

Lewis's face crumples and threatens to cave in. His eyes narrow, like he's trying to make out an almost familiar friend far away in a sunlit distance. 'Sphincter Boys? No . . .'

'Let me explain!' says Danny, but for once he sounds unconvinced.

Luther spins around to face the televisions again, an empty fork halfway to his face. He sees a small dog singing a song extolling the virtues of takeaway Mexican food. 'Jesus H. Christ! How do they do that? It's genius! WHAT A CROCK OF SHIT!'

On the hill, overlooking the airbase, the Hampstead Man lowers his telescope and smiles. Mr Lewis, like a good soldier, was indeed proving himself extensively serviceable to his fellow creatures. 'Mr Lewis's determination might yet see the tongue of good report heard in both our favours,' he thinks. 'Between us, we might yet set things aright, and repair the loss, should Heaven help us in our endeavours.' And then he picks up a shovel and walks back towards his car. He opens the trunk and covers his mouth with his hand. The ground is hard. The night is cool. And he has a grave to dig.

Later, on the hillside outside the hangar, Tracy looks across at Lewis through the flickering flames of a fire. Behind his head, she watches the distant lights of silent trucks pounding Highway 10 east and west between Tucson and New Mexico, speeding along the stretch and stacked up like undirected aircraft at the weigh station. Lewis, it seems, is almost at ease, not quite unburdened, but lying on his back in the scrubby grass, staring upwards. She likes him. She watches him as he watches the stars, pointing out the occasional satellite and naming the constellations, brighter and clearer here than at home, he maintains, and much more beautiful. 'So, Lewis,' she says, initiating conversation again. 'You've been to the moon?'

He pauses, and turns to her, propping his head up on his hand. 'Well, near it, anyway. It sounds unlikely, I know.'

'No. Not at all. Have you orbited any other planets? Jupiter, perhaps. I'm sorry. Jupiter's too far away to reach, isn't it? Now it's my turn to feel foolish.'

Lewis smiles. After an hour or so of being indulged by Luther, not to be taken seriously once more has a familiar, comforting feeling. 'Please don't. And, yes, as far as I can remember, the moon is the only planet I've seen close up, apart from this one, of course.' He raps the dry earth. 'The moon is about the only thing I do remember. And, given that I've been led here on something of a wild goose chase, now I need to go to this Holbrook airbase and see if the Grail *is* there instead.'

'Why bother?' She stubs out a cigarette on the ground and flicks the butt off her thumb and into the flames with a long forefinger. 'I'm no expert, but Luther's theory sounded like the usual paranoid hippie shit.'

'Yes. But then I can lay this whole thing to rest. Move on.'

There's a minute of silence while she considers his answer. And then, 'And what's it like to swing on a star, Moonhead? Did you carry moonbeams home in a jar? Was the stars and stripes still flying up there for all to see? What was it like?'

'Like nothing on earth,' he answers, with a smile.

'Hey, funny guy!' she says. 'And I was hoping you'd say there was no atmosphere.' And under the stars, they both sit and laugh, two bad jokes in search of a punch-line.

*　　*　　*

As the shapeless echo of Luther's listless playing subsides and is replaced by the multi-TV hum, Danny puts down his drumsticks and looks across the hangar. Sid stands behind the shaking old man, encouragingly plucking the appropriate bassline until it's clear that no matter how long he persists, the vibrating notes aren't going to jog any buried memories. The New Round Tabyls' first rehearsal isn't going well. It's thirty years, admittedly, since Luther Peyote last played 'A Look Outside', but, even so, it's only three chords. 'Sorry, boys, it's been a while . . .' he says, setting down a battered, flame-coloured Fender, 'but, hey, I didn't ask you to come here. FUCK YOU! FUCK BOTH OF YOU! I love you guys!' Danny sighs, stands, and walks away, rubbing the back of his neck. Sid leans the black bass Luther had dug out for him against a pile of baked bean tins and crosses to the televisions. Luther watches anxiously, biting at his beard, as, one by one, Sid begins, forcefully, to turn them off. He climbs precariously along the pallet structure the seventy or so sets are balanced on in long unblinking rows, as each screen in turn swallows its images into white dot and darkness. Then, in the silence, Sid drops down to the floor, turns to Luther, takes his hand, and places the long, brown fingers slowly and deliberately on the frets of the neck of his guitar in the simple triangular pattern of a basic D Major chord.

'There.' Luther strums a single downstroke. The chord resonates through the room, trembling a little in the high metal arches, and then travelling heavenwards. Luther looks up to follow the fragmenting notes, suggesting arpeggios as yet unplayed and chord progressions as yet unwritten as they dissolve and die. He shakes his head, a soggy dog trying to work the water loose from its ears. Sid watches, nervous but excited. All Luther's best songs began with a D chord, he recalls, the bassist invariably jamming on detuned open strings as Luther crept up the frets via the D and G strings towards some vague, electrified notion of consummation. It was a simple but brilliant signature of all his early albums, and the first moment, Sid believes, when the ugly caterpillar of garage rock first threatened to bloom into the beautiful butterfly of psychedelia, an evolutionary move that even Danny had on occasion been forced to praise. And hearing the suggestion of the familiar sound, Danny turns back towards its source, a bent old man, looking down astonished at his own hands, as if he had never taken time to consider them before. Luther smiles up at him. He smiles back, and turns his head to one side, asking to be impressed. Sid places an arm around his hero's shoulders and whispers. 'See. You've still got it.'

'The thing is,' Lewis continues, 'if you think you've walked in space, well, everything else seems a little disappointing. I'm dead to this world. Man delights not me.'

'Nor woman neither?' says Tracy, realising as she does that she sounds flirtatious. Lewis closes the line of questioning down.

'I'm afraid not.'

'Perhaps you haven't met the right girl yet,' continues Tracy, trying to change the mood. 'I have an aunt who thinks she was kidnapped by aliens . . .'

'You'll have to introduce me.'

They wait, as their almost-moment evaporates. 'So, what's your story, then, Tracy?'

'Nothing,' she answers swiftly, and then stands and points down towards the hangar. 'Come on. Let's see how the future of rock and roll is shaping up.'

Tracy opens the door to the closing chords of 'A Look Outside'. Danny is rising from the drum-stool to applaud as Luther alternately approaches and retreats from his old Marshall amp, dancing in and out of invisible, screaming waves of electric feedback. He seems lighter, younger, afloat almost. Sid points towards the enraptured old man, coaxing applause out of the new arrivals. 'Thank you, Streatham! And goodnight!' shouts

Danny, coercing Sid and Luther into a bow as he sees Tracy approaching.

'Hey! You guys rock!' she calls out over the dissolving noise. 'Eat shit, Pink Floyd!'

'Who's this Pink Floyd guy?' asks Luther, suddenly distracted, his bewildered self once more. 'Is he some kind of puppet?'

It is late. Luther is dimming the lights at a control switch bodged on to the wall between bare wires and black tape. He sees a small black beetle crawling up the wall, pinches it between finger and thumb, and, when he's sure no one is watching, pops it into his mouth. In the shadows, Danny and Sid are stacking up the gear, marvelling at its antique properties. Lewis approaches the old man as he turns back towards the others. 'Luther. I need to leave. I need to go to Holbrook. I need to know if the Grail's there instead.'

Sid stands and interrupts. 'Mr Lewis. I must apologise again. If Danny and I had thought . . .'

Tracy shoots him a look as he backs away, and she puts her hand on Lewis's shoulder as he goes to take his leave of Luther. But the old man has misunderstood. 'Holbrook's a heavily guarded airbase, Mr Lewis. It's not gonna be easy for us to break in.' Lewis begins to explain that he wasn't asking for help, that he wasn't trying to involve Luther in his quest, but he is silenced with a gesture. 'I knew a guy. Old Indian Bob. A Hopi clown. He'd have found a way. But I ain't seen him so much since he and I got busted back in '71.'

Tracy smiles, and fumbles in her pocket. 'Bob Nequatewa? Here. He said if I needed anything I was to come and find him.' She holds out a crumpled napkin. Bob Nequatewa's address. Luther throws back his head and laughs.

In Sheriff Hopkins' office, Deputy Cowdrey sleeps in his boss's chair, feet up on the desk, snoring lightly. Suddenly he awakes in a blaze of light and reaches for his gun. Littwick stands trembling in the doorway, his finger on the switch, ashen-faced, but it isn't Cowdrey that has startled him. 'Don. Sorry. It's late.'

'Come in. Coffee?'

Littwick shakes his head and nervously removes his glasses, flicking at the frames with shaking fingers. 'Roy, we got a DNA result on a hair found on the gas station clerk.'

'Yeah, and . . .'

'It matches Matthew's DNA.'

Cowdrey sits up straight. 'Hopkins. Uh-huh. I . . . I shouldn't have let him go. Just because he's a sheriff that ain't no excuse to . . .'

Littwick approaches the desk and sits in the other chair. He holds up a specimen between tightly clenched silver tweezers. 'I said it matched Matthew's DNA, Roy . . . but this ain't Matthew's hair.'

Cowdrey puts his head in his hands and groans. In the bright electric light, he sees a black hair, maybe eighteen inches long, casting its slight shadow over the pins and strings of Hopkins' state map. Littwick's hand is shaking, and the outline of the hair trembles across the state, like a great crack opening up from New Mexico to California, threatening to engulf all that they knew, swallow it, and suck it away, as if it had never been.

The Hopi Boy
and the Sun – vi

Riding on the back of the hungry meteor, the Hopi Boy and the Rattlesnake Girl eventually reached the Sun's house, in the place where Holbrook, Arizona now stands. There they found an old woman working on a turquoise, coral, and white shell. She was the Moon, the mother of the Sun.

'Where is my father?' the boy asked.

'He has gone out,' the Moon replied, 'but he will be home soon.'

The Sun arrived in the evening, and the old woman gave him venison and wafer bread. After he had eaten, he asked the boy, 'What do you want here?'

The boy replied, 'I want to know my father.'

'I think you are my son. And when I go into the other world, you shall accompany me,' the Sun said this time. And early the next morning he said, 'Let's go!' He opened a door in the ground, and they went out.

Hopi Indian legend, reported by
Franz Boas in 1922

Thirteen

The Papago Indians had called their village Bac. It meant 'where the water emerges'. And when Father Eusebio Kino arrived in 1692, he added the name of Saint Xavier to the settlement's original title. So Sheriff Hopkins stood, south of Tucson, in the shadow of the white towers of the Mission San Xavier del Bac. He'd been up and down Highway 19 all day, between Tucson and Nogales, watching for the woman and her accomplices as they headed for the border. His instincts told him she would come this way. Cowdrey and Littwick had stripped him of his badge at the gas station, but he still had a patrol car, a rifle and a pistol, and the border patrol guards who manned a road block just north of Tumacacori had promised him they'd keep 'em peeled.

The mission was just off the main road. Hopkins had pulled in to get a coke from one of the Papago concession stands. He knew the building well. The Dove of the Desert, as it was called, was a local point of interest, and he'd brought his daughter here as a little girl as an object lesson in the idiocy of Catholicism. The incense swingers were proud that they'd won over the local savages so easily way back when, but it was easy to see why the Papago had succumbed as swiftly as they did. When the monks first unveiled the gaudy interior of the mission, the Indians must have thought they were in Heaven, with emblazoned icons shining down upon them that far outstripped the impact of any of the artefacts their own hands could have fashioned. They would have had no choice but to worship. So, it was hardly a fair fight. The bright-eyed statue of Mary that stood above the mission's altar was all but a pagan goddess.

Propaganda had its uses, Hopkins had to admit. In the course of his police duties, Hopkins had once met Bob Hammond, missionary broadcaster of a radio show called Voice of China and Asia. He had told him how the Chinese multitudes had been won to communism through mass distribution of cartoon booklets. Which reminds him, he really ought to leave a copy of *Are Roman Catholics Christians?* in the washroom here, before he heads back to the highway.

Danny wakes with a start in the passenger seat. He has a vague memory of passing three thirty-foot arrows buried nose first in the ground, a roadside motel constructed of white concrete teepees, and a sign pointing south to 'Meteor Crater – Planet Earth's Most Penetrating Attraction'. It is late afternoon. The sun is setting on his left, some way behind the railway lines, and they have been driving north all day. Luther swerves abruptly off Highway 40 on to the less well travelled road of Highway 87. 'Christ! Careful, man.'

'Yeah, yeah . . .'

Danny looks over his shoulder. Behind him, Sid, Lewis and Tracy are sleeping in mutually supportive positions on the back seat of the hire car. Danny remembers the long evening of the night before, and an argument that dragged into daylight before they finally settled on a course of action. Most agreed there was probably nothing significant hidden in Holbrook airbase, much as Luther protested otherwise. But the old man had waved ancient photocopied pamphlets at them for proof, and dragged up unconvincing websites, clearly assembled by the borderline mentally ill, from the bowels of his clanking computer. Lewis admitted that he shared everyone's doubts, but said he'd come so far under false pretences he needed to seek out some sense of 'closure'.

Closure. What kind of a word was that? Danny thought it was a peculiarly American term, introduced into the debate by Tracy. She seemed to view Lewis's need to go north and waste everyone's time as a valuable part of his 'cure', as some kind of therapy. Since Sid and Danny were in some way responsible for leading him astray, the least they could do, apparently, was accompany everyone else on their idiot pilgrimage, as if by way of penance. 'Yeah, yeah, you drive and me and Sid will go on our knees. Happy now?' he had snapped. But it was the guilt that finally swung Sid round. And then Danny had no choice. What was he to do? Sit around in Luther's empty hangar, waiting until the next day when he'd only have to go and bail Sid out anyway.

So here he was, being driven to the Hopi Indian reservation by a mad old hippie who hadn't been behind a wheel for the best part of half a century. 'Hopiland includes the oldest continuously inhabited settlement in the United States,' Tracy had told him, appealing to his tourist instincts, like he gave a shit. Still, maybe he could save the day when they inevitably got into trouble, be the hero of the hour, and find a way into Tracy's knickers in the fallout.

Danny fishes around the dashboard debris for cigarettes and lights one, squinting in the windshield-smear-filtered sun. What hideous chain of events had led him to be cooped up in this car full of cunts? The landscape offers no answers. Looking out across the flat empty planes he sees the high rock mesas rising in the north, the home of Luther and Tracy's Native American acquaintance, doubtless some other addled spaz-mystic. Still, maybe the old fart could score them some drugs. Not that Lewis needed any. There'd been long evenings raving round the M25 ten or fifteen years back when Danny himself had felt like he was in orbit, but that twat back there asleep on Tracy's shoulder honestly thought he'd left the planet for real. And, what's more, Tracy seemed to be buying his story, like all she'd ever wanted was her own pet nutcase. Danny had been judged, found wanting, and then rejected, and he felt stupid for letting it get to him. But Lewis had been sitting out there under the stars chatting her up, while Danny was watching Sid trying to teach Luther Peyote a fucking D chord. Some guitar hero he had turned out to be, even with a late spurt of energy in the closing minutes of their so-called rehearsal. Ah, well. 'So? What do you reckon, then, Luther? Do you think it's possible Lewis has travelled through space?'

'We're all travelling through space right now, Danny, you ass,' says Luther, swerving to avoid the newly crushed carcass of a skunk.

'Jesus! Listen, I don't care if you are the godfather of acid rock, just drive carefully.'

'Yeah yeah . . .'

Danny looks up towards the mesas again and snorts dismissively. Americans! They reduce the philosophies of ancient civilisations to bite-sized Little Books of Calm, ready to be plundered for bumper-sticker epigrams, and think any culture more than a hundred years old is some magic fountain of God-given wisdom. Look at the respect they had accorded him in every bar he and Sid had stopped in, just for being Irish, for being a son of 'the old country'. Like that stupid shithole had any answers. If Ireland was so fantastic, why were Kilburn pubs crawling with hod-carriers desperate to get away. He himself hadn't been back in twenty years, though he'd happily play the part expected of him by faux-nostalgic Yanks, so long as they were getting the drinks in. Shame he hadn't thought to bring a leprechaun costume with him, and learn a few dance steps. Then they'd really be in the money. As Luther bounces over a pothole, Danny feels his resentment spilling over. 'I didn't wanna come and find you, you know, granddad. It was Sid's idea. To be honest, Luther, I'm of the opinion that your music's a load of shite.'

The old man seems unmoved. 'So I made some bad albums

in the 70s? But what about *Chainmail Moccasins*? My early stuff rocks.'

Danny takes a drag and thinks. 'OK, OK, your early stuff's OK. But *Satellite Dog* from '74? What the fuck was that all about?'

'I was experimenting with radio interference and random noise, OK? GIMME A FUCKING BREAK! JESUS!'

Danny laughs. 'One great album does not an unsung genius of acid rock make.'

'Right,' answers Luther, fixing him. 'So we're gonna make another one. You guys are where it's at.'

Sure we're 'where it's at', thinks Danny, if where it's at is Streatham High Road. Luther's re-formed Round Tabyls might even be able to get a residency, unless Fat Ian's got himself a new line-up of the Sultans together. But Luther is convinced. 'Danny, I have complete faith in the New Round Tabyls. Once and for all we'll make Jim Morrison look like the FUCKING LIAR he really is.'

'Jim Morrison is dead,' snaps Danny.

'No. Really? That's too bad. When?'

Danny looks out of the window at the first flourishes of the outlying Hopi settlements. Trailer homes and breeze block bungalows stand some way back from the road. At the crossroads with Highway 264, there's an ungassed gas station, and a windowless brick building advertising pottery and *katsina* dolls. There are no people, but skinny dogs range carelessly over roads. Luther turns left, following a signpost to something called Shungopavi, as the highway curls upwards round a cliff. He directs Danny's attention to the view rising behind them, the pre-fab and plywood village of Polacca hugging the bottom of a hill that rises up to a flat plateau. There three separate clusters of sand-brown settlements dot the crest of the mesa, like spines on the back of a sleeping lizard. Stone houses pile up on top of each other, perched precariously on the cliff edge. Their outlines are spiked with wooden poles, the upper ends of ladders that run down through the roofs to each village's myriad underground ceremonial chambers. These are *kivas*, he later learns, closed to whites and women.

'First mesa villages, as I recall. Tewa-Hano, Sichomovi and Walpi,' says Luther. Each settlement is separated from the next by a narrow stretch of uninhabited clifftop. The last village, Walpi, is further, higher and more remote than the others. It clings limpet-like to the end of the mesa, like some subsiding hilltop fortress.

'I ain't been here for years but not much has changed,' the old man continues. 'Sure, there's more cables and cars, and more new housing down there in the valleys, but it's still too quiet. It always seems like they're up to something. Hard to believe you're in the United States, huh?'

And for a moment, Danny feels his irritation start to dissolve away. As they climb upwards the daylight begins its final retreat, and sun, moon and stars are all simultaneously visible in the luminescent blue-black sky. At the top of the hill, another clump of curtained craft shops, with coke machines rusting out front and kids kicking around, and behind them the view now takes in two high mesas of randomly arranged habitations. To the west, the San Francisco peaks shimmer in the fading light, rising high over Flagstaff.

'The Hopi thought gods lived in those mountains,' said Luther, 'now it's miners and skiers.' Once, Flagstaff must have seemed so far, the geographical limit of the Hopi's physical world, where flesh became spirit. Now it was a car drive away. Hopiland was encroached first by the Spanish, then by the Navajo, then by the white man, then by the Navajo again, in alliance with the white man's courts, and then, finally, and perhaps more profoundly, by the more powerful invader of progress. The yellow American road-signs that warn of Slide Areas and Soft Verges seem inappropriate here somehow, artless artefacts of an alien culture, obviously erected in error. Danny finishes his cigarette. Normally he'd throw it out the window, but Luther laughs as he notices him respectfully search for an empty can to put the butt in.

At a corner, Luther slows and turns left, down towards Shungopavi, drifting over the road a little as he checks details on the napkin Tracy gave him. Signs warn that ceremonies are private, photography forbidden, and visitors are to behave in a respectful fashion. A man walks past them on the road, thick-set and black-haired in blue jeans and a work shirt. He carries a nine-inch carving of what looks like a laughing green vegetable with spindly arms and legs.

'These houses weren't here before,' says Luther, pointing at an inconsistent array of shanty shacks and then some almost luxurious, more permanent dwellings; the yards are dotted with jacked-up cars and those omnipresent dogs, 'but Bob will be down in the original part of the village.'

The road narrows and the houses grow denser and older, stone-built structures of indeterminate age now, closing in and obscuring the horizons. Their stylistic uniformity is compromised at irregular intervals by more modern structures that conventional town planning would have outlawed. But this is a village, where people live, not a museum. The architectural aesthetics anthropologists would want to preserve intact are vulnerable to more practical considerations – the need for more living space and the cost of building materials. Old women sit on steps talking, and dogs hopefully trail toddling children across the open space of a central plaza, where stone seat steps rise up around an undistinguished arena. A man steps out from a wooden-framed doorway in a white vest, and sits a child on a plastic tricycle. Eyes look out through a small square window. Some boys jump down off the back of a pick-up truck as it stops in the square, and make for a basketball hoop, incongruously erected near the entrance to a *kiva*. Danny is reminded of somewhere he had not thought of in a long time – home. Of growing up in Ballyporeen, way down south-west of Ireland, of knowing who your neighbours were and playing in the road. Once, when he was five, some American tourists stopped him and his sister in the street to ask the way to the

Ronald Reagan pub, renamed to commemorate the village's most famous alleged descendant. One of them was black, like someone from a TV detective show. They seemed so strange and exotic, their accents so unfamiliar, Danny assumed they must have come from as far away as Cork.

Luther drives slowly so as to minimise the dust thrown up by the wheels, and pulls in by a shack with a sign reading 'Community Office'. 'Danny, I'm going to ask after old Bob. Stay in the car with Sid and don't go wandering off.' Luther turns round and prods Tracy. She sits up and looks around, suddenly thrown half asleep into this new environment.

'Where are we?'

'Hopiland. Come on, and bring Mr Lewis.'

Sid wakes in the car alone. As his eyes become accustomed to the darkness he makes out the walls of the low, ancient buildings, and the flicker of lights behind the small square windows. He hears the barking of dogs. For a moment he is lost, and feels he has woken into a dream. Then he hears Danny's voice outside the car.

'Forty dollars? I'll give you ten. What is it anyway?' Danny is standing at a doorstep, arguing with a seated old man who brandishes a wooden carving of a small, brown figure, with bulbous eyes and ears, waving a tiny feather in one hand, and a miniature knife in the other.

'Mud-head. He's a clown. And he costs forty dollars. Where you from anyhow?'

'Ireland,' answers Danny.

'Uh-huh.'

'You've got relatives there, I suppose.'

'No,' says the man, a little surprised, 'but I have some in Oraibi. That's nearly ten miles up the highway.'

A little way into the village, Tracy and Lewis stand on the roof of a small, squat house, looking across the dark desert plains to the fading outline of the San Francisco peaks, and up at the flickering of the stars. They are so bright here, Lewis feels that if he had seen the stars in this sky, rather than through the fog and cloud of London, he'd have made sense of his memories much sooner, without maps and evenings alone standing in sidings. He shuts his eyes. *The Grail passes over the face of the moon. He reaches for it, flexing the fingers of his space-gloved hand. It drifts closer. It is all but within his grasp.* The shine of the metal dazzles him and he opens his eyes once more.

The silence of the Hopi reservation lends itself to contemplation, punctured only by the sounds, beneath their feet, of Bob and Luther loudly renewing their acquaintance. Tracy remembers Bob's warning, from the day she met him in the diner. She thinks of the boy whose father was the Sun, of how the 'spider woman', apparently, had made her a perfect partner, and of Bob's promise of 'rattlesnake children'. She had found his stories interesting, flattering almost, and was more than a little shocked by how much he had seemed to know about her most secret thoughts and fears. But Tracy hadn't set any more store by his off-the-peg prophecy than she would by an unusually accurate newspaper horoscope. His was a small comfort, one to be instantly forgotten, an anecdote stored up for future use, round a table somewhere, in simpler, safer times. How strange then to be back with him so soon. Still, her situation had not changed, and she had nothing to show for all Bob's reassurances. She feels maybe she should ask him for clarification. But now is not the time. From beneath her, laughter and the slapping of backs, and then Bob's head pokes up through an opening in the roof. Tracy reaches down to pull him up, as Luther follows. 'You're looking at the stars, Mr Lewis,' says the old Hopi. 'Luther tells me you're more familiar with them than most men.'

'Maybe . . .'

'There's *Hotomkan*,' says Bob, tracing a line skywards from Lewis's right eye with a long, straight forefinger.

'Orion,' Lewis suggests, squinting at the sparkling lights.

'And *Choochhokan*, the harmonious stars, the stars that sing together . . .'

'The Pleiades cluster . . .' There is a pause. Bob seems impressed.

'You know your way around the skies, Mr Lewis. But we Hopi were never great fans of you astronauts. You went to the moon. We knew the moon not as a goal to be achieved, but as the Mother of the Sun. We were expecting her to reject you, and shoot you back down to earth, but instead you brought back pictures, and planted your Stars and Stripes . . .'

'Now, Bob . . . that was nothing to do with me,' protests Lewis.

Bob continues. 'In 1967, in one of our clowning performances, I strode out into the plaza, just here, and tied a mouse to the end of a firework, which was painted with NASA symbols. Then we lit the firework. We shot it out of the village, high over the roofs of the houses. People ducked their heads as it flew over them, and then stood up on the steps of the plaza to watch the rocket once more. After the rocket had landed, the people waited in silence to see what would happen next. One of the other clowns ran back into the plaza. He entered from a rooftop and slid down a ladder. He held a mouse in one hand, and a piece of cheese in the other. Everybody laughed. It was judged a fine performance. Back then, we thought it was so foolish, the white man trying to get to the moon. We tried to laugh you out of the sky. But you made it. To the moon. There and back.'

'Not me personally,' Lewis says. 'I seem to remember getting a fairly good look at it, though . . .'

'And was the moon also made of cheese, Mr Lewis?' Bob laughs, and clutches Lewis's shoulder for support. Then he composes himself. 'Tracy, go with Mr Lewis and your two friends up to the motel at the Cultural Center. Find Henry. Tell him I sent you. Meet us back here tomorrow morning, at first light. Give me a night alone with Luther and I'll endeavour to make him of some use to you.'

'Bob . . .' says Tracy, squeezing his hand. 'Thank you.'

'Don't thank me yet. Luther has had an idea and asked me for help. Last time he had an idea and asked me for help, I found myself in prison for six months and he got institutionalised.'

'Yep! What a trip that was!' laughs Luther. 'They blew my mind with their electric shocks! Buzz! Buzz! Buzz! Opened up my third eye, and my fourth, and my fifth, and my sixth, till I finally touched the face of God!'

'Uh-huh. And what's God like, Luther?' says Tracy.

'Get this! He was an old guy, with a white beard! Who'd'a thought it?'

'I appreciate I have arrived rather late in the day, and I'd like to thank you for agreeing to take me on this tour. Believe me, I'll make it worth your while.' On the natural stone bridge that crosses from Sichomovi to Walpi, the Hampstead Man pants for breath as he catches up with the main party. Three day-glo Belgians in shorts follow a beautifully preserved, brown-skinned old woman, of indeterminate age, between the walls of the Hopi homes. 'No photographs, please. And don't enter any *kivas*, or disturb any sites of religious significance.' The stone walls glow softly in the setting sun as she points out various architectural phenomena from underneath her pink umbrella, and says as much as she is prepared to of the village's culture and history. Every now and again, people emerge from houses with pottery, carved wooden figures of men dressed in sacred ceremonial costumes, and children's rattles in the shape of mice or laughing human faces. The Belgians make a polite show of interest and complete the occasional cash transaction.

'This is the best place to buy these,' the Belgian woman tells the Hampstead Man, displaying rather more cleavage and thigh than he would have thought appropriate in a holy place, as she holds up a gracefully carved figure of a slender winged woman. 'The ones you see in Flagstaff and Phoenix are copies, made by the Navajo, who don't even have *katsinas* in their culture.'

'Really?' says the Hampstead Man. 'Then they have learned something of the natural laws of supply and demand. Good luck to them, I say.' And he wanders away from the party.

Unsteadily navigating the cliff-edge path, and trying not to look down as the mesa drops dramatically away to the corn fields below the settlement, the Hampstead Man feels far from home. From what little he has gleaned of Hopi culture and history, he is aware that the vagaries of various invading forces, and the dubious sovereignty of the American state, have had little real impact on life here. Outside events seem insignificant to a people that prides itself on its unbroken ancient cycle of ritual and rebirth. And yet here he is, out of his usual jurisdiction, in a foreign land, attempting to aid the completion of a quest which his superiors believe is of world importance. But the notion of 'world importance', here, in this all but other world, is relative. What difference would it make to these people, or indeed to anyone outside the fellowship of the Brotherhood, if he is successful in his appointed task or not?

At the far western end of the mesa, the Hampstead Man stands and looks over the flat plane to Shungopavi and the white buildings of the Hopi Cultural Center. He fishes in his inside pocket and removes a collapsible telescope. In the middle of a black circle he watches Lewis's hire car heading up the road towards the lodgings Bob had arranged. For a moment he considers letting him go, calling home and saying he lost him somewhere in the south-west, and that it had all been in vain. Then the guide calls him back to the party.

The old woman points out the entrance to a *kiva*, where religious rituals are conducted underground. The Hampstead Man laughs a little. He walks once each week from Westminster to Covent Garden by subterranean routes known to only a few, and charges initiates with loyalty in temples further below the ground than this village was high above the sea.

Then the woman leads them through a tunnel into the main plaza of Walpi. The small square stands on the edge of the cliff, with rows of stone seats around it built into the walls of the surrounding houses. At the western end stands a nine-foot-high rock, a natural feature of the mesa clearly now incorporated into worship. A small bundle of feathers is nestled inside a crack in the stone. 'These feathers, what are they for please?' one of the Belgians asks the woman, poking at the offering with an outstretched Belgian finger. She pretends not to hear and leads the small party onwards.

Watching the Belgian fumbling around the rock, the Hampstead Man bristles with indignation. The woman's pious caution has considerably increased his estimation of her, and her people. Her heart, too, he realises, is the safe and sacred repository of secrets. His anxieties change shape suddenly seem only natural. What was it his school chaplain had told him? Without doubt there cannot be faith. Like he himself, the woman values her tongue. Watching the interfering Belgian, the Hampstead Man finds himself seized by something like sympathy for the put-upon cliff-dwellers. Taking the tourist by the strap of his luminous green rucksack, he forcibly removes him from the area. 'Can't you see, she doesn't want to tell you?' he says to the surprised and struggling lowlander. 'Have a little respect. Some things are meant to remain unknown.'

The tour party winds back through Walpi to the village office at Sichomovi, where the Belgians humbly thank the guide and climb into their car. The Hampstead Man dawdles by a display explaining the Navajo–Hopi land dispute, waiting for them to leave. 'You did me a great service today, madam,' he says to the woman, as she returns refreshed from a room at the rear. 'You have strengthened my resolve.'

'Thank you. I am glad you enjoyed your visit.'

'*May your oblations of piety be grateful as the incense, your love warm as its flame, and your benevolence diffusive as its fragrance,*' he continues, pressing an unprecedentedly large tip into her wrinkled hand. '*May your heart be as pure as the altar, your thoughts and actions acceptable as the sacrifice laid thereon, and may the exercise of your charity be as constant as the ever-recurring wants of the fatherless and the widow.*' The old woman looks up at him, blankly. '*And may the hope of Heaven's approbation be your encouragement and the testimony of a good conscience your sufficient reward.*'

'The village is closing soon,' she says. 'You'd best get off the reservation or find somewhere to stay.'

During the night, a trail of ants has climbed the table leg from a crack in the wall on to a paper plate of half-eaten *piki* bread. The insects break off wafer flakes of the blue cornbread roll, and pass it back down the chain, to some subterranean storage cellar. Tracy wakes and watches them at work as the first shafts of the morning sun filter through the windows of her room. In her sleep she had dreamed of the local creation myth, which she'd seen pasted up on a wall in the museum next to the restaurant; of the Hopi emerging ant-like from the underworld in a blinking procession, into the fertile lands above them, and promising to make good the tenure entrusted to them. It had been another long night.

The Hopi Cultural Center was a bright white building, set on the side of the 87, north of Shungopavi. Behind the restaurant and museum, little courtyards of rooms spread east into scrubby trees and sand in the shadow of a disused water tower. The usual dogs patrolled the ground, falling into step beside visitors and begging hopefully wherever they went. Tracy suspected the building's real purpose was an attempt to corral and control the inevitable tourists. They were going to come whatever, but the presence of some accommodation and a place to eat would go at least some way towards restricting their often intrusive ramblings.

It was as they sat and ate mutton stew and cornbread round a table in the restaurant that Danny had turned weird. When he learned there wasn't a bar in the building, or in fact anywhere on the reservation as a whole, Tracy had watched his irritation spill out into a more general unpleasantness. Why were they driving to the airbase anyway? Couldn't Lewis just phone up for a space ship and fly them there? And maybe they should ask at the desk if there's a discount for 'nutters'. He had told Tracy she should bail out now, ditch the mental case, and go south with him to live the high life in Mexico, far away from this gang of losers. Sid tried to calm him while Lewis sat silent and stoic, staring at his stew. Finally Danny threw down his spoon and stood up and left. Out of the window they watched him stomping off into the darkness towards a small wood spotted with tourists' motor homes. Dogs ran playfully around him, leaping up to lick his face, unaware that they were unwanted, while he swore back at them with an unfamiliar tongue. And that was when Sid, Lewis and Tracy, all started to laugh, uncontrollably, well beyond dusk and into darkness.

Later, as she wandered back to her room across the courtyard, paced by a little white puppy, Tracy had looked up and seen Sid and Lewis standing on the roof, staring out across the black landscape. She had climbed up some steps to join them. They were sucking soft drinks through straws and smoking. Sid had offered her a cigarette. She took it. To the east they could just make out the dark silhouettes of the second and first mesas, and the glow of lights clustered around at the bottom of the cliffs. Sid smiled. 'A week ago I was in Balham, with my so-called life in shreds. But look at this place. Whatever happens, I'm glad I came out here with you two.'

'Yes,' Lewis had said. 'We've seen something of the world.'

Tracy had envied them for a moment. Once they'd both settled their own private scores they'd be free, one way or another. But she was shackled to something she felt she'd never be able to shake off. She saw as far ahead only as the border and a few months of relative peace before her past started to gain on her once more. To slow down for a moment, and stand on a roof smoking and taking in a view, only emphasised the restless chaos that usually filled her life. She dare not pause for breath. Sid offered her his straw. She slurped on it, and felt the bubbles fizz in her nose. 'You need to go to bed, boys. We've got an early start. And there's no telling what state Luther's going to be in.'

Having raised a disgruntled Danny, still sulking, in the early light, Tracy checks out. Bob had somehow arranged to take care of their bill, and Tracy indulges herself with an orange juice from the last of her dwindling cash supply. The boys bundle into the car and they drive to Shungopavi to collect Luther from Bob's house. Lewis sits next to her, in the front seat, silent with anxious anticipation.

Outside Bob's house, Tracy knocks on the wooden door. No one answers. 'He's sussed us out, Old Obi Wan Kenobi,' shouts Danny. 'He's fucked off for good before everything really goes tits up.'

Suddenly, a voice. 'Let's go.' It's Luther. He stands at the rear of the car, having emerged unseen from somewhere, round-eyed and shaking a little. He smells bad, and when he smiles, they see that his teeth have been coated with clay. No one feels entitled to ask why. Danny shrugs his shoulders and shuffles along the seat to make a space for the near comatose old man, occasionally staring meaningfully at Sid. Sid ignores him. Tracy slips the car into gear and they head south to the alleged airbase of Holbrook, the sun rising behind them over the huddled villages of the Hopi reservation.

Half an hour later, Luther wordlessly points the way off the highway, along a dirt track signposted to Joseph City. There are No Trespassing signs, and ominous black aircraft intermittently swoop low over their vehicle, quietly dive-bombing the empty desert in endless rehearsals of as yet unplanned assaults on unborn Arab enemies. In the back seat, Sid and Danny watch nervously as Luther sticks out his clay-coloured tongue, and touches it repeatedly with the tip of his finger. 'I am one hundred per cent confident we are in safe hands here,' says Danny, catching a doubtful flicker in Lewis's eyes.

On their left, a lone white mailbox suddenly breaks the uniformity of the landscape, and Luther leans forwards and points at an all but indecipherable dusty trail leading west beside it. A sign informs drivers that unauthorised visitors may be shot without warning. 'Use of Deadly Force is Authorized'. Danny pointedly reads it aloud. 'That's "deadly force", folks. Deadly. As in "dead".' Lewis looks around for advice, but Luther smiles benignly and, reassuringly, touches everyone in turn on the shoulder or the knee, flicking his brown caked tongue in and out exploratively over his dirty teeth. Tracy drives on.

On the road ahead, the way is blocked by an unmanned wooden barrier. 'Stop here,' says Luther, suddenly breaking his silence, 'and go and see what's over the hill.' Luther walks away from them, towards the barrier, and points the rest of the group towards a rising bank of earth. Sid gestures for the others to keep low, with a second-hand signal learned from Viet Nam movies, and scurries up the incline. 'Oh, yes. You're fucking Rambo now,' says Danny to no one in particular, walking obstinately upright as the others do their best to hug the ground. Lying at the top of the bank they look out over the flat plain.

Though unmarked as such a size on any maps, Holbrook airbase stretches out before them in all its undeniable immensity. Black saucer-shaped aircraft taxi in and out of hangars, and small phalanxes of soldiers march briskly between buildings. A barbed-wire-topped fence surrounds the complex, studded with guard towers and cameras, and concrete tunnels sweep down towards underground chambers. Even Danny is surprised, and drops down to the ground accordingly. 'Jesus! This is insane.'

'Yes,' says Lewis. 'But if Luther is to believed, somewhere behind that fence lies the key to my identity.'

'Listen, I wish I'd told you the key to your identity back in London, mate,' Danny snaps. 'You're fucking mental. Can we go now?'

Tracy turns to take issue, but is interrupted by a sound from the road behind them. At the barrier, Luther is in conversation with the end of a rifle, pointed out of the passenger-side window of a soft-top white Cherokee Jeep. Lewis notes that base security has clearly been put into the hands of civilian contractors, perhaps to minimise legal complications should deadly force indeed be required. Sid stands, as if to run down and offer some kind of useless, flyweight assistance, but Tracy gently restrains him. As they watch, the gun is lowered and, one by one, five men climb out of the vehicle, clad in anonymous green camouflage fatigues and slowly begin to undress.

'Well,' says Lewis, 'it seems Luther has made five perfect strangers take off their clothes without any resistance.'

'Now that, I grant you, is a skill worth having,' says Danny, entranced, as they scuttle down the hill.

'I got us some fancy new threads!' Luther points at a pile of green uniforms. Beside them are the five men, dazed and in their underwear, but instilled with enough rigorous training to maintain an illusion of dignity, standing smartly at attention in a parody of parade. Luther throws Danny a tow rope, liberated from the back of the vehicle.

'Book 'em Danno.' Danny begins to tie up the confused, semi-naked security men, who offer no resistance and helpfully place their hands behind their backs in an accommodating fashion. 'What's that then, Luther? Old Jedi mind trick?'

'Nope,' says Luther, steadying himself as he pulls the stolen clothes over his own, 'Old Bob has invited the snake spirits into my soul. I'm hypnotising my prey.'

'Uh-huh. Like a snake would,' says Tracy, realising that Luther is serious.

'Yep. You got it.' Lewis and Tracy share a quizzical look and begin to change their clothes.

At the junction with the dirt track and the road to Joseph Town, the Hampstead Man sits on top of his vehicle. He munches a piece of *piki* bread, and brushes the falling flakes off his pressed white shirt. Back down the highway, a heavy-set, wide-necked man had welcomed him into his trailer home. A hand-painted sign outside had proclaimed it the 'Secret Airbase Information Office'. Offered his choice of conspiracy theory literature, the Hampstead Man had seen a book on the Freemasons' control of world government, and he bought a few copies for friends back home. The man insisted there was something sinister afoot in Holbrook airbase. He had shown him captured satellite photographs that proved, quite frankly, nothing, before signing him up to a right-wing libertarian mailing list for further discussion of various implausible phenomena. But Lewis had gone to Holbrook airbase nevertheless, and the Hampstead Man was duty-bound to observe his movements. So now he raises his telescope and watches the transformed group climb into the jeep. He reaches into an icebox next to him, pulls out a bottle of champagne and pops the cork which thuds dully on to the dirt. Some might say his celebration was a little premature. But as the frothy liquid flows into a paper cup, the Hampstead Man considers how young Mr Lewis has undertaken and faithfully discharged, with integrity and zeal, the duties of the high office to which he has found himself elected. The Hampstead Man raises his glass as if to congratulate his distant quarry. After all, he recalls from the appropriate texts, *he who faithfully performs his duty, even in a subordinate station, is as justly entitled to esteem and respect as he who is entrusted with supreme authority*. Chin chin! And he clinks his glass against the empty air.

At the airbase's first manned checkpoint Luther tucks his beard into his collar, leans out of the window of the jeep, and calmly calls over a guard. A young soldier approaches from an office in front of the wire fence. Behind it, Tracy can see black planes circling on a runway and distant men running around and shouting. Danny leans forward. 'We're dead,' he says, prodding Lewis, 'and it's your fault.' Sid pulls him back into his seat and Lewis barely registers his taunts, far away in his private fears. They crane their necks to listen as Luther says something to the guard, who then walks purposefully away.

'Patience, my friends. He's just finding out where we need to go,' explains Luther.

'We're going to jail obviously, mate, unless Tracy turns this thing around and gets us out of here now.' Danny remains unconvinced.

An officer approaches the car from behind the sentry post, and Luther gets out of the car to meet him. Watching through the window, the others see the man's initially brusque hostility melt almost immediately, as he calls for the guard to issue five passes. The officer stands and watches Luther return to the car, and cheerily waves it on as the gate is raised and Tracy drives forwards into the bustling base. Luther distributes the passes.

'He says it's official policy to deny any government interest in the Holy Grail, but has suggested we visit the Project Arimathea HQ in Hangar 18. Even under the influence of my powers he's still maintaining a state of plausible denial, but these passes will get us in.'

'Luther . . .' begins Tracy, sounding doubtful.

'Don't question me, please. It's necessary for me to believe I can do this or Bob's magic won't work.'

Lewis winces and looks out of the window as he feels a sweat break out all over his body, evaporating a little and then condensing in the clammy layer between his own clothes and the stolen uniform. As the jeep wends its way between stationary aircraft, shiny metal huts, rows of hangars, brick barracks and bored personnel, Lewis wonders if it has all been worth it. Within minutes he will face confirmation that he is either involved in the most obscure conspiratorial cover-up of the post-war era, or that he is positively insane. He feels a strange gratitude for the support of these new-found friends, even for Danny's begrudging presence. But as they approach Hangar 18 he worries that these sudden acquaintances might be some part of the greater picture that has been hidden from him. Are they too just paid observers? Lewis would have questioned the sudden aid and interest of any respectable or useful-looking characters, but this group of rootless eccentrics were such unlikely accomplices as not to have aroused his suspicions. Trying to break into an airbase on a whim under the influence of Native American magic seemed like the kind of thing Luther would have done any weekend. Which is, of course, why the bedraggled old hippie would make the perfect double-agent. How long before his new companions suddenly leaped from the jeep and left it to explode, with him strapped into the back seat? Lewis feels Danny's hand on his shoulder.

'Hey, spaceman. Just so as you know, if I never have time to tell you later, I hate you for getting me into this. I hope there's no Grail there and you are revealed for the psychotic twat you so obviously are, OK.'

'Thank you. I'll bear that in mind.' Danny's for real at least, thinks Lewis, reassured. No one could counterfeit that level of hostility.

As she drives across the compound, Tracy looks back at Lewis and the two British musicians. In coming here, to Arizona, they have rushed forwards to confront their fears. With every turn of the jeep's wheels, Lewis is closer to a resolution, good or bad, of his anxieties. And in finding old Luther, Sid and Danny have at least taken steps to address their own impending obsolescence. But even here, helping relative strangers to steer their way through this suicidally dangerous situation, Tracy is still only playing for time. Somehow, assisting a dubious stranger to break into a secure government compound in a search for a long-lost historical treasure is easier than dealing with her situation. She'd rather face off an armed soldier than take stock and face the facts.

A jet screams through the sky above them. 'Stop here,' says Luther. 'This is Hangar 18.' They get out of the vehicle.

Luther leaves the group at the jeep, and crosses to the entrance to the hangar, a freshly painted and perfectly maintained mirror-image of his own home. They watch him brandishing their passes at a security guard, and then he beckons them forwards. They enter easily into the building, the young soldier paying them no attention as he stares distractedly at his boots, pointing them towards a lift, and mumbling something mysterious under his breath. 'I hope it's as easy to get out as it was to get in,' Sid mutters.

Luther presses the button and they wait. Military personnel of various ranks and ages pass them by, hurrying along the striplit corridor, oblivious to the unauthorised visitors. The lift arrives and they enter, Danny stepping aside to allow a red-haired female soldier out first. Even in disguise, he can't resist trying to get her attention. Sid snatches him by the arm and pulls him into the lift. In silence, Luther punches in a number. 'You'll find our selection of non-existent holy relics in the basement, sir,' says Danny, and jabs Lewis in the ribs. The lift begins to sink down the shaft. Lewis feels his stomach shift, and can't work out whether it's due to the effects of gravity, or a palpable sense of his own impending destiny. He shuts his eyes. *The Grail passes over the moon. The space-gloved hand opens and closes as it slips away from his grasp, drawn into another, more powerful orbit.*

Luther suddenly staggers a little, and falls into Tracy's arms. She feels him soaked in sweat, and unnaturally hot, boiling over like a sick child.

'Luther. What's wrong?'

'I think the snake people need to go home,' he says, his tongue flickering in and out of his muddy mouth. 'I can feel them slipping away.'

Sid and Tracy stand Luther and steady him as the lift comes to a stop. The pneumatic hum subsides, and everyone turns and looks at Lewis, willing him forwards. 'This is it, Moonhead,' says Tracy. 'I think you should go first.' Lewis stiffens, sucks in his stomach, and steps up to the doors as they slowly start to hiss open.

'*Suddenly the hall was lit by a sunbeam which shed a radiance through the palace seven times brighter than had been before.*' There is a blinding whiteness, a night-time headlight dazzle shot through a magnifying glass the size of the sun. Lewis raises his hand to shield his eyes as he feels himself falling forwards. *The Grail passes over the moon.* Then, as he lowers his hand to look, trembling with anticipation, fearful with the threat of fulfilment . . . he sees nothing. Before him, an enormous empty room, whitewashed from floor to ceiling, with a white tiled floor, and powerful arc lights blazing from the white panelled ceiling, fully the length of a football field, a perfect cube of anti-chromatic nothing. Nowhere has ever seemed quite so convincingly vacant. This clear absence of any Grail, or of any Grail-like thing, or of any thing at all, is quite clearly not negotiable. This expanse is utterly empty; like Roslin chapel, like the Cathar castles of southern France; as lacking in significance as the landscaped clues of Gorges du Verdon in Provence; as hollow as Glastonbury's mythical boasts; barren like del Monte castle, like Narta Monga and Genova Cathedral; a vacant vastness, its meaninglessness amplified by its unnecessary immensity. This is a lesson in emptiness, the journey of a million miles hereby ending in a perfect vacuum, a brilliantly realised, unbeatable anticlimax. As their eyes adjust to the light, Lewis's companions look doubtfully at each other. He walks out of the lift and collapses on to the floor, his head in his hands. Afraid to move, they stand and stare at him as he beats his fists on the tiles a moment, and then shivers into stillness. A single sob bounces around the white walls and finally dissolves. Danny breaks the silence. 'Right. There's no Holy Grail, then. Ah, well. Shall we meet this time next year in Scotland and see if we can't dredge up the Loch Ness monster!'

'This is your fault. Your damn stupid fucking fault,' says Tracy, running forwards to help. 'Lewis! It doesn't matter. Walk away! Get up and walk away.'

Sid and Danny follow her out into the room, Luther trailing unsteadily behind them, licking and picking at his clay-coated teeth, as if he's forgotten how the sticky substance that clogs his mouth ever got there. The lift doors close and they hear it rise back to the surface. Tracy kneels and cradles Lewis's head in her hands. He stares at the empty room with empty eyes. *The Grail slips out of his hands, growing ever smaller in the blank void as it drifts from him a final time.* Will this be the last time he suffers this recurring nightmare, or will he be forced to replay images of this supreme moment of humiliation and failure for the rest of his life? Every time he shuts his eyes to sleep, will he be reminded that he was not whoever he thought he was, that he had not done whatever he thought he had done, that he had lived an unknown life and had nothing to show for it, least of all a legendary holy treasure? *The Grail disappears behind the sun, lost for ever.* A clatter. The lift doors open. Twelve soldiers stand facing them, fully armed and pointing rifles.

'Raise your hands!'

Luther turns and stands at the front of the group. 'I'll deal with this.'

Fixing the soldiers in his gaze he confidently issues his command, 'Lay down your weapons and return to your posts.'

The soldiers stand unmoved and silent, the interlopers trained in their sights. Everybody looks at Luther. 'Sorry. I guess I'm all snaked out,' he shrugs, and steps aside. 'It happens. This isn't an exact science.'

Danny pushes past him. 'I'll take 'em out then. You lot run for it. Come and kiss me, Tracy.' There is a pause, rendered more painful by the unwavering concentration of the soldiers. Nothing happens. 'Ah, well. Suit yerself.' Danny rushes towards the armed men, braying a battle cry. Tracy covers her eyes. Two of the soldiers step forward, rifle butts raised, and effortlessly club him to the ground, as the others walk forwards with handcuffs ready.

'Danny!' yells Sid, but a soldier is already holding him back.

'Hey, didn't you used to be Luther Peyote?' says a young corporal, fastening Luther's limp hands behind his back.

'Nope. Luther Peyote was eaten by piranhas. Way up-river in the Amazon jungle.'

'Yeah? Well, my mom has all your stuff. It's cool. Could I

please have your autograph?' But nobody has a pen. 'Never mind. I'll give you an address. Write to my mom. It'll blow her mind.'

The men march them out of the chamber, carrying Danny on a stretcher. Lewis looks back into the vast empty space behind him, and wonders what lies ahead.

Abby lets herself into Sid's flat using her old key. She's timed it so she knows Andy his flat-sitter will be out, and begins to cast her eye around Sid's familiar mess and new layers of rubbish brought in by the temporary tenant, looking for things she feels are rightfully hers. Peter Rugg pushes in behind her and heads straight for an overturned ashtray. She's persuaded herself that she's brought him along on her day off just to keep him out of trouble, but she secretly doubts her own motives. Maybe she was just lonely. As Peter picks through the cigarette butts on the carpet, she sets about filling a cardboard box with a kettle, a toaster, a coffee percolator, and various cups and plates. In the bedroom, she strips a sloping shelf of green- and orange-spined paperback books that Sid would never miss, should he ever return, and harvests a handful of soaps and perfumes from the forgotten recesses of the bathroom.

'Ah-ha! Jackpot!' She hears Peter getting agitated in the front room and assumes he must have found a particularly exciting piece of discarded smoking material. As an academic exercise as much as anything, she'd often taunted Sid by comparing his many streaks of obsessional behaviour with those of her patients. But now Sid's not there as a daily yardstick indicating the first, and more socially acceptable, steps on the road to full-blown mental illness, Peter Rugg and her other patients seem somehow further removed from her. With his charming, but ultimately irritating, delusional belief that, one day, he would make it as a musician, Sid had provided her with ongoing evidence of the thin line separating an insanely unrealistic outlook on life from simple insanity. And as she sees Peter standing near her home computer holding the stub of something up to the light he suddenly seems like an utterly unsalvageable subject.

'Look!' says Peter, pointing at an ashtray on the table by the computer, 'top quality grass your old boyfriend smoked, Doctor, but the bouquet is wrong. This is no good to me.' Abby ignores him and lifts up the ashtray. Underneath it, one of Sid's stupid druggy books lies open and coffee-ringed. She sees a black and white picture of an astronaut standing on the surface of the moon, and, on the opposite page, a diagram showing a religious relic in orbit around the planet. She sighs at the stupidity of it, and at all the immature ephemera of Sid that spills out over every surface.

'Come on, Peter,' she says, handing him the cardboard box. 'Take this down to the car for me and then we'll go and have a milkshake, eh?'

'Sorry about all this, Danno,' whispers Sid, as he shuffles hand-cuffed in the seat. His friend is awake now, with blue bruises blossoming on his face. Sid has brought Danny here, from Balham, to fulfil an adolescent fantasy. Now they are chained to chairs in a secret military installation whose overseers seem unlikely to respect whatever rights they're still technically enti-tled to. Beyond the boundaries of the base there are thousands of acres of desert where unwanted intruders can easily be disposed of, and nobody back home has the slightest idea that either of them is here. The signs all along the highway said that deadly force was authorised. They can hardly say they weren't warned.

'Ah, fuck it, Sid. It's been, how can I say, a good craic. And, by the way, in case I don't get the chance to say later, I'm sorry about what happened with the Lemon Pies too.'

Sid suppresses a gasp. Danny has never broached the subject seriously before. 'Forget it,' he says. 'It doesn't matter. Playing with Timothy Waterhouse would probably have been even worse than the Sultans of Streatham.'

'Spare me,' hisses Tracy. 'You sound like Butch and Sundance.'

On the other side of the office, General Lamoreaux has been sitting silently staring at the five captives for minutes now. There's a set of black plastic blinds behind his head, but the midday sun slides between the slats and makes the prisoners squint. The soldier sucks on a cigar, rubs his square jaw, sighs heavily at his guests, narrows his eyes, stands, and speaks. 'The Holy Grail? In space? I feel for you people, I really do.' Tracy stares at the floor. Lewis stares at the ceiling. Luther, still a little unstable, stares at a blue pencil eraser. And Danny and Sid shrug and squirm like schoolboys. 'Jesus, we've got better things to worry about here, I assure you. International terrorism, for example! Or the fundamentalist Muslim states' development of nuclear capability!' He pauses to let the point sink in. Then he laughs. 'And, most significantly, the annual budget cuts! I'd love the luxury of trying to steal a mythical religious relic from space, I honestly would, but really, think for just a second about the sheer stupidity of what you're suggesting. That all this, this whole compound and all the millions of dollars' worth of equipment contained in it, has been used to try and find a tiny cup containing the blood of Christ. I'd like to try and justify that to Congress . . .'

Lewis raises his head and speaks, spluttering as a cloud of cigar smoke hits him full in the face. 'But . . . I saw it. I've been there. I walked in space.' The general stoops and squares up to him.

'Really. Now, Mr Lewis, by the powers invested in me etcetera I could detain you here indefinitely, beat you to a pulp on a daily basis, and still come out smelling of roses. But this is only a simple military installation and you clearly need psychiatric help.'

'That's what I keep telling him,' mutters Danny.

Tracy speaks. 'What are you going to do with us?'

'If it were up to me, young lady, I'd lock you all up and ⸍row away the key. But we've found that if we bust the ass ⸍very pot-head conspiracy theorist who breaks on to our ⸍ty looking for non-existent alien cadavers, salvaged

UFOs and the reanimated corpse of John F. Kennedy, we're swamped by the media, and the whole tedious process only begins again. Normally there's a six hundred dollars apiece spot fine, but given that you five unarmed civilians somehow managed to penetrate every layer of this installation's defences, I think it might be best for all of us if we just forget the whole matter. And I mean . . . forget.'

The general gestures towards a sentry, who has been standing behind their seats throughout the interview. Tracy rubs her wrists as her handcuffs are unfastened. 'That's it?'

'That's it. Now, get outta here. But if I see so much as one late-night cable TV interview about any of this you'll all wake up dead, got it? We'll be watching. And know this, people, I can and will carry out my threat. Remember, I have armies of genetically engineered alien ninjas at my personal disposal, and you'll recall how efficiently my secret right-wing cabal disposed of Martin Luther King back in '68? I'm sure you've all read the appropriate literature.' The general permits himself a smile, and Lewis suddenly feels his fears disappear, to be replaced by a deep, soul-destroying shame.

'Did you believe him?' Tracy asks Lewis, as he slumps in the passenger seat next to her. He doesn't answer, and just gazes out of the window. 'Well,' she says, smiling at him. 'It was kinda fun, anyhow. It's not every day a girl gets to see the inside of a secret military installation and then be interrogated by a high-ranking government official . . .'

There's a pause. 'Now what?'

'I don't know . . .' Lewis answers, looking back towards the base, and the room where he had finally realised he was wrong. 'I really don't know.' Tracy slows the car to a stop, pulls off the road on to the dusty verge, pulls him towards her and kisses him. When Danny opens one eye to watch a minute later, Lewis's head is still clamped between her hands. He nudges Sid.

'Once more, history repeats itself. The English seize again

that which rightfully belongs to the Irish.'

'Well, looks like the best man won.'

'Women love that little lad lost bit. I think he made the whole Moonhead thing up for sympathy.'

Sid laughs. 'Danny, *you* made the whole Moonhead thing up. Now that actually *is* irony. In a way that playing in a Dire Straits covers band as some kind of joke just isn't.' Danny pauses a moment to consider the veracity of Sid's theory, and then reluctantly assents.

'Oh, yeah. Well, that's the last time I read a book. There's no justice, I tell you.'

Behind the headrests, Lewis and Tracy stare silently at each other, she pushing her hair back off her face with a shaking hand, and him closing his eyes as if to try and preserve the memory of the moment. Luther leans over the boys, suddenly semi-coherent once more, and puts his finger to his lips. 'Never mind, son. Go back to sleep. I think they need to talk.'

'You're sure it was him?' The priest leans forwards from the armchair. His simple black robe mirrors the clothes of the two younger priests who sit listening, but his age and bulk make it clear he is their superior.

'Positive, Father,' answers the general, pouring a Scotch and setting it on the table, 'and he still has almost complete memory loss. He does not suspect anything any more.'

The fat priest takes the drink and swirls the ice around. 'You should have eliminated him while you had the chance, despite the risk of exposure. You're certain he's no danger to our work?'

The general opens a packet of cigarettes and offers them around. The two junior priests decline but their leader takes one. 'I am certain, Father. To kill him would only arouse suspi-
ion.' The youngest priest leans in and lights the cigarette.
ho knows, he may yet come in useful. And I convinced his
plices that Project Arimathea is nothing more than a
umour. Everything is under control, I assure you.'

The old priest sucks on the cigarette and considers. 'And the Grail?'

'The Grail is still out there, in the desert, somewhere, in the shuttle we shot down. But don't worry. Our best men are working on it round the clock. We'll find that crash site sooner or later.'

The priest swallows a mouthful of Scotch. 'Good. Then you won't mind if I give the Vatican your personal assurance of success.' The priest stands and shakes hands with the general. The two young priests lean in close to watch as their fingers entwine in an ancient handshake.

Outside in the corridor the three clerics gather their cassocks and walk towards the exit. A hospital trolley passes them on their way out, wheeled by two masked surgeons. The youngest priest looks down at its passenger and gasps, tugging at his companion's sleeve to confirm what he has seen. A white-faced, opal-eyed, spindly figure, positively not of this earth.

The Hopi Boy
and the Sun – vii

Seating himself on a stool of crystal, the son*
took a fox skin and held it up. Daylight
appeared. After a while he put the fox skin down
and held up the tail feathers of a macaw, and
the yellow rays of sunshine streamed out. When
at last he let them down, he said to the boy,
'Now let's go!'

The Sun made the boy sit behind him on the
stool, and they went into another world. After
travelling for some time, they saw people with
long ears, Lacokti ianenakwe, *and if bluebird*
droppings fell on those people they died. The
boy jumped down, took a small cedar stick, and
killed the bluebirds. Then he roasted them over
a fire and ate them.

About noon they came to another town, and
they saw a whirlwind moving along. When
wheat straw was blown against the legs of the

---

* Boas uses the word 'son' here. But the story would seem
to make more sense if we substitute the word 'Sun'. Is it
possible he made some kind of phonetic error in tran-
scribing the tale?

people they fell dead. The boy jumped down, gathered up the wheat straw and tore it up.

Then they came to another town, where the Hopi boy saw people with very long hair down to their ankles, cooking a thin mush in a large pot, and when it hit a person, he died. The boy jumped down, dipped the mush out of the pot and ate it with onions. But he lived and travelled on.

Hopi Indian legend, reported by
Franz Boas in 1922

Fourteen

'You're really going, then?' Sid stands in the late afternoon shadow of Luther's hangar as Lewis and Tracy load up Tracy's car.

'Yes,' says Lewis. 'South. To Mexico. There's nothing more for me here. And Tracy should be safe down there.' Luther approaches from the building. Danny follows, carrying coffees in empty baked bean cans.

Lewis takes one from him. 'You've been very kind, Luther.'

'It was nothing,' says the old man, 'as it turned out.'

Tracy kisses Luther and Sid, each in turn. Lewis shakes both of them by the hand. Luther presses a small packet into his palm. Lewis holds it up to the light. It's a plastic bag of powdered cacti buttons.

'A gift for the future. Use sparingly in search of insight. It made me the man I am today.'

Lewis's gratitude is almost convincing. As the transaction is completed Danny beckons Tracy into the doorway. 'Are you sure you know what you're doing?' he says, taking her hand in his. 'You hardly know this guy, but he's clearly not the most balanced individual. What makes you think he won't top himself like all the others when you break the news?'

Tracy takes stock. 'I don't know, Danny. But he thinks he's walked in space. He should be unshockable.'

'You're a brave woman. Good luck.' And he takes her in his arms, and hugs her, and kisses her just a little too long, until Sid notices, and makes a disapproving face that convinces him to desist.

The car climbs the hill out of Luther's empty airbase. The New Round Tabyls' infant first line-up watch it disappear, and, as the final cloud of dust settles and dies, Luther looks to the boys. 'Practice time, guys. You gotta show me more shapes, Sid. We have a show in Tucson next weekend.'

Sid's mouth opens and words almost form. 'Don't get excited, son. We're bottom of the bill on a new acts showcase in a club that's all but closed. I made a phone call and reconnected with the one promoter who remembered me as anything other than a liability.'

Sid embraces his suddenly sane hero, feeling a surge of pride, until Luther waves him off, wriggles free and re-enters the hangar. Danny spits on to the ground and smiles, secretly, so that no one will see. Then he follows them inside.

Having headed west to shop for supplies in Tucson, Lewis drives south out of town on Highway 19. Tracy sits next to him, the window open and her hair billowing behind her in the breeze. Nogales will be a good place to cross the border, she had told him. It's busy, and the guards are unlikely to ask too many questions. There's a checkpoint and a high metal fence bisecting the village, but so much passing tourist trade that nobody white tends to get stopped going south. Half a day after their adventure at Holbrook, Lewis is still struggling to make some sense of what he has learned, and Tracy sympathetically indulges the cyclical arguments that he self-consciously spills forth.

'Even if there is a Holy Grail, I'm not going to be the one that finds it, am I?' he says, smoking his fifteenth cigarette of the journey. Then, as he stubs it out in the ashtray, a strange kind of calm, which has been threatening to break through the gloom all day, seems to settle on him. 'Now there's no way I can prove who I was. So it can't matter what I ever did or didn't do, on this planet or any other.' An endless procession of six-foot cacti slides past the window, and, on their right, the white towers of the Mission San Xavier del Bac rise out of the desert from behind the habitations of the Papago Indians, long since subdued by shiny saints and relics. Lewis looks down at the speedometer: 90 kph. But it feels, for a moment, as if everything has stopped. Tracy's fluttering hair hangs suspended in the air, and the sunlight stiffens as light flickers on the windshield. On the radio, the Bobby Fuller Four freeze mid-phrase in the chorus of 'I Fought The Law', and spiralling cigarette smoke surrenders its upwards climb like a ruined castle tower staircase. Roadside tumbleweed trembles in stillness and a half-formed breath hangs unexhaled on the edge of his lips. Lewis looks across at the woman at his side, smiling back at him, and at the road ahead, sloping south down to a new life. What if some mail-shirted figure suddenly rose up out of the cacti scrub and offered him the Grail, polished up and ready on a silver presentation plate? As he watches Tracy watching him, he wonders if, now, he might not just walk away from it, and he realises, 'All that matters now . . . is now.'

Tracy laughs as things lurch back into place. 'All that matters now is now? That's so "Zen".' She makes inverted commas in the air. But he forgives her. This must be the beginning of love. 'So what name do I call you now, then, Mr Lewis?'

'I'll have to stick with A.R.Y. Lewis, I suppose,' he shrugs, as the once crushing weight of those five unwanted syllables grows yet a little lighter.

'Please! I preferred Moonhead,' she laughs. 'Will that make you happy?'

And he laughs in return. Lewis realises that, yes, it could make him happy. He was happy when he and Tracy had sat around the fire, at night, above Luther's hangar; he was happy when he listened to Bob Nequatewa naming the stars of the south-western sky; and he was happy when he and Sid had stood on the roof of the Hopi Cultural Center, and looked out over the land. He'd been happy, for the first three times in his short mental life-span, and all before he'd even known there wasn't a Holy Grail in Holbrook. When he finally admitted to his airforce interrogator that the relic wasn't to be found, it had seemed at the time to set him back. But then he had been happy again, only hours later, when Tracy had kissed him, unexpectedly, in the car, somewhere north of Coronado.

'Yes,' Lewis says, 'I am happy. And you?'

'Me?'

'Yeah. What will it take to make you content?' he continues. 'What's your story, Tracy?' Tracy knew Lewis had realised she was on the run. The boys back at Luther's let that much slip. But she's told him nothing more, and she shudders at the thought of turning everything sour, so near to safety and a chance to begin anew. She thinks Lewis, if anyone, will understand her need to shake off her story and start afresh. He seems at the point of beginning the same process himself, but, as she shuts her eyes, the same ghosts haunt her still. And Lewis, next to her and suddenly satisfied, was he to be one more?

'I don't have a story, Mr Lewis.'

'Come on,' he says, pressing the point. 'I don't even know your second name.'

'You don't need to,' she says turning away. 'You're already too close for your own good. Bad luck follows me like a sick dog.'

Lewis feels the fragments of glass bite into the back of his neck before he hears the gunshot. The rear window explodes and he momentarily loses control of Tracy's car, careering over the roadside and back on to the blacktop. Behind them a police siren blares into life and a patrol car accelerates into their back bumper, shoving them sideways. Lewis steers at speed towards an exit, over the dry bed of the Santa Cruz river, and down the road towards the white edifice of the Mission San

Xavier del Bac. Another gunshot cracks out across the desert as the police car rams them once more. Tracy grips her seat for support and looks behind her, as the car rolls off the road between spindly trees and through a low wooden fence. In a dusty paddock pot-bellied pigs squeal and run for cover. Catholic monks in black robes and local Papago farmers run out from low white adobe buildings to protect their joint investments. A priest jumps to their right as a pig scurries left from under the wheels. The car circles a small stone-walled well to smash through a flimsy wooden gate. It slides sideways out into the wide empty space in front of the church. Lewis looks to his right, dazzled and distracted by the big white building, and the car collides with a small sign detailing the times of mass. Pigs run out of the farm, over the dirt road, and into the square. Tracy kicks open her door and slithers out into the sunlight, wiping a small smear of blood off her forehead. She looks up at the towers of the church, as they shimmer in the setting sun, and remembers.

At school, they'd learned all about the Mission San Xavier del Bac, or the White Dove of the Desert, as the locals called it. Her father used to come here to pray for especially powerful divine information, as if the Catholics had a more direct route in times of real need. He'd drag her with him to admire the architecture, even as he quietly admonished the genuflecting priests for their gaudy, heretical icons. Tracy sees Lewis, standing in front of her face, shaking her shoulders, but she's somewhere else. She feels him take her by the arm, and pull her towards the Mission steps, perhaps hoping to lay claim to some right of sanctuary. She sees the patrol car swerve between the building and a wooden-walled complex of Papago-run concession stands, through a cluster of six or seven startled pigs, to block off their escape route. Behind her, through the open doors of the Mission, white arches lead back to the altar. A statue of Mary, in a freshly laundered blue linen dress and golden crown, stands flanked by painted red plaster. 'Thou shalt not make any graven image, or any likeness of any thing that is in heaven above, or that is in the earth, or that is in the water under the earth,' her father had said, as he led her by the hand along the central aisle. She feels Lewis stand in front of her on the steps. The door of the patrol car opens, and someone begins to emerge, rifle first.

'You ain't no part of this, boy. Yet. Step away.' Tracy shuts her eyes. Blood congeals in her lashes. 'I'm giving you a chance, boy. She's a killer and you're probably next. You're lucky I came along.'

'I won't step away,' says Lewis, shielding Tracy behind him.

'Well, you was warned.' Tracy hears the click of the rifle reloading. 'Step out into the sunlight, girl. Let me see what I've been chasing these past ten years.'

The mission bell tolls seven times behind them. Tracy hears the grunting of the bewildered pigs. She opens her eyes, and though Lewis struggles briefly to stop her, she walks down the steps towards the sheriff. Hopkins looks at the woman, squinting in the sun, and then, slowly, lowers his rifle in open-mouthed surprise. He thinks momentarily of the map in his office, of the coloured strings and coloured pins, of the complex theories and suspect lists he'd struggled to formulate, when all the time . . .

'Aw no!' he murmurs. 'Tracy? Is that you?'

Tracy stands still, facing him square on. She wipes the blood off her forehead once more, and looks the sheriff straight in the eye.

'Yes. Dad.'

Hopkins winces a little, and looks down at the ground for a few long seconds. Then he raises his rifle, his finger fidgeting on the trigger, the head of his long-lost daughter fixed firmly in his sights. He remembers the scent he'd picked up after the shoot-out at the gas station. He knew it from diaper changing and the smell of her room, where he had sat alone long after she'd left. And every time he'd taken a description from some confused witness, or measured a footprint, or picked up some discarded item of her personal property, he knows now that he had been struggling to paint himself a picture of her. How Littwick and Cowdrey would laugh, that all the while Hopkins' mysterious quarry had been someone so close to home. The woman is older now, and a little heavier, but still bears some traces of that sweet little girl. She's not changed much, Hopkins thinks, since the last time he'd seen her. The day she'd announced she was pregnant, an hour or so before he kicked her out of the door, and threw her things out after her, Grace pounding his chest with her fists as she struggled to make him stop. Tracy sees her father shake a little, and strengthen his grip on the rifle. But she doesn't move. She simply stands still, as if inviting him to shoot her. Hopkins's finger twitches on the trigger. Tracy walks towards him, puts her hand on the barrel of the rifle, and presses her forehead up against it. Their eyes lock. If there was one thing he could undo, Hopkins thinks, one mistake he could erase from his life, this woman would be it. And now the good Lord has offered him the opportunity to do so.

Lewis is halfway down the steps, diving to push Tracy aside, as the shot rings out. He pulls her to the ground with him, but already knows he must have been too late, landing heavily on her in the dirt. At the same moment Hopkins cries out and drops his rifle. He stumbles backwards to fall down into the midst of a curious herd of pigs, clutching at his arm. Tracy raises her head. She runs a finger along the grazing on her temple, and looks out, over her father's prostrate body, between the legs of the snuffling pigs, to a shape at the far side of the square.

At the corner of the road, in the shadow of the trees, a figure sits mounted on a white horse. The heat haze fuzzes the evening air at her eye level and Tracy can't quite be sure of what she sees; the rider seems to be naked, but for a small loincloth and a hat that tapers to two yellow tassels. His body is painted in a series of concentric black and white stripes. In his left hand he holds a bow that he looks a little too old and feeble to use, and when he smiles Tracy realises, through the sand and blood and sun, that she knows him. Bob Nequatewa tugs on the reins. The horse turns. The rider rounds the corner, and canters slowly along the dry bed of the Santa Cruz, the horse walking onwards where the water once flowed . . .

Tracy stands and looks down at her father. He wriggles amongst the snuffling pigs and clutches at an eagle-feathered arrow buried in his right forearm. Lewis hands her the rifle. He squeezes her shoulder and steps back towards the Mission. Hopkins raises his head and splutters up at her.

'You little bitch. Come on, then. Come on. Kill me. I should have guessed. I should have guessed it'd be you.' Tracy raises the rifle. She studies the scowling man through the sights. 'Well, you have to hand it to the good Lord. He sure knows how to punish a man. Come on, then. Come on. Kill me. You know you want to. Just kill me.'

Tracy watches him writhe a while. Twenty years later he looks no different. Right now, her father is wounded, angry, proud, but still afraid. And yet he had always been a little afraid. The almost monastic life he had inflicted on her as a child reflected not a concern for her, but a fear that she might somehow embarrass him, had she been allowed to roam. He'd left her no choice but to flee. She sometimes wondered if her body had grown the baby by itself as a means of escape. When she miscarried on her first day in Mexico, it was as if the unborn had somehow agreed to set her free. In rare moments of regret, her father was a convenient figure to blame for her troubles. But now, as he lay before her, scared and bleeding a little, she couldn't find it in herself to hate Matthew Hopkins as much as he hated her. Something like pity grapples with something like disgust, causing gag reflexes at the back of her throat and threatens a flow of tears.

Tracy takes aim, squeezes the trigger, and fires. A pig dies squealing, skin and blood exploding over her father's aston- ished face. The other pigs panic and run, stumbling over the still shaking corpse of their fallen fellow. She fires again, and another pig falls halfway between her crashed car and the concession stand. The other pigs wheel around randomly and run back towards her, one breaking off towards the broken gate. She fires two shots in succession, one straight into the forehead of an approaching animal, the other wounding the escaping pig in a hind leg, but not quite killing it, leaving it to stagger in squealing circles. Matthew Hopkins shivers in spasms on the floor, as she steps over his body, shoulders the rifle, and fires two more shots at the fleeing farm animals. The first pig dies within feet of the shelter of the stockade of shops. The other manages a run to the road, until it lies down on the tarmac, kicking its legs. Tracy throws down the gun. Around her the expiring pigs squirm and twitch. Her father begins to uncoil from the crash position, taking his fingers out of his ringing ears. Lewis takes Tracy's hand, and kisses her. He leans down and lifts the pistol from Hopkins's holster. The sheriff offers no resistance. Lewis walks up to the patrol car and shoots out each tyre in turn, and then fires the final two shells into the body of the pig Tracy had merely wounded. Hopkins climbs up on to his knees and watches, bewildered.

'Dad,' she says. 'That there is Mr Lewis, an escaped English mental patient I met while he was in Coronado, searching for the Holy Grail. He and I are heading to Mexico to start a new life. I hope you will give us your blessing.'

Hopkins stares ahead, stone-faced and stunned. Tracy bends down and kisses him, but he doesn't even meet her eye.

'Goodbye, Dad. And, by the way,' she pulls the briefcase out of the car, opens it, holds it above her head, and hurls the contents out into the air, 'I think some of these are probably yours.' The little comic books flutter up on the breeze like a sudden swarm of butterflies, red, blue, green, orange, purple, brown and black. Some catch the wind and whirl out over the square. Others fall to the ground and hop in fits and starts over the dust towards her father, still kneeling in the dirt. Hopkins looks down and sees his own handwriting staring up at him. 'Please pass this on to a friend when you have finished with it.' Tracy closes the case and climbs into the car. Lewis reverses out from the crumpled sign and drives back over the river. Behind them, Matthew Hopkins struggles to stand in the middle of a square strewn with empty cartridges, breeze-blown booklets, and the bleeding carcasses of pigs. As the car rounds the corner and is gone, he mumbles under his breath.

'He sure knows how to punish a man.'

Danny follows Luther's donkey through the cacti. He feels the good humour that had started to creep up on him that afternoon beginning to wane. The sun scalds his bare scalp. He and Sid have already nearly stepped on a snake apiece. 'Don't worry,' Luther had said, sat high above ground in the saddle, 'nineteen times out of twenty they're dry bites. Venom's too good to waste.' Danny has had enough fucking about. Granted, Sid's stupid reclaim-a-rock-star scheme had actually worked, up to a point, but now he just wants to get on with rehearsing, and let all the Holy Grail shite settle. As for Tracy – there'd be other girls, especially once they got gigging properly, but few, he suspects, with such a broad-minded attitude. Ah, well.

Three hours back, Luther had suddenly laid down his guitar in the middle of reminding himself of a basic blues riff. He had started slapping his head and stamping around, struck by a profound notion. Sid had rushed to restrain him, but the old man easily shook him off. 'Of course,' Luther had shouted, 'the great white bird, the great white bird!' and rushed out to saddle the mule.

Sid hadn't wanted to follow the crazy old man out into the desert either, but he'd argued with Danny that they really ought to protect their investment. Once Luther had got whatever this white bird was out of his system, maybe they'd be in a better position to concentrate on retraining the old geezer in simple chord shapes. For a moment Sid thought about calling Abby, but he wasn't ready to confront her until he had something substantial to show for his departure. And so he and Danny had snatched up a water bottle and run out into the sun, chasing the trotting mule and its deranged rider. But three hours later, as Danny dodges his second snake and blunders into a spiny cactus that bites into his lower leg, he finally snaps. 'OK, Luther, thanks for showing us the sights and all, but would you mind telling us what the fuck is going on. If this is some band bonding exercise I'd rather do it over a few beers, you know.'

Luther brings his mount to a stop, and looks round surprised, as if he'd forgotten he was being followed. 'See, I just recalled,' he begins. 'Once I was tripping with some Apache medicine men, out east of the state line. They told me 'bout a Great White Bird, sleeping in the sand beyond the mountains, down in the hidden valley between Rodeo and Portal. Meant nothing to me back then, but sometimes it takes years to see the shapes in the smoke.'

Danny scowls at Sid, looking as if he's about to punch out the psychedelic pensioner.. But Luther rides ahead, and then calls back to them from the top of the hill, 'Hey, I think we're nearly there.' And he disappears down over the ridge.

'What the fuck is he on about, Sid?' shouts Danny, cresting the small rise in Luther's wake. 'This had better be . . .' His words tail away. Below them is a small flat plain, bordered by boulders and cacti, hidden from Highway 18 and sheltered in permanent shadow by a circle of cliffs. Fragments of twisted metal are strewn across the space. The sparse vegetation is blackened by bush fire. Sid and Danny climb carefully down the rocky path, and then pick their way over a wreckage of wing tips and windows, cogs and canisters, wheels and melted plastics, arranged at random from impact. And then ahead of them, buried in the sand where it had sunk itself, they see an unmistakable shape. The nose-cone of the Space Shuttle rises from the rocky ground, flightless, broken and at rest. The white paint has peeled, the dust has rendered the hull a drab brown, and persistent desert plants poke up through the crumpled metal of the wrecked wings. But there's something breathtaking about the spacecraft none the less. It manages a defiant nobility even in this prostrate position.

Over a week ago, Sid and Danny had confirmed Lewis's deluded story with unlikely evidence hijacked from a handful of paranormal pamphlets and excitable websites. But smashed and battered before them lies an undeniable physical manifestation of all the absurd allegations the alleged astronaut had sought to verify. It's probably for the best that Lewis is long gone, Sid thinks. This would blow his already fragile mind. The sun sets and the shuttle skeleton stretches its shattered shadow across the sand towards them. Danny runs a hand over his scalp. Sid sniffles and wrestles with imminent weeping. 'They actually did it. Those maniacs. They actually did it.' A way ahead of them, Luther dismounts and kneels, as if in penance.

Sheriff Matthew Hopkins sits on the steps of the Dove of the Desert. He winds a piece of white cloth around his wound. He watches the locals drag away the last of the pig carcasses and sweep up the holy litter. Hopkins had refused the help of the priests and Papagos, and told them not to call anyone for assistance. Once he's figured out how to get home from here, he'll use whatever influence he still has left to smooth things over, and have the case closed. No one need ever know a thing. And what's a few pigs between friends?

As he ties off the makeshift bandage, a black limousine pulls into the square. A large, elderly Catholic priest climbs out, followed by two younger acolytes. 'Ah, Father Kino's folly,' gasps the bulky cleric. 'Isn't it beautiful? We couldn't possibly pass through this region without stopping to see it.' And he leads the two younger men towards the steps.

'Excuse me, sir, are you hurt?' one of the priests says to Hopkins as they pick their way past him. The sheriff looks over his shoulder to the older priest.

'Father do you believe in divine retribution?'

The priest crosses himself. 'The Lord moves in a mysterious way His wonders etcetera . . . Why?'

Hopkins shifts his weight and leans on the outstretched palm of his good hand. 'I haven't seen my daughter in twenty years. Then she turns up out of nowhere, with an English guy who she says she met while looking for the Holy Grail.' The older priest looks worriedly at his acolytes. 'Then I get shot in the arm by an Indian I busted back in 1971. It just seems too much of a coincidence.'

'Nothing must jeopardise the success of Project Arimathea,' the fat priest says. The youngest removes a pistol from the folds of his cloak. He points it at Hopkins's head. The sheriff springs up and shoves his way between the priests, running over the square towards the concession stands. The first bullet misses, the second catches him in the left leg and he falls down just beyond the limousine. The three priests walk towards him, all wielding weapons now. Hopkins lies on the floor, looking up into the sky. The Mission bell chimes again. As the three faces crowd his field of vision Hopkins waits for his life to flash before him. But it doesn't. Instead he just feels nauseous, wonders if Deputy Cowdrey has changed the answerphone message yet, and finally wishes he'd said something fatherly to Tracy before she left. But he is out of practice, and he'd never been that good at finding the right words. The priests level their guns.

'You are absolved,' announces their leader, as they unload their weapons into Matthew Hopkins's head.

In the valley between Rodeo and Portal, Danny and Sid sift through the shuttle smash. Luther sits on a rock, his head in his hands, mumbling astonished exclamations under his breath. Danny calls Sid over to a fallen and blackened saguaro cactus. It must once have stood forty feet at least. He kicks at the rotting pulp and there, beneath it, nestles a small black, coffin-shaped box, no more than two feet long, and half buried in the sand. The boys drag it out from under the broken saguaro. At the top end of the lid there's an etching of a leaf, and then a compass in raised relief. Below it, something like the letters U, L and N, on a brass plate, and perhaps the number 3,000, but written backwards. As they stare at the lid, their sweat drips down on to it, making little circular marks in the dust. A shadow falls over the box. Luther stands behind them.

'Dare we?' says Sid, tugging at the tightly sealed lid.

'Dare we not?' answers Danny, as Luther hands him a pocketknife.

Kneeling round the box, they take it in turns to break each section of the seal, working anti-clockwise. With a crack, the wood shifts its position a little. Danny and Sid take either end, squeeze their fingertips under the rim, and lift the lid. It comes away easily and they throw it aside into the sand. Danny reaches into the box, scrabbles around a little, and then, without angelic accompaniment, without so much as a crack of thunder, or the echoing sound of the voice of God, he simply raises a small wooden cup up into the fading sunlight. It's an unprepossessing, practical vessel, without decoration of any sort, its mouth sealed over with a circular disc of black wax. Danny shakes it. Dried flakes of something old and undisturbed rattle inside.

'Well . . . fuck me sideways. The fucking Holy fucking Grail. Now we're really in trouble.'

Luther bursts into tears and sits down in the sand.

Tracy had taken a ticket, and parked the car in an empty lot on the north side of Nogales, with no intention of ever coming back to collect it. 'Take heart,' Lewis had said to her, as she lifted her bag out of the trunk. 'Everything you ever feared is twenty miles back up the road with no means of transport and a non-fatal flesh wound.'

'I hope he's OK, I really do.'

'I know. And so you've set yourself free. It's finished.' But Tracy knows otherwise.

In the queue at border control they stand alongside a mixture of tourists, bargain hunters and Mexicans laden with bags. The air smells of gasoline and cooking, and through the fence they can already see a bustling crowd of street vendors, selling food, plastic wind-up toys, canned drinks. The futurist concrete edifice of the border building contrasts with the patchwork shop-fronts either side of the fence. Pressing with all its might against every inch of the flimsy fortification, Mexico feels like a boil ready to burst.

'Well, Mr Lewis,' says Tracy, squeezing his hand, as they pass unhindered through the cool shadows of the office and then out into the fading light, 'this has been a hell of a first date so far.' Putting her passport into her back pocket, she places her bag between her feet and looks down the main street of Nogales. Boys and beautiful girls, bearded men and bent old women in black rags run over the cracked road surface, between cars and pick-up trucks accelerating in and out of the country. The road seems endless and immense, and she knows this will be a one-way journey. She shakes herself free of her thoughts as Lewis picks up her bag. 'It's gonna be hard to top a gun battle with an estranged parent, though, Mr Lewis. What do we do now?'

They walk on into the town, looking for a bus station or somewhere that feels safe to stay. They push effortlessly through the endless approaches of salesmen offering them carvings, Coca-Cola and prescription drugs, as if nothing can touch them. The hawkers flutter past them like leaves in a breeze. As they amble aimlessly into town, Lewis realises that neither he nor Tracy has a plan beyond crossing the border. This was as far as it went. Unspeaking, they breathe in, and through the masking mesh of Mexican smells, they catch the scent of freedom. The evening wind feels wet on Lewis's arms as he searches his pockets for cigarettes. 'Wait here a sec,' he says, entering a shop on the street corner. 'I'm going to get some fags.'

Tracy leans against a lamppost and looks down at a blanket laid out on the pavement below her. Carvings of devils and tentacled demons, spotted with dots of multicoloured paint, rise up from the striped rug, and a woman squatting down by it begins to recite a price list. Tracy leans down to look, but straightens swiftly, as she feels the point of a pistol in the small of her back. 'Madam. I wonder if you'd care to join me for tea,' says an English accent in her ear, as a hand seizes her elbow and leads her across the street.

Lewis emerges from the shop and strikes a match. He sees Tracy waving to him from under the awning of a bar opposite. The match burns away to nothing in his fingers, and he drops it as fire touches flesh. She is sitting outside in the shade with someone, white-suited now and far from home, but familiar none the less.

'The blood of Christ, man! The blood of Jesus sweet Jesus! In a cup!' Luther raises the grail, over the face of the rising moon, and stares up at it.

They had been there for hours now. Sid approaches his entranced hero, placatory and concerned, feeling all his hopes and dreams gradually fading out of focus. He came here to form a band. He took a detour to the empty cellar of a top-security installation to clear both his conscience and a way forward. But just when he thought things were about to go his way, Sid finds he's caught up as an intermediary in an ethical debate about the future of the most sacred legendary artefact on the planet. 'Luther,' he says, weakly, 'do we really need this?'

'The blood of Christ?' splutters the old man, holding the wooden cup to his heart. 'Do we really need the blood of Christ?'

'We've got the New Round Tabyls to think of now, Luther, haven't we, Danno?'

'Yes,' says Danny, standing wearily from a rock where he'd fallen to earth earlier in the argument. 'And caring for the most famous mythological relic of the Christian religion is hardly the kind of distraction we want on the road to rock and roll success now, is it, Sid?' Danny, in his uncomplicated way, has already suggested a far simpler future for the Grail. He wants to sell it.

Sid snaps and pokes him in the chest, pushing him back

down. 'Danny – shut it, just once, shut it.' Danny stands and begins to circle Luther as Sid pleads with him. 'For the first time in our lives we've got something we can really believe in, something we're committed to, and now this!' And Sid gestures towards the most divine totem with the expression of a man who has just found the cat has shat in his bed.

Danny stands before Luther, pointing at the Grail. 'Yeah? And I'm committed to flogging this piece of holy crap to the highest bidder. Gimme it!'

'No!' Luther holds the Grail tighter. Danny charges him and wrestles him to the ground, grasping at the wooden cup. Luther wriggles free, kicks a cloud of sand in Danny's face, and heads up the hill. Danny springs to his feet and rushes after him.

'Danny!' shouts Sid, and gives chase.

In the courtyard of a Nogales café bar, the Hampstead Man gestures for Lewis to join him. 'Ah, Mr Lewis. We met on the Heath, remember? Please, sit down.' Lewis notices a flash of metal under the table as Tracy takes his hand. A waiter emerges from a leafy doorway out of the darkened bar. 'Three teas, please,' the Hampstead Man barks at him. 'Well, isn't this delightful? You didn't find the Holy Grail, then, I take it?'

'Who are you and what do you want?'

'If you know anything about its whereabouts, now really would be the time to speak up. How can I put it? Let's say . . . the supreme order of Masonry has hitherto been highly appreciated and its good reputation well established.' Lewis feels his heart begin to race. 'This consideration alone, were there not others of greater magnitude, should be sufficient to induce you to preserve and perpetuate our honourable tradit-ion.' The words thud dully in Lewis's ears, like the sound of a familiar name he can't put a face to. The Hampstead Man continues. 'But, when to this is added the pleasure which every philanthropic heart must feel in doing good, in diffusing light and knowledge, and in cultivating the virtues, I cannot doubt that your future conduct, and that of your successors, will still further enhance the lustre of your justly esteemed reputation.' The man looks expectantly at Lewis. He says nothing. There is a pause. The tea arrives. 'Ah, tea! I'd be mother,' says the Hampstead Man, licking his lips, 'but it would mean putting down the gun which I have aimed squarely at your young lady. I'd have preferred a drawn sword, of course. The pistol is a matter not of ritual but of common sense.' The Hampstead Man gestures at the tea with his free hand. 'Would you pour, dear?' Tracy does so, and passes round the cups in silence. 'You really have no recollection, do you, Mr Lewis? The Americans that brought you down were so devilishly efficient.'

Tracy looks up at Lewis, biting her lip. 'Lewis . . . this man says he knows who you are.' Lewis shakes a little and sets down his cup. Only hours ago, he had all but rationalised away the gnawing need to know. As he crossed the border with Tracy he had felt himself approaching a state of grace. His real identity was as nothing now. He was ready to scrub away the doubts and make something of himself unhindered by anxieties about his past. And yet here it was once more, in the form of a frightening fat man, trying to claw him back even as he finally slipped its clutches.

'Indeed, Mr "Lewis",' the man goes on, dabbing at his red face with a little white hanky, 'you have me to thank for your very survival. They were all for chopping out your tongue upon your reappearance, in case you should recover your memory. But having survived being shot down and ejecting into the stratosphere, I rather thought you deserved a little clemency. You found the money I popped into your pyjamas, of course. "Must we mutilate him so?" said I. "He *is* our brother." You haven't touched your tea. Sugar?'

'So,' says Lewis, brushing away the proffered sugar bowl, 'you're here to finish me off. Whoever I am.'

'My stars, no!' the sweating man exclaims, mid-sip. 'Ironically, when the Worshipful Master became aware of your travel plans he was delighted. It appeared your half-formed suspicions might lead us to the prize that had eluded all of our finest agents for so long. But, alas, it was not to be. Oooh, this tea is a disgrace. They'll never learn, will they? I don't know which is worse. Throwing it into Boston Harbor or stewing it so.'

Mindful of the pistol beneath the table, Lewis leans in close to the Hampstead Man's face. 'It's too late. It doesn't matter to me any longer. Do you understand? I've decided. I don't even want to know.'

'Really!' the man answers, holding Lewis's gaze. 'And are you not a little curious, Mr "Lewis"? Wouldn't you just like to know your real name?'

'What's in a name?'

'Oh, you tease! Your date of birth, then?'

'Why?' says Lewis, backing off. 'Am I eligible for some astronaut pension?'

'Oh!' laughs the Hampstead Man, clutching at Tracy's forearm for support. 'I see they didn't manage to erase his sense of humour, did they, dear? Smashing! But Mr "Lewis", wouldn't you even like to know whether you *really* walked in space? It would be such a tale to tell one's children.'

'I've made a decision.' Lewis lifts the fat man's hand from Tracy's arm. The Hampstead Man bristles.

'Well, aren't you a lucky little boy,' he spits. 'How lovely for you to be able to just forget it all in an instant and start all over again. Wouldn't it be simply marvellous if we could all shirk our responsibilities so. If you think for a moment I'm going to allow you the satisfaction of . . .' The man trails off, his eyes rolling a little, as he sits back into his chair. 'Excuse me. I seem to have come over all queer. Oh, dear me.' The Hampstead Man loosens his tie, dabs at his face, and falls off his seat. With a clatter the gun slides out over the terrace. A crowd of drinkers stand and point at it. A woman screams. Tracy grabs Lewis's hand, pulls him out into the street and they break into a run, dodging traffic as they flee south across the city.

'What happened?' says Lewis, doubled up, pausing for breath on a street corner.

'You know that little pack of powder Luther gave us?' answers Tracy, smiling. 'I slipped it all into his tea.'

At the edge of a cliff, overlooking a canyon, Luther stops running. In daylight, the sun would paint the canyon walls in a thousand shades of orange and red, but the gathering darkness simply emphasises its unknowable emptiness. Behind him, in the moonlight, he can make out Sid following Danny through a miniature forest of barrel cacti and prickly pears. Luther looks over the edge, but there's no way he could climb down the cliff, even if he could have seen where to put his feet. As Danny squares up to him, Luther holds the cup up into the sky once more. 'The blood of Christ!'

'Yeah, yeah. Give it to me granddad. Now!'

Luther backs away, his feet feeling for the edge of the canyon. 'It's Lucifer, Danny, the light angel! The devil's clock has struck midnight! He's standing you on the cliff edge and tempting you with wealth!'

Danny considers this for a moment. He'd been raised a Catholic and there's certainly something about the day's events, and the situation he now finds himself in, that evokes long buried religious resonances. Still . . .

'Oh, fuck off! Give it to me!' Danny smacks Luther round the face. The old man goes down screaming and drops the Grail. Danny catches it in mid-air and retreats to the cliff edge. Luther lies on the ground, moaning. Sid arrives, breathless and wheezing.

'Why, Danny, why do you want it?' he shouts, helping Luther up. 'So we can run away again as usual?'

Danny spits, and laughs. 'We? Who said anything about sharing? The way I look at it, maybe the good Lord owes me this one.'

'Danny. You are standing on the edge of a precipice,' says Luther through a mouthful of blood and a few broken teeth.

'Yeah? We all are. Literally.'

Luther approaches him once more, carving crosses into the night air with a shaking hand. 'The blood of Christ, Danny! Don't you see? It's a sign! It must be sacrificed?'

'Uh?'

'That's it,' continues Luther, gesturing towards Heaven. 'He's giving us life! The blood of Christ.'

'Yeah. And for all the good it's done us. Centuries of false hopes and squabbling.' Danny looks at the vessel in his hands, rattles the flakes of dried blood and presses it to his ear, like a summer holiday schoolboy listening for the sea in a shell. 'Can you hear me, you stupid heavenly cunt? I'm going to sell your last mortal remains at auction and finally someone will get some use out of you.'

Luther winces. 'Don't you see. I've been dead for thirty years, and he's sent you two to raise me once more!'

Sid staggers towards him. Danny shouts, 'Enough!' and he stretches his arm out into the darkness of the canyon, holding the flimsy cup out over a drop of some thousand feet or so. The three men stand still, locked in an impasse. The wind blows. A coyote howls. Somewhere a wild horse whinnies. Luther sneezes. The moon shines down. The dull wood of the Grail does not reflect its light.

The Hampstead Man surfaces from behind the table of the bar, and scrabbles for his gun. He sees it on the ground behind him, and reaches for it over a sweeping stretch of empty stone and between a forest of feet. Something isn't right. He sweats, snatches up the weapon, feels its cool weight in his hand, and staggers, faint and bleeding, out into the street. His feet feel unfamiliar and heavy, as if he was schlepping through sticky mud. But he looks down and sees only cracked tarmac, and the stunning brown brown-ness of his shoes. Then his feet become light and fluffy, the pads of his toes pumped up on tiny springs, the wind whistling past them at light speed as he raises each in turn to walk forwards, the blood pumping down his enormous legs to power them. He sees cripples begging, a one-eyed cat, a row of comic books in a newsagent's window about a masked wrestler, and two sick dogs fighting. He knows that one of the dogs will die, and all but weeps. Unaccustomed to commanding his incredible new feet, the Hampstead Man trips and falls once more, coming to rest against a wire meshed fence, several thousand miles away on the other side of a narrow thoroughfare. As he leans into it he feels the fence give, and the whole street seems to surge inwards with it. At the point where his fingertips meet the mesh, the fence transfers its flexible properties to him, and he too bends out into the wobbly world, billowing into the air like a cotton kite. Presumably this tension and energy have always been present, he thinks, but somehow he had previously found a way, subconsciously, to subdue it. He is horrified, and not a little thrilled by this state of affairs.

The Hampstead Man has always had a respect for order, both social and natural, and it was this that had first attracted him to the Craft. It had been an enormous comfort to know that the Great Architect had a grand design. But all around him, he feels the evidence of this design dissolving into a beautiful and exhilarating chaos. This mess is unmappable. The earth beneath his feet resonates at random from the footfalls of the crowd, and, whenever he looks up, the evening sky flashes unstructured firework displays of fading sunlight and rising stars, splattered out across the heavens with a flagrant disregard for disciplined organisation. The Hampstead Man feels the urge to sing, as if invoking a charm against all this witchcraft. He had risen in the east, from Whitechapel up to Whitehall. He is not yet ready to see himself sink in the west.

> *Now the evening shadows closing,*
> *Warn from toil to peaceful rest,*
> *Mystic arts and rights reposing,*
> *Sacred in each faithful breast.*

Bouncing back from the fence, the Hampstead Man merges into a delicious flow of bodies, sucking in their juicy heat as they push him through the gates of a market. Men jabber and point, waving wooden carvings and soft-drink bottles which have been artfully melted into new shapes. Maybe. He isn't sure. Everything seems to be taking new shapes. The open mouths of dozens of little shops surround him. Silver and glass gleam out of their darknesses. He cannot remember where he entered, not only the market, but the wider scheme of things. It does not matter, once he gets his bearings, because a Lodge may be resumed, upwards or downwards, in any degree in which it has been previously opened, provided that the degree in question has not been formally closed. And it has not yet been formally closed.

> God of Light! Whose love unceasing,
> Doth to all Thy works extend,
> Crown our Order with thy blessing,
> Build; sustain us to the end.

The shapes of the tumbledown shops suddenly irk him. This market is poor architecture. Wooden door-frames rub up against roof supports, windows wilt, and the shop opposite him, selling a selection of multicoloured masks which laugh and call out to him through the somehow less realistic faces of traders and tourists, is leaning at a disgraceful angle. The Hampstead Man approaches the doorway and throws his weight against the wall, pushing it forcibly back into shape. He raises a stray brick to knock off all superfluous knobs and excrescences; to further smooth and prepare the stone; to adjust the rectangular corners of buildings; to assist in bringing rude matter into due form; to lay and prove the horizontals; to adjust uprights while fixing them on their proper bases; and thus by square conduct, level steps, and upright intentions, hoping to ascend to those immortal mansions whence all goodness emanates. The Hampstead Man pounds the surface of

266

the droopy wall with the crumbling brick for what seems like hours. But, today, rude matter is obstinately resisting its due form.

The shopkeeper turns at the sound of splintering plaster and pulls him away. The Hampstead Man falls to the floor. But the friendly floor anticipates his arrival, cushions the impact, and flings him bodily back up into the air. 'It is customary at the erection of all stately and superb edifices, to lay the first or foundation stone at the north-east corner of the building,' says the Hampstead Man to the shaking shopkeeper, who is scrabbling around in a desk drawer. 'And you, being newly admitted into Masonry, are placed at the north-east part of the Lodge,' and he pulls him from behind the desk, pushing him across the room, knocking over a pile of striped blankets and a little bamboo ladder, 'figuratively to represent that stone, and from the foundation laid this evening may you raise a superstructure perfect in its parts and honourable to the builder.' The shopkeeper struggles free and strikes the Hampstead Man across the forehead with a hammer he'd pulled from the drawer. 'Be careful not to gavel too heavily!' he shouts, falling out of the shop, as blood painlessly trickles down his face, tickling his cheeks, the air biting deliciously into the greedy wound. 'Happy have we met! Happy may we part! And happy meet again! Keep within hail.'

The problem there, you see, had been finding the north-east part of the Lodge. For what is East, and what is North? They are constructs of the deceitful compass, laid over chaos to make sense of it, so it would seem now, and thus can they truly be said to represent the relative position of the room itself? Who is to say that rude matter has a due form? Maybe it has all been in vain? But, if this is the case, then how can he do his duties? How can he mark the sun at its meridian, to call the brethren from labour to refreshment, and from refreshment to labour, that profit and pleasure may be the result? And how may he mark the setting sun, so to close the Lodge by command of the Worshipful Master, after having seen that every brother has his due, if he does not know where the sun will set?

Silently, the Hampstead Man invokes the assistance of the Great Architect of the Universe, that the rays of Heaven may shed their influence, to enlighten him once more in the paths of virtue and science. He feels the air around him harden into the door of a high castle, and knocks three times on its invisible solid surface. But there is no reply. The Grand Geometrician is no longer at home.

He finds himself in another shop, the roof hung with wooden skeletons that quiver and dance before him. He sees a shelf at eye-level, a lamb, a Devil, a naked Adam and a naked Eve. There is the Virgin Mary, a laughing sun, and a skeleton giving birth to another skeleton which has burst through its stomach from a womb-like wound. There are a thousand different figurines, all the dead of the earth dressed in their finest clothes, staring back at him out of the sockets of their small white skulls. He backs into the middle of the shop, flattening shelves of overpriced pottery, searching for the point within the circle from which every part of the circumference is equidistant. The earth constantly revolving on its axis in its orbit round the sun, and Freemasonry being universally spread over its surface, it necessarily follows that the sun must always be at its meridian with respect to Freemasonry. But where is the sun, and where is the meridian, and where is the centre of the circle?

It was not so many years ago that he felt he had gained the summit of a winding staircase, but now the staircase is crumbling beneath his feet. Freemasonry had enabled him to distinguish and appreciate the connection of the whole system, and the relative dependency of its several parts. He had long since become resigned to the will of the Great Architect of the Universe, and, proceeding onwards, still guiding his progress by the principles of moral truth, he had long ago been led to contemplate the intellectual faculty. Finally, he had traced its development, through the paths of heavenly science, even to the throne of God Himself. But, the Hampstead Man now observes, as a blue-winged moth the size of his fist flitters past his face and up through the azure ceiling of the roof out into the grey-green sky, when he had knocked for him only seconds ago, the throne of God was bare. Years ago, in gentler climes, the secrets of Nature and the principles of intellectual truth had been unveiled to his view. To his mind, thus modelled by virtue and science, Nature presented one great and useful lesson more. She had prepared him, by contemplation, for the closing hour of existence; and now, when by means of that contemplation she had conducted him through the windings of his mortal life, Nature at last instructs him how to die.

He hears the voice of his Worshipful Master, and he is the kneeling candidate once more: 'Let me now beg you to observe that the Light of a Master Mason is darkness visible, serving only to express the gloom which rests on the prospect of futurity. It is that mysterious veil which the eye of human reason cannot penetrate, unless assisted by that Light which is from above. Yet, even by this glimmering ray you may perceive that you stand on the very brink of the gulf into which you have descended, and which, when this transitory life shall have passed away, will again receive you into its cold bosom.'

But it was not 'the Light which is above' that had revealed this to the Hampstead Man, but a light from below, beyond, from without and within him, which suddenly reshapes everything and resists rearrangement. The lights of glass vases on the shop shelves in front of him shine more brightly, and illuminate the rude matter around them in more profound detail, than the glimmering ray of which he had learned. And the cold bosom he had formerly feared suddenly seems inviting, like the fence and the shop floor, a soft and forgiving friend he was simply yet to meet.

> By Thy glorious Majesty –
> By the trust we place in Thee –
> By the badge and mystic sign –

Hear us, Architect Divine!
So Mote It Be.

He plucks up a crucifix with a gore-spattered Jesus slowly expiring on it, and he rushes out of the shop, trailing shattered trinkets and leaving behind him the screams of shocked and shaken craftswomen. He kneels down in the street outside and holds the crucifix up to the cascade of stars above his face. Jesus flickers and burns. A crowd surrounds him. For a moment, he wonders if one of the faces is familiar, a white man watching him and making notes. And he finds himself, at last, at the centre of a circle, but knows now that this is mere coincidence. The Hampstead Man pulls the pistol from his pocket, pushes the barrel into his mouth, and squeezes the trigger.

'Danny. What are you going to do?' Sid stands as close to Danny as he dare, the canyon edge the last point of detail before a vast darkness. Danny looks back at the two men behind him, their images becoming indistinct in the fading sun, and down once more at the wooden cup, wobbling in his shaking fist. He sees Sid, and still recognises behind the gathering weight of years, and the wilting of his hair, the face of the mere boy who kept him late at Lemon Pies rehearsals, coaxing him into Keith Moon rolls and promising him that one day they would be the rhythm section by which all others would be judged. And in Luther, he sees almost a little of himself, of something that might have been mutated into something that wasn't. And he looks out at his own, now insubstantial, shadow, slipping into darkness on the canyon wall beyond the great gulf. It's a hundred metres high at least, but a trick of the light none the less, an outline shaped and shaded by circumstances, by the rocks that ripple beneath it and the action of the receding rays of sunshine above it. It is moulded by random geology and the last light. It knows nothing of its own self. And soon the shadow shape of him is gone, as if it never had been, leaving only the blank cliff, and the throbbing empty dark.

'I'm gonna do what we all should've done years back. Let everything go, let it all go at last!' Danny leans back, raises the Holy Grail in his right hand as Sid readies himself to intervene, and then he calmly hands the cup back to Luther. 'Come on, man, set us free.'

The Hopi Boy
and the Sun – viii

Finally the Hopi boy and his father the Sun came
to the house of the Sun in the east. There the
Sun's sister gave them venison stew for supper.

In the morning the Sun said to the boy, 'Go
ahead! I am going to follow you.' The boy
opened the door in the ground and went out.
He sat down on the crystal stool, took the fox
skin and the macaw feathers, and held them up
to create the dawn. As he did, the people of
Laguna, Isleta, and the other eastern pueblos
looked eastward and sprinkled sacred meal. The
sun behind him said, 'Look at the trails, the life
of the people. Some are short, others are too
long.'

In the evening the Sun returned to his house
in the west. By then the boy wanted to go back
to his own people, so the Sun's mother made a
trail of sacred flour, and the boy and the
rattlesnake-woman went back eastward over it.
At noon they came to the rattlesnakes' home.
The rattlesnake-woman said, 'I want to see my
father. After that, let's go on.' They entered her

house, and she told her father that the Hopi boy was her husband. And then they resumed their journey.

That evening they arrived in the Hopi village. The boy made straight for his grandmother's house, but an old chief said, 'Look at that handsome man going into that poor home!' He invited the boy into his own house, but the boy replied, 'No! I'm going here.' The war chief said, 'We don't want you in that dirty house.'

'The house is mine,' the boy replied, 'so tell your people to clean it up. When all of you treated me badly, I went up to the Sun and he helped me.'

And the people of the village set about cleaning the boy's grandmother's house.

Hopi Indian legend, reported by
Franz Boas in 1922

Fifteen

In the lobby of a cheap hotel some way south of Nogales, Lewis walks back to Tracy from the check-in desk. With one key.

'We're sharing a room, then?' she says, pointedly.

'I'm sorry. I didn't mean . . . I've been presumptuous. Forgive me.'

'I thought you understood,' she says, pressing her hands to his face. 'I told you. I'm poisoned water. You'd be taking your life in your hands.'

'I don't care,' Lewis answers, forcing her fingers free. Tracy knows this is her last chance to walk away. She can be free here, but to hope to be happy would surely be pushing her luck.

'Well, I do care. And I care about you too much to allow this to happen. It's gone too far . . .' Lewis turns and raises his voice, and the desk clerk looks away embarrassed. 'So join a convent, Tracy. Join a convent and I'll go back to London alone and we'll never know . . .'

'Lewis. Listen to me.' Once more Tracy begins her usual speech, but this time it has a resigned air, and lacks the defiance that characterised it last time she was called upon to recite it, days earlier, on the highway with Sid and Danny. 'I've loved many men in the last ten years, and every single one of them is lying somewhere between here and Los Angeles, throats slit, wrists slashed, necks broken, arms and legs separated from their bodies by speeding locomotives, heads crushed by passing trucks, guts contorted by deadly poisons, hearts broken and dead, all dead, every one of them dead.'

Lewis puts his finger to her lips, silencing her. 'Tracy Hopkins, please, I've walked on the moon. I'm unshockable.'

And Tracy stares up into his eyes, for a very long time. She takes the key from his hand.

'Come on, then. Let's go.'

Luther shrugs, stares a final time at the wooden relic, and then hurls the Holy Grail over the cliff. 'Here's to a united Ireland!' says Danny, under his breath. The cup's trajectory is not as clean a line as he'd have liked, he could probably have made a better show of it himself, but the Grail is gone none the less. The three men squint to watch it fall, but the tiny brown cup disappears all but instantly into the cavernous night sky. They put their hands to their ears and listen. The seconds pass. Maybe the cup will never land, snatched up in mid-flight by guardian angels and returned to its rightful owner. Then there is a dull pop, the sound of wood splintering on stone. Below them on the canyon bed, the cup lies unseen and cracked among the stones, the wax seal broken. A rattlesnake hisses at it and retreats under a rock. The slightest of breezes gathers speed along the dry river-bed, and conjures a small cloud of red dust from its broken mouth, whipping the particles up into a growing column of crimson cloud.

They turn silently away from the cliff edge. Danny puts his hand on Luther's shoulder. 'I'm sorry I hit you back there, Luther.'

Luther looks back towards the canyon. Wide-eyed, he tugs on Sid's sleeve. In the darkness they hear a whistling of wind, and looking up at the white face of the full moon, they see a shadow start to cross it. First the moon seems speckled, as if someone had flicked paint at it from the bristles of a brush. Then it begins to change, slowly and almost imperceptibly, from left to right, as a cloud of something passes over it. And for a brief moment the moon is full and round and red all over, staring down at them out of the black sky. And then it is white once more. The three men turn and walk wordlessly away, each wondering if he alone had imagined that which they all had seen.

As the moon outside her hotel window resumes its normal colour, Tracy throws back her head and cries out. Her mouth opens and closes silently for a few seconds, before she falls back into bed beside Lewis. He pulls her close to him on the white sheets, beneath the brown blankets.

Later that night, when she wakes once more, Tracy sees Lewis standing across the room from her. He is looking out of the window, staring out at the night sky. And then he slowly closes the shutters and finally shuts out the stars. Behind him, Tracy is sitting up in bed, her arms open wide, ready to receive him at last.

In the office that now bears his name, Sheriff Cowdrey prepares a final draft of the speech he's due to deliver at Matthew Hopkins's funeral. Then he stands, walks to the wall, and slowly unpicks the mass of pins and coloured cotton that has sprawled for more than a decade over the sheriff's office state map. He crumples the refuse into a ball and drops it into a waste bin. The case is closed.

And in a secret, black and white checkered room, beneath the streets of Covent Garden, but a little above sewer level, intelligence reports harvested from Mexico are handed to a committee of ashen-faced men. If ever it was about to be found, the great prize, it seems, is gone once more, their lifeline severed. Their most trusted servant is dead by his own hand, at sunset, in a city square. He rose in the East. He set in the

West. Lewis is lost to them now, too, they all agree as one, and, striking his name from the records, and cancelling the Hampstead Man's account, they turn their immeasurable minds to more pressing matters, and draw their plans against less insubstantial targets. *So mote it be.*

Six days later in London, Abby Quinton settles down at her desk for her weekly consultation with Peter Rugg.

'Well, Peter, here's an unexpected and mysterious treat. There's a letter for both of us, care of the hospital, postmarked Mexico.'

'Mexico,' says Peter Rugg, looking up from a plastic bag of cigarette ends. Abby opens the letter and hands him a small parcel marked with his name. He begins tearing at it, as she feels around the envelope for whatever else it may contain, and pulls out a Polaroid photograph.

A man and a woman are standing with the sea behind them, dressed in shorts and sunglasses, smiling into the camera. The woman, Abby observes, seems confident and relaxed, leaning against the man's shoulder with easy intimacy, having just finished laughing at some shared joke. The man, she realises after a minute of frustration at his familiarity, is Mr Lewis. The astronaut. But here he exudes a contentment that she has never seen in any of their consultation sessions. She flips over the photograph, looking for clues, and sees the handwritten message. 'Goodbye and thank you. Please make sure Mr Rugg gets his present.'

She looks up. Peter is inhaling the musky scent of the burned remains of a tightly rolled joint with uncharacteristic satisfaction. 'That's the one,' he says, standing up and throwing his precious plastic bag of dog-ends into a waste bin. 'Finest Mexican weed. Right. I've got things to do, people to see.'

Abby jumps up from behind her desk and follows Peter Rugg out into the corridor. 'Mr Rugg, you can't just discharge yourself.'

'I can, love,' he laughs back at her. 'I'm cured.'

Abby pursues him towards the exit, feeling another certainty slip away. Back in her office, her answerphone picks up a message she's in the process of missing. There's the sound of crowd noise, like someone is holding the receiver up into a busy public place, and then a distant American voice, announcing something over a p.a. system.

'Ladies and gentlemen . . . I don't know how to tell you this but . . . here's Luther Peyote, and the *New* Round Tabyls!'

The Hopi Boy
and the Sun – ix

The evening after the people of the village had cleaned his grandmother's house, the boy appeared before the council and told all that had happened to him. Then he gave melons and wafer bread to the poor. Every evening after sunset the women would come with their dishes, and he would offer them venison stew and peaches. He said to the chief, 'I teach the people the right way to live. Even if you are my enemy, I must show you how to behave well.'

Twin children, a boy and a girl, were born to his wife. They had the shape of rattlesnakes, but they were also humans.

Hopi Indian legend, reported by
Franz Boas in 1922

Credits